Biopolitics, Governmentality and Humanitarianism

This book critically analyses the changing role and nature of post-Cold War humanitarianism, using Foucault's theories of biopolitics and governmentality.

It offers a compelling and insightful interpretation of the policies and practices associated with 'new' humanitarianism in general, as well as of the dynamics of two specific international assistance efforts: the post-2001 conflict-related assistance effort in Afghanistan and the post-2000 Chernobyl-related assistance effort in Belarus.

The central argument of the book is that 'new' humanitarianism represents a dominant regime of humanitarian governing informed by globalising neo-liberalism and is reliant on a complex set of biopolitical, disciplinary and sovereign technologies. It demonstrates that, while the purposes of humanitarian governing are specific to particular contexts, its promise of care is more often than not accompanied by sovereign and/or biopolitical violences.

Making an important contribution to existing scholarship on humanitarian emergencies and humanitarian action, on biopolitics and governmentality, this book will be of much interest to students and scholars of humanitarianism, critical security studies, governmentality and International Relations generally.

Volha Piotukh holds a PhD in Politics and International Studies and is currently Postdoctoral Research Associate at Durham University.

Routledge Critical Security Studies series

Titles in this series include:

Securing Outer Space
Edited by Natalie Bormann and Michael Sheehan

Critique, Security and Power
The political limits to emancipatory approaches
Tara McCormack

Gender, Human Security and the United Nations
Security language as a political framework for women
Natalie Florea Hudson

The Struggle for the West
A divided and contested legacy
Christopher S. Browning and Marko Lehti

Gender and International Security
Feminist perspectives
Edited by Laura Sjoberg

Reimagining War in the 21st Century
From Clausewitz to network-centric warfare
Manabrata Guha

The New Spatiality of Security
Operational uncertainty and the US military in Iraq
Caroline M. Croser

Human Security as Statecraft
Structural conditions, articulations and unintended consequences
Nik Hynek

US Domestic and International Regimes of Security
Pacifying the globe, securing the homeland
Markus Kienscherf

Biopolitics, Governmentality and Humanitarianism

'Caring' for the population in Afghanistan and Belarus

Volha Piotukh

Routledge
Taylor & Francis Group

LONDON AND NEW YORK

First published 2015
by Routledge
2 Park Square, Milton Park, Abingdon, Oxon OX14 4RN

and by Routledge
711 Third Avenue, New York, NY 10017

Routledge is an imprint of the Taylor & Francis Group, an informa business

British Library Cataloguing in Publication Data
A catalogue record for this book is available from the British Library

Library of Congress Cataloging in Publication Data
Piotukh, Volha.
Biopolitics, governmentality and humanitarianism : 'caring' for the
population in Afghanistan and Belarus / by Volha Piotukh.
    pages cm. – (Routledge critical security studies series)
    Includes bibliographical references.
    1. Humanitarianism–Political aspects–Afghanistan.
    2. Humanitarianism–Political aspects–Belarus. 3. Biopolitics–
    Afghanistan. 4. Biopolitics–Belarus. 5. Foucault, Michel,
    1926–1984–Political and social views. 6. Afghanistan–Politics and
    government–2001– 7. Belarus–Politics and government–1991– I. Title.
    HV555.A3P56 2015   361.609478–dc23
    2014043128

ISBN: 978-0-415-85545-7 (hbk)
ISBN: 978-1-315-88968-9 (ebk)

Typeset in Times New Roman
by Wearset Ltd, Boldon, Tyne and Wear

Printed and bound in Great Britain by
TJ International Ltd, Padstow, Cornwall

Contents

Acknowledgements

As many would attest, every book is a journey, with too many steps, stops, challenges, obstacles, *eureka* moments, inspirations and influences to list them all. My journey towards this book, in terms of exposure to the issues I am addressing in it, started back in Belarus, when I was Lecturer in International Law teaching in the broad area of Human Rights and International Humanitarian Law. The next important stage of the journey was MA studies at the University of Manchester, which, despite countless challenges, was one of the best experiences of my life, the time when I could feel myself grow every day. This experience was made possible by the Joint Open Society Institute/Chevening/The University of Manchester Scholarship. I would like to thank all my tutors at Manchester, but, in particular, Dr Veronique Pin-Fat and Dr Elizabeth Dauphinee, for it was them who introduced me to Michel Foucault's work, saw some potential in me and encouraged me to continue my academic studies.

This book is largely based on my PhD research generously supported by the University of Leeds (Joint ORSAS/Lupton and Tetley International Research Scholarship), for which I am very grateful. I would like to express my gratitude to my PhD supervisors, Prof. Alice Hills, Dr Ricardo Blaug and Dr Deniol Jones, and to my examiners, Dr Stuart McAnulla and Prof. Mark Duffield. I would also like to thank all the academic and support staff of the School of Politics and International Studies (POLIS) of the University of Leeds who made my time there as a PhD student and a Teaching Assistant such a rewarding experience. While teaching at the University of Leeds, University of Westminster and UCL, I delivered several research-based lectures to MA students. Their response to, and engagement with, my ideas and arguments was very helpful and is much appreciated.

Many people made this research project possible by agreeing to volunteer their time to share their experiences/insights in interviews and/or to facilitate interviews with others for the case studies on the assistance efforts in Afghanistan and Belarus, and I am deeply appreciative of their kind assistance. They cannot all be named here, and most of them expressed a preference to remain anonymous, but I know who they are, and they continue to speak to me through the pages of this book.

Earlier versions of Chapter 1 were presented as *'Power over Life: the Concept of Biopolitics in Foucault, Agamben and Esposito'* conference papers at the

'Towards a Philosophy of Life: Reflections on the Concept of Life in Continental Philosophy of Religion Conference', Liverpool, June 2009, and at the *'Special Workshop on Biopolitics at the IVR XXV World Congress of Philosophy of Law and Social Philosophy'*, Goethe-University, Frankfurt am Main, Germany, August 2011.

Earlier versions of Chapter 2 were presented as conference papers: *'Humanitarian Action and the War on Terror: Some Preliminary Thoughts on a New Biopolitical Nexus'* at the *4th Northern PSA Postgraduate Conference*, University of Edinburgh, June 2008; *'The "New" Humanitarianism as a Biopolitical Project'* at the *12th Annual PSA Postgraduate Conference for Central and Northern England (CANE)*, Nottingham University, November 2008.

Earlier versions of Chapter 3 were presented as conference papers: *'Population as a Battleground for War: The Dangers of Securitisation and Militarisation of Humanitarian Assistance in Afghanistan'* at the *'Responsibility to Rebuild: Linking Governance, Infrastructure and Democratisation Workshop'*, Sussex University, June 2010; *'Problematisations that Matter: the Power/Knowledge Nexus and the post-2001 Assistance Effort in Afghanistan'* at the *'Conflict, Intervention and the Politics of Knowledge Conference'*, Manchester University, November 2010; *'Biopolitical Triage, Necessary Killing and Inevitable Abandonment: Understanding Securitisation and Militarisation of Aid in Afghanistan post-2001'* at the *'Global Insecurities Conference'*, Leeds University, September 2011; *'Foucault in Afghanistan: Problematisations that Matter and the Biopolitics of Securitisation and Militarisation of Aid'* at the *'Radical Foucault Conference'*, University of East London, September 2011.

Earlier versions of Chapter 4 were presented as conferences papers: *'Foucauldian Applications: Biopolitics, Governmentality and the Chernobyl Accident'* at the *'Thinking (With)Out Borders II: The St. Andrews International Political Theory Conference'*, University of St. Andrews, July 2010; *'Foucault in Chernobyl: Biopolitics, Governmentality and the Assistance Effort in Belarus'* at the *'Foucault and Habermas Workshop'* at the *2011 MANCEPT Conference*, Manchester University, September 2011; *'The Chernobyl Accident: Understanding Its Wider Impact on the People of Belarus'* at the *13th International Congress of the International Radiation Protection Association (IRPA)*, Glasgow, May 2012; *'Problematisations that Matter: Politics of Expertise in the Chernobyl-Related Assistance Effort in Belarus'* at the *22nd International Political Science Association (IPSA) World Congress of Political Science*, Madrid, Spain, July 2012.

I would like to thank the organisers of the above events for the opportunity to present work in progress, and panel chairs, discussants and participants for their insightful comments and questions and stimulating discussions that helped me shape my ideas and arguments.

At Durham University, I am incredibly fortunate to work with Prof. Louise Amoore, who is a fantastic colleague and mentor and a constant source of inspiration. I am profoundly grateful to her for her kindness and wisdom, for her work ethic, for being so considerate and so generous with her time and advice, for supporting me through my work on the manuscript and for several close readings of draft chapters and invaluable comments and suggestions.

I am also grateful to the three anonymous reviewers, whose constructive criticisms and useful suggestions have undoubtedly helped to improve the manuscript. I would like to acknowledge the team at Routledge, and, in particular, Andrew Humphrys, Annabelle Harris and Hannah Ferguson, and to thank them for believing in me, for their guidance and for their patience and professionalism in ensuring the completion of this project.

Finally, I would like to thank my parents and my husband Peter for all the love and support they have given me over the years. My every achievement, no matter how small, is also theirs. I would like to dedicate this book to them.

June 2014
Leeds, UK

Abbreviations

ACBAR	Agency Coordinating Body for Afghan Relief and Development
ANSO	Afghanistan NGO Safety Office
ARS	acute radiation syndrome
CAP	Consolidated Appeal Process
CERF	Central Emergency Revolving Fund
CHARP	Chernobyl Humanitarian Assistance and Rehabilitation Programme
CIMIC	civil-military co-operation
COIN	counter-insurgency
CORE	Cooperation for Rehabilitation
DAC OECD	Development Assistance Committee of the Organisation for Economic Co-operation and Development
DHA	Department of Humanitarian Affairs
DFID	UK Department for International Development
DoD	US Department of Defense
DPA	UN Department for Political Affairs
DPKO	UN Department for Peacekeeping Operations
ERC	Emergency Relief Co-ordinator
FAO	Food and Agriculture Organisation
HDI	Human Development Index
HPG	Humanitarian Policy Group (ODI)
HTS	Human Terrain System
HTT	Human Terrain Teams
IAC	International Advisory Committee
IAEA	International Atomic Energy Agency
IASC	Inter-Agency Standing Committee
ICRC	International Committee of the Red Cross
ICRIN	International Chernobyl Research and Information Network
IDP	Internally Displaced Person
IFRC	International Federation of Red Cross and Red Crescent Societies
IGO	international intergovernmental organisation
IHL	International Humanitarian Law
INGO	international non-governmental organisation

IOM	International Organisation for Migration
IPECA	International Programme on the Health Effects of the Chernobyl Accident
ISAF	International Security Assistance Force
JDP	Joint Doctrine Publication
MFA	Ministry of Foreign Affairs of the Republic of Belarus
MSF	*Médecins Sans Frontières*
NGO	non-governmental organisation
NPP	nuclear power plant
NSP	National Solidarity Programme
NSRC	National Society of the Red Cross
ODA	Official Development Assistance
ODI	Overseas Development Institute
OEF	Operation Enduring Freedom
PMCs	private military/security contractors
PRTs	Provincial Reconstruction Teams
QIP	quick impact projects
SDC	Swiss Agency for Development and Cooperation
SF	Strategic Framework (for Afghanistan)
SG	the Secretary General (UN)
SRSG	Special Representative of the Secretary General
UK MOD	UK Ministry of Defence
UN	United Nations
UN GA	United Nations General Assembly
UN OCHA	United Nations Office for the Coordination of Humanitarian Affairs
UNAMA	United Nations Assistance Mission in Afghanistan
UNDP	United Nations Development Programme
UNHCR	United Nations High Commissioner for Refugees
UNICEF	United Nations Children's Fund
UNSC	United Nations Security Council
UNSCEAR	United Nations Scientific Committee on the Effects of Atomic Radiation
WFP	World Food Programme
WHAM	'winning hearts and minds'
WHO	World Health Organisation

Introduction

To approach our present as though it were reducible to a unitary explanation is to approach it sloppily, without concern for detail, without responsiveness to the practices and the archives among which we live.

(May, 2005: 72)

A critique is not a matter of saying that things are not right the way they are. It is a matter of pointing out on what kinds of assumptions, what kinds of familiar, unchallenged, unconsidered modes of thought the practices that we accept rest.

(Foucault, 1988: 155)

Humanitarian action, both normative and material, has its roots in several traditions – such as charity, assistance to war victims, disaster relief and human rights – and its origins can be traced back to ancient civilisations and all major world religions (e.g. Hoffman and Weiss, 2006; Rieff, 2002; Smyser, 2003; Walker and Maxwell, 2009). During its evolution, it has had many expressions, such as the humanitarian colonialism of the nineteenth century and the assistance and protection of war victims enshrined in the 1949 Geneva Conventions and 1977 Additional Protocols. For most of the twentieth century, however, humanitarian action represented a rather modest vocation, undertaken by a select few (e.g. Delorenzi, 1999; West, 2001; Collinson and Elhawary, 2011; Kahn and Cunningham, 2013).

Following the end of the Cold War (since the early 1990s), the nature of humanitarian assistance has been radically changing (e.g. Duffield, 2001; Macrae and Leader, 2000; Rieff, 2002; Macrae, 2001, 2002; Mills, 2005; Hoffman and Weiss, 2006). The rise of 'new' humanitarianism has been seen as a departure from the traditions of a principled and limited life-saving effort, following the humanitarian imperative of providing assistance wherever it is needed; a departure so significant that it provoked the following lamentation:

when humanitarianism can mean anything and everything – relief, human rights, refugee protection, charity, conflict prevention, conflict resolution, nation building – what does it exemplify if not the principle of entropy?

(Rieff, 2002: 272)

Attempts to account for the changes in the nature of post-Cold War humanitarianism have been numerous (e.g. Duffield, 2001 onwards; Hoffman and Weiss, 2006; Keen, 2007; Fassin and Pandolfi, 2010; Barnett, 2011); however, further theoretical engagement is warranted with a view to critically examining the policies and practices associated with 'new' humanitarianism, their conditions of possibility and their implications. Indeed, the complexity of post-Cold War developments and associated changes in humanitarian action call for an approach that pays close attention to constellations of rationalities and technologies of power, constellations that inform and sustain these changes, including their effects at different levels. This also makes complementary analysis of specific assistance efforts indispensable. In fact, the resultant heterogeneity, both temporal and contextual, would justify the use of the term 'humanitarianism(s)' and suggests drawing on Michel Foucault's work for it is especially well-suited for examining the 'how' of power, including specific regimes of governing. What follows is a discussion of the theoretical and methodological choices and considerations underpinning the analysis undertaken in this book and a reflection on its main themes and arguments.

Examining regimes of governing: biopolitics and governmentality in a broader context

Michel Foucault is well recognised for the significance, originality and productive nature of his work on power (e.g. Moss, 1998; Prado, 2000; Kelly, 2008; Downing, 2008; Richmond, 2010; Saar, 2011). In the last decade, the expanding Foucauldian scholarship has proved the continued relevance and fruitfulness, and reaffirmed the overall importance, of Foucault's thinking on power. Here, the development of a framework for analysing post-Cold War humanitarianism has been informed by the belief that an engagement with Foucault's later thinking on biopolitics and governmentality should take place within a broader theoretical context of his thinking on power. Indeed, it has been suggested that '[o]ne cannot understand Foucault's account of biopolitics ... unless one first addresses Foucault's generic understanding of power' (Dillon, 2010: 63). I not only take this suggestion seriously by using Foucault's thinking on power as a horizon, or a broader context, for the analysis, but also take it further in several important ways: first, by arguing in favour of examining Foucault's account of biopolitics within a broader framework of governmentality (drawing on Dean, 1999; Senellart, 2007; Lemke, 2011; Walters, 2012 and others); second, by distinguishing between substantive and perspectival sides of governmentality (drawing, in particular, on Walters and Haar, 2005; Joseph 2010; Walters 2012) and by using the former to evaluate specific policies and practices, while operationalising the latter to establish a productive way of doing so (informed by Foucault, 1987 and drawing on Dean, 1999; Miller and Rose, 2008; Nadesan, 2008; Collier. 2009; Bröckling, Krasmann and Lemke, 2011; Walters, 2012 and others); and, third, by combining different levels of analysis to better understand a transnational (or, as argued here, globalising) regime of governing (drawing on Dillon, 1995; Dean, 2002; Rose, O'Malley and Valverde, 2006; Rosenow, 2009; Joseph, 2010; Jessop, 2011; Weidner, 2011; Kiersey, 2011; Walters, 2012 and others).

In terms of Foucault's broader thinking on power, the analysis in this book acknowledges that power for Foucault has several key characteristics: impersonality and ubiquity; relationality; decentredness and multidirectionality; strategic nature; productive nature; and coexistence with resistances (as identified by Kelly, 2008). These characteristics are interrelated; thus, since power is not possessed by anyone and not rooted anywhere, it has no centre and permeates the whole social fabric. In Foucault's words, power only exists in power relations: 'power is neither given, nor exchanged, nor recovered, but rather exercised, and … it only exists in action' (Foucault, 1980a: 89). As '[p]ower is co-extensive with the social body' (Foucault, 1980d: 142), it produces multiple effects (Foucault, 1980e), and not just negative ones (Foucault, 1980d). The productive nature of power is emphasised in the following observation:

> it seems to me that the notion of repression is quite inadequate for capturing what is precisely the productive aspect of power…. What makes power hold good, what makes it accepted, is simply the fact that it doesn't only weigh on us as a force that says no, but that it traverses and produces things, it induces pleasure, forms knowledges, produces discourse.
>
> (Foucault, 1980c: 119)

As Chapter 1 shows, awareness of this productive side of power is especially important for our understanding of biopolitics as a life-promoting and 'caring' technology of power, and for accounting for the success of neoliberal governmentality. It is also crucial for appreciating both positive and negative effects of biopolitical governing, something that is also shown to be characteristic of contemporary humanitarianism. Importantly, for Foucault, power relations are never about total domination, and they always presuppose a possibility of resistance; indeed, 'there are no power relations without resistances' (Foucault, 1980d: 142). While the issue of resistance does not take centre-stage in the examination of 'new' humanitarianism in general or of the two localised assistance efforts, it represents a background theme, to which I return in the Conclusions.

In Foucault's work, the relational and decentred nature of power also implies a reassessment of the centrality of the state, although it does not imply that it should be ignored completely. Rather, 'the State, for all the omnipotence of its apparatuses, is far from being able to occupy the whole field of actual power relations' (Foucault, in Smart, 1985: 123–124). The ability to move beyond the state in analysing various regimes of governing will be shown to be crucial for using governmentality as a perspective (Chapter 1) and for analysing transnational regimes of governing (Chapter 2). It should be noted that Foucault's earlier focus was on the so-called 'microphysics of power', as he advocated studying mechanisms of power at the point of their application, where their effects were produced (Foucault, 1980b). However, given that mechanisms of power operate at different levels, from the local to the global, and are inter-related, additional levels of analysis are necessary:

> One must ... conduct an ascending analysis of power, starting, that is, from its infinitesimal mechanisms, which each have their own history, their own trajectory, their own techniques and tactics, and then see how these mechanisms of power have been – and continue to be – invested, colonized, utilized, ... transformed, displaced, extended ... by even more general mechanisms and by forms of global domination.
>
> (Foucault, 1980b: 99)

It was Foucault's theorising on biopower that signalled the move towards analysing the macrophysics of power, and his theorising on governmentality provided even more opportunities for that (Moss, 1998).

One of the difficulties associated with using Foucault's work is that he never developed theories as such. Foucault himself rejected the notion that what he did could be seen as theory production (Hamilton, in Smart, 1988: 9; Brich, 2008), hence my use of the term 'theorising' throughout. In addition, Foucault privileged detail analysis over theory production (Gordon, 1980), which is reflected in his writing, as he produced 'singular works, which were for him experimental pieces of thought, from which he then moves on' (Kelly, 2008: 3). Despite these reservations, it was Foucault's expressed intention that his work should be used to aid particular studies (Kelly, 2008). Using Foucault's work implies using 'theory as a toolkit' in the following way:

> (i) The theory to be constructed is not a system but an instrument, a logic of the specificity of power relations and the struggles around them; (ii) ... investigation can only be carried out step by step on the basis of reflection (which will necessarily be historical in some of its aspects) on given situations.
>
> (Foucault, 1980d: 145)

These insights acquire further specificity within Foucault's genealogical approach, which also invites another, more methodological, contextualisation, which has been crucial for the framework of analysis used in this book. As Lloyd and Thacker (1997: 2) pertinently point out, with Foucault we should not expect a methodology that can be applied in a variety of disciplines, and, in the absence of such a 'ready-made' methodology, we 'must actively and creatively use his work and ideas'. In this respect, it should be noted that genealogy is considered Foucault's 'greatest epistemological import' (Prado, 2000: 11; also Apperley, 1997; Brown, 1998). Foucault famously described genealogy as 'meticulous, and patiently documentary', operating 'on a field of entangled and confused parchments, on documents that have been scratched over and recopied many times' (Foucault, 1991: 76). Genealogy serves as an alternative history, a history 'suspicious of grand narratives and seismic shifts, single causes for historical change and value-laden teleologies of progress' (Downing, 2008: 15). Instead of origins, genealogy is more interested in the conditions of possibility of events and reveals their contingent nature. In this way, our present becomes not a necessary outcome of a progressive linear development, but 'a result of struggles and relations of force and domination' (Mahon, 1992: 112; also Smart, 1985).

Genealogical analysis is interested in the present, and 'Foucault's approach to history is to select a problem rather than a historical period for investigation' (Kendall and Wickham, 1999: 22). What this means is that something that 'appears ... normal or true' is questioned as to 'how it came about in the light of contingency and power' (Vucetic, 2011: 1301). This is one sense in which genealogy is a critique of the present (Gordon, 1980; also Mahon, 1992). The other sense in which genealogy is a critique is that 'it considers it desirable to transgress the limits of the present' (Nilson, 1998: 78). In this way, '[g]enealogy separates out, from the contingency that has made us what we are, the possibility of no longer being, doing, or thinking, what we are, do, and think' (Mahon, 1992: 82).

Genealogy is an effective history, which, unlike traditional history, is focused on events 'in terms of their most unique characteristics, their most acute manifestations' (Foucault, 1987: 231). Effective history is also one that affirms 'knowledge as perspective' (Foucault, 1987: 232). In doing so, effective history appreciates that knowledge 'is grounded in a time and a place', as well as the 'preferences and passions' of the genealogist (Smart, 1985: 57–58). Building on the 'Neitzschean insight ... that the truth cannot be separated from the procedures of its production' (Mahon, 1992: 11), genealogical analysis does not engage in the search for truth, but reveals the discursive conditions and power effects behind the regimes of truth. Therefore, it is not sufficient to focus on the formal elements of discourse, as its co-constitutive relationship with the practices should also be considered (Howarth, 2002). Indeed, genealogical investigations allow us to identify dominant discourses and the practices they engender, along with their position with respect to other discourses and practices, which, in turn, makes it possible to identify and operationalise excluded alternatives (Howarth, 2002).

As far as the use of genealogy is concerned,[1] Vucetic (2011: 1300) draws attention to the 'three Es' of genealogy: episodes, examples and effectiveness. Episodes serve the purpose of breaking down the history of the phenomenon, and each episode is presented through examples, which are based on discourse analysis of documentary evidence. The choice of episodes and examples is governed by logic similar to that behind the selection of cases for a case study (see below). While genealogical accounts are not linear, they still appreciate traces from the past without which there would be no continuities and, therefore, no need to engage in genealogical analysis. Importantly, although Foucault did not provide strict rules for a genealogical inquiry, genealogies are still evidence-based (Vucetic, 2011). Here, the general direction provided by the genealogical approach is used in the context of the chosen theoretical and analytical perspectives. While Chapter 1 further discusses the affinities between governmentality as a perspective and problematisation and genealogy, what need some clarification here are the key considerations informing the way in which these strands of theorising have been operationalised in this book. In approaching a regime of governing, the book argues, it is advisable to appreciate productive nature of the analytics of government (see Foucault, 1987; Dean, 1999; Miller and Rose, 2008), as it allows examining different elements of a regime, along with their relationships and effects. In so doing, a particular attention should be paid to the dominant problematisations and their role in creating the conditions of possibility for and sustaining specific practices. Thus, the analysis of 'new' humanitarianism as a regime of governing underscores, *inter alia*, the significance of particular agendas, such as the coherence agenda or integrated approach to peace, in transforming the ways in which humanitarian crises were to be addressed. In turn, the analysis of the specific assistance efforts shows how the ways in which these particular crises and their consequences were framed informed both the assistance offered or withdrawn, and the construction of those to be assisted. In addressing the assistance practices, in line with the topological analysis (Collier, 2009) and following Dean (2002), Rosenow (2009), Walters (2012) and Death (2013) among others, attention is paid to the combinations and interplays of different technologies of power and their effects. In fact, it is this focus that allows analysing transnational regimes, while appreciating their complexity, which often resists clear-cut categorisations and unitary explanations. Indeed, this is shown to be true in the case of humanitarian governing, especially when the importance of different contexts is fully considered.

Selecting and studying cases: 'new' humanitarianism and specific assistance efforts

Case studies provide an opportunity to take an in-depth, nuanced approach (e.g. Gerring, 2004, 2009; Yin, 2009). Indeed, case studies are always contextual (e.g. Yin, 2009) and are associated with 'holistic analysis' and 'thick' descriptions (Gerring, 2009: 49). Not surprisingly then, Foucault's genealogy is reliant on cases (Vucetic, 2011). Here, the choice of cases in terms of particular assistance efforts was guided by the nature of the phenomena of interest and the chosen theoretical perspective. Another important consideration was the need for cases to be representative, at least in some sense, of a larger group (e.g. Walton, 2005; Wievorka, 2005; Gerring, 2009). Despite the uniqueness and originality of each case, in order for it to count as one, it needs to be a 'case' of something else. In this sense, humanitarianism is both a transnational regime and one of many types of international response to crises, while the assistance effort in Afghanistan is an example of an assistance effort in a conflict environment, and in Belarus – of an assistance effort in a non-conflict environment.

In addition to being representative in a general sense, cases should also be theoretically decisive in some way (Ragin, 2005: 2). Genealogical analysis usually focuses on 'hard/least likely, easy/most likely, maximum variation or anomalous/extreme/deviant/outlying or paradigmatic' cases (Vucetic, 2011:

1301). In this respect, both localised assistance efforts are the least likely cases in the sense that they are very far removed from the context analysed by Foucault. These assistance efforts can also be seen as extreme, with the assistance effort in Afghanistan shaped by a high-profile external intervention, while the one in Belarus represents a very limited response to a forgotten emergency. Finally, the cases chosen can be seen as different as possible, to allow mapping out and analysing very different combinations of various rationalities and technologies of governing, as well as identifying any possible similarities (for obvious reasons, I have not attempted comparing these cases in a conventional way, although a certain degree of implicit comparison has been unavoidable).

Importantly, the issue of cases being representative is also linked to the fact that cases are not merely empirical, and do not exist out there in their unity, waiting to be investigated; rather, cases are better understood as products of the process of 'casing', which implies interplay between a particular theory and empirical evidence (Wievorka, 2005). Thus, one could only talk about 'new' humanitarianism because of the intention to analyse it as a regime of governing; the same applies to particular assistance efforts, whose unity is shaped by the theoretical and analytical frameworks, which also defined the main aspects/elements to be investigated. The fact that the cases chosen are in some way representative, does not invite unlimited generalisation, however. Furthermore, far-reaching generalisations would be contrary to the spirit of any Foucault-inspired inquiry, and especially a genealogical one, which is suspicious of, and questions, grand narratives.

In choosing cases, a distinction between intrinsic and instrumental cases (Stake, 1998) is helpful, with the former being chosen due to an interest in a particular case, while the latter are examined to get an insight into an issue or refine a theory. Here, 'new' humanitarianism and specific assistance efforts serve as both intrinsic and instrumental cases. The fact that case studies are designed for studying situations 'when the boundaries between phenomenon and context are not clearly evident' (Yin, 2009: 18) makes them especially suitable for studying regimes of governing. With theory elaboration at stake, choosing cases that allow for variation in both the unit of analysis and the level of analysis can be particularly effective (Vaughan, 2005; Gerring, 2009). Importantly, as discussed above, governmentality as a perspective also combines macro- and micro-levels of analysis, while a genealogical approach is attentive to local interplays of power, and implies a focus on processes and developments, which requires sustained analysis over a period of time. This, along with the focus on what particular assistance efforts in different contexts can tell about the nature of humanitarian governing, has suggested the use of a complex, embedded case study, with 'new' humanitarianism simultaneously serving as a case and as a context (bigger whole) for the other two, more localised, case studies, with all of them considered over a certain period of time (at least a decade). The time focus was also informed by genealogy as a history of the present, with problems raised by present-day phenomena serving as the starting point of analysis. Thus, for 'new' humanitarianism, the time period under consideration is the post-Cold

War period, from the early 1990s onwards, with the acknowledgment of the post-2001 shifts. The specific time frame for Afghanistan is from 2001 to 2011 (from the start of the US *Operation Enduring Freedom* to the beginning of troop withdrawal); for Belarus – from 2000 to 2011 (from the publication of the 2000 UN OCHA (United Nations Office for the Coordination of Humanitarian Affairs) Report *Chernobyl: a Continuing Catastrophe* to the 25th anniversary of the accident). Overall, the chosen time frame also allowed for a better appreciation of the relationship between the transnational and local in terms of the former creating the conditions of possibility for the latter (e.g. coherence agenda of the 1990s and aid securitisation in the post-2001 Afghanistan; resilience agenda of the early 2000s and 'non-material' assistance effort in Belarus), but also the latter informing the former (e.g. the impact of the Afghanistan experience on practices of aid securitisation and militarisation elsewhere).

In the last two decades, several Foucault-inspired accounts of humanitarian governing have been produced; e.g. Hendrie (1997); most notably, Duffield (2007 onwards), but also Branch (2009), Kelly (2010), Reid (2010) and Ophir (2010) among others. This book builds upon, and engages with, these accounts, but is distinct in the objectives, scope and approach it takes. More specifically, I am as interested in how Foucault's work can inform our understanding of transnational phenomena in general, as in making sense of the changing nature of humanitarian action post-Cold War. While the former preoccupation has been explicated, the latter is in need of some elaboration.

First, as has already been mentioned, in an attempt to grasp the complexity of humanitarian governing, this book engages in its analysis at different levels, and is also interested in the interplay between them.

Second, I am particularly interested in the relationship between sovereignty and biopolitics and in the production of negative biopolitical effects (or biopolitical violences), as well as the role that the expert knowledge plays in this process (professionalisation of humanitarian action as a feature of 'new' humanitarianism is important in this respect, but so is the authority of international expert bodies, as the case study on the Chernobyl-related assistance effort attests). This calls for a focus on the conditions of the possibility for specific regimes of humanitarian governing, which suggests viewing 'new' humanitarianism as a particular historical articulation of humanitarianism. In analysing the conditions of possibility, due attention is paid to the convergences between wider opportunities/constraints and particular rationalities and technologies of governing that have led to significant transformations. Thus, as far as the rise of 'new' humanitarianism is concerned, the book stresses the convergence between the opening created by the end of the Cold War that allowed for the spread of neoliberal governmentality and new, more ambitious, agendas for humanitarian action. In tracing the early evolution of 'new' humanitarianism, the books draws attention to other developments and convergences that led to this regime becoming dominant. With respect to the Chernobyl-related assistance effort in Belarus, a lack of resources has had an impact on the way in which the tensions between biopolitical governing informed by different rationalities (i.e. socialist and neoliberal) have been resolved, while for the post-2001 assistance effort in Afghanistan, both previous history of aid securitisation and a high-profile military intervention bringing with it an abundance of resources have contributed to making possible a wide range of practices of aid militarisation and securitisation. Furthermore, I argue that invisibility (achieved in different ways in different contexts) played a key role in creating conditions of possibility for biopolitical violences that characterise humanitarian governing, which, depending on the context, included containment, endangerment and abandonment of those affected by the humanitarian crisis.

Finally, while a certain degree of generalisation is inevitable when attempting to analyse a transnational regime of governing, it needs to be stressed that I do not suggest that 'new' humanitarianism represents a totality of humanitarian governing, unchallenged and unopposed. Instead, it is argued here that 'new' humanitarianism is a dominant regime of humanitarian governing, a regime that is characterised by its own tensions and contradictions. This clarification is important in terms of accounting for resistances and envisaging alternatives and is equally applicable to the analysis of particular assistance efforts.

Overview of the research process

This book's overall narrative is informed by extensive literature and document analysis, semi-structured expert interviews, observations and field visits. The analysis builds upon and bridges many areas of scholarship, including the ever-expanding body of work on humanitarianism, the growing number of studies informed by Foucault's theorising on biopower, biopolitics and governmentality, and the current literature on the conflict-related assistance effort in Afghanistan. Furthermore, the analysis of the two specific assistance efforts has covered a significant amount of 'grey' literature produced by specific humanitarian agencies. This literature has aided mapping out the positions of various actors, identifying issues of relevance, and provided necessary background information for expert interviews. The need to engage with grey literature has also been informed by the nature of the overall theoretical and methodological approach, with its focus on conflicting problematisations.

The analysis of the particular assistance efforts has also required insight into their dynamics that can only be obtained by interviewing those directly involved in the assistance interventions in question. The majority of the interviews have been expert interviews (four interviews with Chernobyl clean-up workers, or 'liquidators', have been conducted in the form of personal history). Such an approach does not imply a deliberate disregard for the opinions and perceptions of the intended aid beneficiaries; rather the choice of the respondents was informed by the nature of inquiry with its focus not on the public perceptions of assistance, but on the rationalities and technologies of governing used in assistance interventions. In choosing respondents with respect to each of the assistance efforts, the following categories have been considered for inclusion: (1) main humanitarian 'players'; (2) intergovernmental and non-governmental organisations; (3) single- and multi-mandate organisations (as well as a 'Dunantist'[2] – type organisation); and (4) where possible, an emergency-specific organisation. The interviews have been predominantly semi-structured in format and active in nature, i.e. they have been treated as a site of meaning production, with the aim not to elicit the preformed and pure meaning possessed by interviewees, but to co-construct the meaning during the interview (see Holstein and Gubrium, 2004). The overall approach has been informed by constant critical reflexivity and transparency regarding the research project and the way in which it is to be conducted (see Kvale, 1996).

Most of the expert interviews on Chernobyl-related assistance effort were conducted over the three visits to Belarus in April 2008, May–June 2009 and December 2009–January 2010. The last of these trips also included two visits to the areas affected by the accident, one of which was a visit to the exclusion zone in Gomel region, now occupied by the Polessky State Radiological and Ecological Reserve, where we saw the resettled village of Babchin. This visit allowed for a much better understanding of the impact of the accident on a major agricultural area and an area of outstanding natural beauty, of the Reserve's role and activities, and of the drama of people evacuated from their homes with no opportunity of return. A close engagement with the assistance effort in Afghanistan began on 16 December 2009 at the Panel discussion *Humanitarian assistance in Afghanistan: Where to now?*, organised by the British Agencies in Afghanistan Group (BAAG) in co-operation with the Canadian High Commissioner in London. Representatives of agencies directly involved in the assistance effort, along with representatives of the Humanitarian Policy Group of the Overseas Development Institute (ODI) and of the UK Department for International Development (DFID), took part in the discussion. The event has proved to be incredibly useful in terms of understanding the humanitarian situation in the country and the dynamics of the assistance effort, mapping out the positions of various actors, and commencing the recruitment of experts for interviews, the majority of which were conducted over the 2009–2010 period.

Organisation of this book

Chapter 1 is the main theoretical chapter that establishes the theoretical and analytical framework of analysis. It introduces and engages with Foucault's theorising on biopower and biopolitics and places it into a wider frame of governmentality, with the special focus on liberal and neoliberal governmentalities. It also provides a critical overview of biopolitics and governmentality studies with a view to establishing productive ways of operationalising Foucault's conceptual and methodological tools for the analysis of the international. In particular, the chapter demonstrates that Foucault's theorising on biopolitics and governmentality can inform analysis of transnational regimes of governing.

Chapter 2 provides an analysis of 'new' humanitarianism as a dominant regime of humanitarian governing, including its conditions of possibility, i.e. the crucial convergences between post-Cold War developments in the international environment and the rise of the new agendas for humanitarian action. It also uses the analytics of government to examine the processes of institutionalisation of this regime and knowledges, technologies and divides on which it is reliant.

Chapters 3 and 4 focus on the analysis of the specific assistance efforts. Chapter 3 critically examines the post-2001 conflict-related assistance effort in Afghanistan (with the focus on aid securitisation and militarisation) in terms of the dominant problematisations and knowledges informing them; strategies and technologies of governing used in the assistance interventions (broadly conceived); and the ways in which people in need of assistance were constructed. The chapter argues that, in the post-2001 Afghanistan, assistance provision has been instrumentalised and to a significant extent incorporated into the war effort, which has combined biopolitical concerns with sovereign violence. In particular, the assistance effort has been characterised by the displacement of the humanitarian imperative with imperatives informed by counter-terrorism or counter-insurgency and stabilisation, and by the use of the biopolitical rhetoric of care and protection to justify the war effort, obscure civilian casualties, and endangerment and abandonment of those in need.

Chapter 4 critically examines the post-2000 Chernobyl-related assistance effort in Belarus (with the focus on health consequences of the accident). In particular, the chapter shows that the dominant problematisations of the accident and its health consequences have created the conditions of invisibility for those affected and have informed the assistance effort characterised by such strategies as neoliberal responsibilisation and mentality change aimed at transforming individuals and communities living with the aftermath of the accident, who have been constructed as dependent, passive and irresponsible victims, into self-reliant, active and entrepreneurial survivors.

The central argument advanced in this book is that 'new' humanitarianism represents a dominant regime of humanitarian governing informed by globalising neoliberalism and is reliant on a complex set of biopolitical, disciplinary and sovereign technologies. While the purposes of humanitarian governing are specific to particular contexts, its promise of care is more often than not accompanied by sovereign and/or biopolitical violences, something that we need a better appreciation of if we are to be able to counter them.

The Conclusions, in turn, go beyond summarising the key elements of the analysis to engage the issue of resistance to the dominant policies and practices of humanitarian governing and to invite a further discussion about possible alternatives.

Notes

1 See also Walters (2012) and Koopman (2013).
2 Named after Henry Dunant, the founder of the International Committee of the Red Cross (ICRC), and defined as an organisation with traditional, humanitarian assistance-only, mandate that follows the ICRC's set of principles (as a minimum, neutrality and independence).

12   *Introduction*

References

Apperley, A. 1997. Foucault and the problem of method. *In*: M. Lloyd and A. Thacker (eds). *The impact of Michel Foucault on the social sciences and humanities*. Basingstoke: Macmillan, pp. 10–28.

Barnett, M. 2011. *Empire of humanity: a history of humanitarianism*. Ithaca: Cornell University Press.

Branch, A. 2009. Humanitarianism, violence, and the camp in Northern Uganda. *Civil Wars*, **11**(4): 477–501.

Brich, C. 2008. Review. Brent Pickett. On the use and abuse of Foucault for politics. *Foucault Studies*, **5**: 105–107.

Bröckling, U., S. Krasmann and T. Lemke. 2011. From Foucault's lectures at the *Collège de France* to studies of governmentality: an introduction. *In*: U. Bröckling, S. Krasmann and T. Lemke (eds). *Governmentality: current issues and future challenges*. London: Routledge, pp. 1–33.

Brown, W. 1998. Genealogical politics. *In*: J. Moss (ed.). *The later Foucault*. London: SAGE, pp. 33–49.

Collier, S.J. 2009. Topologies of power: Foucault's analysis of political government beyond 'governmentality'. *Theory, Culture & Society*, **26**(6): 78–108.

Collinson, S. and S. Elhawary. 2012. *Humanitarian space: a review of trends and issues* [online]. [Accessed 7 June 2014]. www.odi.org.uk/sites/odi.org.uk/files/odi-assets/publications-opinion-files/7643.pdf.

Dean, M. 1999. *Governmentality: power and rule in modern society*. London: SAGE.

Dean, M. 2002. Powers of life and death beyond governmentality. *Journal for Cultural Research*, **6**(1): 119–138.

Death, C. 2013. Governmentality at the limit of the international: African politics and Foucauldian theory. *Review of International Studies*, **39**(3): 763–787.

Delorenzi, S. 1999. *Contending with the impasse in international humanitarian action: ICRC policy since the end of the Cold War*. Geneva: ICRC.

Dillon, M. 1995. Sovereignty and governmentality: from the problematic of the 'New World Order' to the ethical problematic of the world order. *Alternatives: Global, Local, Political*, **20**(3), pp. 323–368.

Dillon, M. 2010. Biopolitics of security. *In*: J.P. Burgess (ed.). *The Routledge handbook of security studies*. London: Routledge, pp. 61–71.

Downing, L. 2008. *The Cambridge introduction to Michel Foucault*. Cambridge: Cambridge University Press.

Duffield, M. 2001. *Global governance and the new wars: the merging of development and security*. London: Zed Books.

Duffield, M. 2007. *Development, security and the unending war: governing the world of peoples*. Cambridge: Polity Press.

Duffield, M. 2008. Global civil war: the non-insured, international containment and post-interventionary society. *Journal of Refugee Studies*, **21**(2): 145–165.

Duffield, M. 2010. The liberal way of development and the development-security impasse: exploring the global life-chance divide. *Security Dialogue*, **41**(1): 53–76.

Fassin, D. and M. Pandolfi (eds). 2010. *Contemporary states of emergency: the politics of military and humanitarian interventions*. Brooklyn, NY: Zone Books.

Foucault, M. 1980a. Two lectures. Lecture one: 7 January 1976. *In*: C. Gordon (ed.). *Power/knowledge: selected interviews and other writings 1972–1977. Michel Foucault*. Harvester Press Limited, pp. 78–92.

Foucault, M. 1980b. Two lectures. Lecture two: 14 January 1976. *In*: C. Gordon (ed.). *Power/knowledge: selected interviews and other writings 1972–1977. Michel Foucault.* Harvester Press Limited, pp. 92–108.

Foucault, M. 1980c. Truth and power. Interview with Alessandro Fontana and Pasquale Pasquino. *In*: C. Gordon (ed.). *Power/knowledge: selected interviews and other writings 1972–1977. Michel Foucault.* Harvester Press Limited, pp. 109–133.

Foucault, M. 1980d. Power and strategies. Interview with the editorial collective of *Les Révoltes Logiques*. *In*: C. Gordon (ed.). *Power/knowledge: selected interviews and other writings 1972–1977. Michel Foucault.* Harvester Press Limited, pp. 134–145.

Foucault, M. 1987. Nietzsche, genealogy, history. *In*: M.T. Gibbons (ed.). *Interpreting politics*. Oxford: Basil Blackwell, pp. 221–240.

Foucault, M. 1988. Practicing Criticism, or 'Is it really important to think?' May 30–31, 1981. Didier Eribon interview. *In*: L. Kritzman (ed.). *Foucault, Politics, Philosophy, Culture*. London: Routledge.

Foucault, M. 1991. Governmentality. *In*: G. Burchell, C. Gordon and P. Miller (eds). *The Foucault effect: studies in governmentality*. Chicago: University of Chicago Press, pp. 87–104.

Gerring, J. 2004. What is a case study and what is it good for? *American Political Science Review*, **98**(2): 341–354.

Gerring, J. 2009. *Case study research: principles and practices*. New York: Cambridge University Press.

Gordon, C. 1980. Afterword. *In*: C. Gordon (ed.). *Power/knowledge: selected interviews and other writings 1972–1977. Michel Foucault.* Harvester Press Limited, pp. 229–259.

Hendrie, B. 1997. Knowledge and power: a critique of an international relief operation. *Disasters*, **21**(1): 57–76.

Hoffman, P.J and T.G. Weiss. 2006. *Sword and salve: new wars and humanitarians crises*. Maryland: Rowman and Littlefield.

Holstein, J.A. and J.F. Gubrium. 2004. The active interview. *In*: D. Siverman (ed.). *Qualitative research: theory, method and practice*. London: SAGE, pp. 140–161.

Howarth, D. 2002. An archaeology of political discourse? Evaluating Michel Foucault's explanation and critique of ideology. *Political Studies*, **50**: 117–135.

Jessop, B. 2011. Constituting another Foucault's effect: Foucault on states and statecraft. In: U. Bröckling, S.

Joseph, J. 2010. What can governmentality do for IR? *International Political Sociology*, **4**(2): 202–205.

Kahn, C. and A. Cunningham. 2013. Introduction to the issue of state sovereignty and humanitarian action. *Disasters*, **37**(S2): S139–150.

Keen, D.J. 2007. *Complex emergencies.* Cambridge: Polity Press.

Kelly, M.G.E. 2008. *The political philosophy of Michel Foucault*. London: Routledge.

Kelly, M.G.E. 2010. International biopolitics: Foucault, globalisation and imperialism. *Theoria*, **57**(123): 1–26.

Kendall, G. and G.M. Wickham. 1998. *Using Foucault's methods*. London: SAGE.

Kiersey, N.J. 2011. Neoliberal political economy and the subjectivity of crisis: why governmentality is not hollow. *In*: N.J. Kiersey and D. Stokes (eds). *Foucault and International Relation: new critical engagements*. Abingdon: Routledge, pp. 1–24.

Koopman, C. 2013. *Genealogy as critique: Foucault and the problems of modernity*. Bloomington, IN: Indiana University Press.

Krasmann, S. and T. Lemke (eds). *Governmentality: current issues and future challenges*. London: Routledge, pp. 56–73.

14   *Introduction*

Kvale, S. 1996. *InterViews: an introduction to qualitative research interviewing*. London: SAGE.

Lemke, T. 2011. *Biopolitics: an advanced introduction*. Albany: New York University Press.

Lloyd, M. and A. Thacker. 1997. Introduction: strategies of transgression. *In*: M. Lloyd and A. Thacker (eds). *The impact of Michel Foucault on the social sciences and humanities*. Basingstoke: Macmillan, pp. 1–9.

Macrae, J. 2001. *Aiding recovery?: The crisis of aid in chronic political emergencies*. London: Zed Books.

Macrae, J. (ed.). 2002. *The new humanitarianisms: a review of trends in global humanitarian action*. HPG Report 11. London: Overseas Development Institute.

Macrae, J. and N. Leader. 2000. *Shifting sands: the theory and practice of 'coherence' between political and humanitarian responses to complex political emergencies*. HPG Report 8. London: Overseas Development Institute.

Mahon, M. 1992. *Foucault's Neitzchean genealogy: truth, power and the subject*. Albany: State University of New York Press.

May, T. 2005. Foucault now? *Foucault Studies*, **3**: 65–76.

Miller, P. and N. Rose. 2008. *Governing the present: administering economic, social and personal life*. Cambridge: Polity Press.

Mills, K. 2005. Neo-humanitarianism: the role of international humanitarian norms and organisations in contemporary conflict. *Global Governance*, **11**: 161–183.

Moss, J. 1998. Introduction: the later Foucault. In: J. Moss (ed.). *The later Foucault*. London: SAGE, pp. 1–17.

Nadesan, M.H. 2008. *Governmentality, biopower, and everyday life*. London: Routledge.

Nilson, H. 1998. *Michel Foucault and the games of truth*. Basingstoke: Macmillan.

Ophir, A. 2010. The politics of catastrophization: emergency and exception. *In*: D. Fassin and M. Pandolfi (eds). *Contemporary states of emergency: the politics of military and humanitarian intervention*. New York: Zone Books, pp. 59–88.

Prado, C.G. 2000. *Starting with Foucault: an introduction to genealogy*. Oxford: Westview Press.

Ragin, C.C. 2005. Introduction: cases of 'What is a case?' *In*: C.C. Ragin and H.S. Becker (eds). *What is a case? Exploring the foundations of social inquiry*. New York: Cambridge University Press, pp. 1–17.

Reid, J. 2010. The biopoliticization of humanitarianism: from saving bare life to securing the biohuman in the post-interventionary societies. *Journal of Intervention and Statebuilding*, **4**(4): 391–411.

Richmond, O.P. 2010. Foucault and the paradox of peace-as-governance versus everyday agency. *International Political Sociology*, **4**(2): 199–202.

Rieff, D. 2002. *A bed for the night: humanitarianism in crisis*. London: Vintage.

Rose, N., O'Malley, P. and M. Valverde. 2006. Governmentality. *Annual Review of Law & Social Sciences*, **2**: 83–104.

Rosenow, D. 2009. Decentring global power: the merits of a Foucauldian approach to International Relations. *Global Society*, **23**(4): 497–517.

Saar, M. 2011. Relocating the modern state: governmentality and the history of political ideas. *In*: U. Bröckling, S. Krasmann and T. Lemke (eds). *Governmentality: current issues and future challenges*. London: Routledge, pp. 34–55.

Senellart, M. 2007. Course context. *In*: M. Foucault. *Security, territory, population. Lectures at the Collége de France, 1977–78*. Basingstoke: Palgrave Macmillan, pp. 369–401.

Smart, B. 1985. *Michel Foucault*. London: Routledge.

Smyser, W.R. 2003. *The humanitarian conscience: caring for others in the age of terror.* Basingstoke: Palgrave Macmillan.

Stake, R.E. 1998. Case studies. *In*: N.K. Denzin and Y.S. Lincoln (eds). *Strategies of qualitative inquiry*. London: SAGE, pp. 86–109.

UN OCHA (United Nations Office for the Coordination of Humanitarian Assistance). 2000. *Chernobyl: a continuing catastrophe* [online]. [Accessed 15 March 2008]. www. reliefweb.int/ocha_ol/programs/response/cherno/qms.pdf.

Vaughan, D. 2005. Theory elaboration: the heuristics of case analysis. *In*: C.C. Ragin and H.S. Becker (eds). *What is a case? Exploring the foundations of social inquiry*. New York: Cambridge University Press, pp. 173–202.

Vucetic, S. 2011. Genealogy as a research tool in International Relations. *Review of International Studies*, **37**: 1295–1312.

Walker, P. and D. Maxwell. 2009. *Shaping the humanitarian world*. London: Routledge.

Walters, W. and J. H. Haahr. 2005. *Governmentality and political studies. European Political Science*, **4**: 288–300.

Walters, W. 2012. *Governmentality: critical encounters*. London: Routledge.

Walton, J. 2005. Making the theoretical case. *In*: C.C. Ragin and H.S. Becker (eds). *What is a case? Exploring the foundations of social inquiry*. New York: Cambridge University Press, pp. 121–137.

Weidner, J.R. 2011. Governmentality, capitalism, and subjectivity. *In*: N.J. Kiersey and D. Stokes (eds). *Foucault and International Relation: new critical engagements*. Abingdon: Routledge, pp. 25–49.

West, K. 2001. *Agents of altruism: the expansion of humanitarian NGOs in Rwanda and Afghanistan*. Aldershot: Ashgate.

Wievorka, M. 2005. Case studies: history or sociology? *In*: C.C. Ragin and H.S. Becker (eds). *What is a case? Exploring the foundations of social inquiry*. New York: Cambridge University Press, pp. 159–172.

Yin, R.K. 2009. *Case study research: design and methods*. London: SAGE.

1 'Working with Foucault after Foucault'[1]

Biopolitics, governmentality and the international

> A whole series of objects were made visible for possible forms of knowledge on the basis of the constitution of the population as the correlative of techniques of power. In turn, because these forms of knowledge constantly carve out new objects, the population could be formed, continue, and remain as the privileged correlate of modern mechanisms of power.
>
> (Foucault, 2007: 79)

> The debate over how Foucault's work is best used ... is entangled with a series of debates over how his work is best interpreted.
>
> (Pickett, 2005: 1)

Introduction

In the last two decades, Michel Foucault's theorising on biopolitics and governmentality has been very influential in many social science disciplines. The proliferation of biopolitics and governmentality studies has generated many debates and even disagreements about how Foucault's original ideas can/should be interpreted and used. In this book, Foucault's theorising on biopolitics and governmentality, firmly positioned within his broader thinking on power, informs the analysis of humanitarian governing at different levels. Accordingly, this chapter is intended to establish the theoretical framework for this analysis. The ever-expanding field of biopolitics and governmentality studies, and a lack of consensus on a number of key issues, suggest that there is significant value in going back to and re-reading Foucault's own work, as well as in examining the secondary scholarship.

As far as the concept of biopolitics is concerned, Esposito (2008: 13) argues that Foucault's redefinition[2] of the concept 'has opened a completely new phase in contemporary thought'. Foucault's original account, and its readings by Agamben (1998), Hardt and Negri (2000), and, most recently, by Esposito (2008), have led to multiple accounts of biopolitical governing.

While considering Foucault's account of biopower and biopolitics, this chapter emphasises its appreciation of the differences between sovereignty and biopower (discipline and biopolitics) and of the complex nature of biopolitics (as having both positive and negative potential). The relationship between sovereignty and biopolitics is also addressed, especially because it is important for elucidating the central paradox of biopolitics, i.e. how a life-preserving and life-promoting power can turn lethal, and because it has been argued (e.g. Agamben, 1998; Esposito, 2008) that this relationship is undertheorised in Foucault. His reconceptualisation of racism is shown to be important for this discussion. Agamben's and Esposito's readings of Foucault are briefly engaged in order to emphasise some important differences between their accounts and that of Foucault, as well as elucidating some crucial aspects of Foucault's approach.

Foucault considered biopolitics in a wider framework of governmentality, and his account of governmentality can primarily be found in *Security, Territory, Population* and *The Birth of Biopolitics*. He did not use the term *governmentality* consistently and it appears to have several different meanings (e.g. Walters, 2012). Here, an important part of the discussion is focused on Foucault's account of liberal and neoliberal governmentalities as specific rationalities of governing.

The third section of the chapter is devoted to an exploration of the ways in which Foucault's theorising on biopolitics and governmentality has been used for studying the international (global) domain. The purpose of this exercise is three-fold: first, to provide an overview and critically engage with a broad range of studies; second, to identify important substantive insights of relevance; and, third, to establish the most productive ways of operationalising Foucault's theorising with respect to international concerns. A critical overview of the international biopolitics and governmentality studies provides evidence in support of the contention that Foucault-inspired investigations have been boundary-expanding, in both methodological and empirical terms (e.g. Richmond, 2010; also Pasha, 2010; Walters, 2012; Death, 2013; Zanotti, 2013). On the basis of this, I argue in favour of simultaneously applying the two strands of Foucault's theorising, and positioning them within his broader thinking on power, as well as in favour of empirical investigations.

Foucault on biopower and biopolitics

In *The History of Sexuality*, Foucault famously argued that, since the classical age, power has undergone a profound transformation, where 'the right to take life or let live' was replaced by the right 'to foster life or disallow it to the point of death' (Foucault, 1998: 138). In other words, the sovereign power, capable of inflicting death, was replaced by a new power, taking care over life, with death becoming its limit. Equally important was his clarification, made in *Society Must Be Defended*, that it is not that

> sovereignty's old right – to take life or let live – was replaced, but it came to be complemented by a new right which does not erase the old right but which does penetrate it, permeate it.... It is the power to 'make' live and 'let' die.

> (Foucault, 2003: 241)

This clarification means that sovereignty was not replaced by biopower, nor did the right to kill disappear, having been replaced by the right to make live. Biopower evolved in two basic forms: discipline, centred on the individual body as a machine, associated with the emergence of such institutions as medicine, education, and punishment; and control, focused on the population (birth, morbidity and mortality rates, life expectancy and longevity, etc.) (Foucault, 1998). Importantly, 'unlike discipline, which is addressed to bodies, the new nondisciplinary power is applied ... to man-as-living-being; [and] ultimately, ... to man-as-species' (Foucault, 2003: 242). Unlike discipline, or anatomo-politics of the human body, which is individualising, biopolitics is massifying (Foucault, 2003: 243). Again, it is important to emphasise that, although it developed at a later stage, biopolitics did not replace discipline, and both remained intimately linked, being 'the two poles around which the organisation of power over life was deployed' (Foucault, 1998: 139).

The main differences between discipline and biopolitics are in the level and scale of operation, as well as in the mechanisms deployed (Foucault, 2003: 242). The concept of population is key to understanding biopolitics as a specific technology of power. According to Dean (1999), three main elements of the concept of population should be considered. The first has to do with a different concept of the governed, as we are not talking about 'subjects bound in territory who are obliged to submit to their sovereign', but rather of the 'members of population' (Dean, 1999: 107; see also Foucault, 2008c: 161). Indeed, Foucault stressed that, with biopolitics, there was a move away from understanding humans as humankind to understanding them as human-species (Foucault, 2007: 75). The second characteristic of a population is that it represents an entity defined in its relation to processes which can be known; for instance, a birth rate, a life-expectancy or a mortality rate (Foucault, 2008c). Indeed, according to Blencowe (2012: 4), 'the "bio" of "biopolitics" ... refers to "trans-organic" serial phenomena that take place at the level of the population'. The knowledge of the population is derived from techniques of observation, including statistics, and numerous institutions utilise this knowledge with a view to regulating a population. In other words, biopolitics accesses the population through calculative techniques that make visible regularities that can only exist at the level of population. Finally, given that a population is a collective entity, the knowledge of it is 'irreducible to the knowledge that any of its members have of themselves' (Dean, 1999: 107) and also irreducible to the knowledge about each of its members. As Lemke (2007: 4) explains:

> Foucault's concept of biopolitics assumes the dissociation and abstraction of life from its concrete physical bearers.... This procedure makes it possible to define norms, establish standards, and determine average values. As a result 'life' has become an independent, objective and measurable factor and a collective reality.

It follows, he suggests, that biopolitics is reliant on the knowledges generated by such disciplines as biology, demography and epidemiology, which make analysis of life processes, and therefore, governing, possible. In this respect, Dillon (2005: 38) stressed that Foucault's account of biopolitics is 'historico-epistemological', for which 'a complex epistemological transformation in the interpretation and scientific study of life' is of crucial importance. Drawing on Foucault but moving beyond him, Dillon also alerted us to the flexible, adaptable and constantly changing nature of biopolitics, as it follows changes and adaptations of populations, as well as changes in life sciences (Dillon, 2005, 2008; Dillon and Lobo-Guerrero, 2008).

Importantly, mechanisms of biopolitics, unlike those of discipline, are not aimed at modifying individuals, but rather at establishing equilibrium, maintaining an average and compensating for variations at the level of population. These are security mechanisms 'installed around the random element inherent in a population of living beings so as to optimise a state of life' (Foucault, 2003: 246). When elaborating the differences between disciplinary mechanisms and those of security, Foucault suggested that, first, while '[d]iscipline is essentially centripetal' in that it 'concentrates, focuses, and encloses', 'security apparatuses … are centrifugal' in that they constantly expand and integrate new elements. Second, while 'discipline … regulates everything' and 'allows nothing to escape', 'security … lets things happen' (Foucault, 2007: 44–45). Finally, like legal systems, discipline operates through permission and prohibition, but it focuses on prescribing what must be done at every moment. Security, on the other hand, tries to grasp things in their 'naturalness', in their effective reality and make them function (Foucault, 2007: 44–47). While sovereignty relies on law for its institution, both discipline and biopolitics are reliant on norms. However, these norms are established and function in a different way: with discipline, a norm is a given, a starting point, while with biopolitics the norm emerges as an 'interplay of different normalities' (Foucault, 2007: 63), which is at the heart of the process of normalisation. The power acting through the norm is an administrative power, that of 'the experts and interpreters of life' (Foucault, in Ojakangas, 2005: 17), and it is this power that will be shown to characterise the 'new' humanitarianism as a regime of governing.

For Foucault, the 'reality' or 'naturalness' of the population suggests that it 'is not a datum', but rather 'it is dependent on a series of variables' (Foucault, 2007: 70), produced through complex interactions with its milieu. The notion of milieu came to biology via physics and accounted for 'action at a distance', that is 'the medium of an action and the element in which it circulates' (Foucault, 2007: 20–21). As such, the milieu combines both natural and artificial givens to produce effects on those living in it. The significance of this notion[3] has to do with the appreciation that 'life is not a given but depends on conditions of existence within and beyond life processes' (Lemke, 2014: 11), as well as with the fact that security mechanisms make milieu their focal point of application by establishing 'a hold on things that seem far removed from the population, but which, through calculation, analysis, and reflection, … can really have an effect on it' (Foucault, 2007: 72). This points to the ability of security mechanisms to govern indirectly and at a distance. Given that natural processes require a degree of freedom in order to function, freedom of circulation is indispensable for security. Security requires freedom to operate, and, therefore – one of the most provocative of Foucault's ideas – 'freedom is nothing else but the correlative of the deployment of apparatuses of security' (Foucault, 2007: 48). Consequently, 'the security problematic of circulation' (Dillon and Lobo-Guerrero, 2008: 280) revolves around 'organizing circulation, eliminating its dangerous elements, making a division between good and bad circulation, and maximizing the good circulation by diminishing the bad' (Foucault, 2007: 18). This security problematic of circulation is a crucial element of multiple regimes of governing the international, including that of humanitarian governing.

Given that, for Foucault, neither discipline replaces sovereignty, nor biopolitics replaces discipline, population management 'makes the problem of the foundation of sovereignty even more acute', while also making discipline 'more important and more valued' (Foucault, 2007: 107) than ever before. As a result of them operating alongside each other, there exists 'a ... mutable and complex manifold in which different formations of power are continuously at play in different ways throughout different aspects and different formulations of life' (Dillon and Neal, 2008: 13). This, however, does not sufficiently explain the relationship between sovereignty and biopower or answer the question – given that the basic function of biopolitics is 'to improve life, to prolong its duration, to improve its chances, to avoid accidents, and to compensate for failings' – how can a power like that kill? (Foucault, 2003: 254). This question exposes what may seem a paradox of biopolitics – that the care of life can become the administration of death (Enoch, 2004: 54), or that 'the reverse side of biopolitics is thanatopolitics' (Foucault, 2000b: 416). For Foucault, the reclaiming of the death function is operationalised through racism, whereby racism functions as 'a way of introducing a break into the domain of life that is under power's control: the break between what must live and what must die' (Foucault, 2003: 254). It is, in essence, a way of 'separating out the groups that exist within a population' (Foucault, 2003: 255). Another important function of racism is the establishment of a positive relation of the type: '[t]he very fact that you let more die will allow you to live more'. While it is a familiar relationship of war, Foucault (2003: 255) argues that it functions in a new way:

> The fact that the other dies does not mean simply that I live in the sense that his death guarantees my safety; the death of the other, the death of the bad race, of the inferior race ... is something that will make life in general healthier ... and purer.

In this biological relationship the enemies who need to be eliminated are threats, either external or internal, to the population; and racism is the precondition for exercising the right to kill (Foucault, 2003: 256). And it is race war that can be 'waged on behalf of the existence of everyone', where 'entire populations [can be] mobilised for the purpose of wholesale slaughter in the name of necessity' (Foucault, 1998: 137).

With racism, even death is 'experienced as a maximisation of life, an aug-mentation of capacity and experience' (Blencowe, 2012: 96). However, 'killing' in a biopolitical context does not have to be limited to murder as such – it can be anything from exposing someone to death, to political death, expulsion, aban-donment and other types of social death. What is crucial in this respect is sub-jecting the population to constant processes of division and separation with a view to identifying those elements (groups) that can have positive or negative effect on the life of the population as a whole, promoting and supporting the former and preventing, containing or eliminating the latter (Dean, 1999), or, indeed, allowing them to die. This suggests that, like sovereignty, biopolitics is 'also a politics of life and death' and that '[w]hat differentiates biopolitics from sovereign politics is a change of correlation of life and death, not some escape from the inevitability of that correlation' (Dillon, 2008: 167–168).

Dissatisfaction with the perceived lack of elaboration of the relationship between sovereignty and biopolitics in Foucault's work has led to a number of attempts to 'correct' and/or 'complete' his account, most prominently by Agamben (e.g. 1998, 2002) and Esposito (2008). Neither contribution is dis-cussed here in detail,[4] as they do not serve as the basis for the analysis; instead, I will make just a few points emphasising the differences between these later accounts and that of Foucault. Thus, Agamben focuses on what Foucault argu-ably did not fully emphasise – 'a persistent and illimitable sovereign power dealing death' (Agamben, 1998: 9). Unlike Foucault, who treated sovereign power and biopower as distinct, Agamben considers them to be two sides of the same coin. For him, 'the production of a biopolitical body is the original activity of sovereign power' (Agamben, 1998: 6). So, if for Foucault the entry of biolog-ical life into politics represent a historical transformation, for Agamben the pol-itics are originally biopolitics (Vaughan-Williams, 2009: 22). For Agamben, sovereignty operates by suspending the law and creating a zone of indistinction between outside and inside, where an expendable form of life – 'bare life' – is produced. Agamben's revelation of bare life as the nexus between sovereignty and biopolitics leads to the claim that it is the camp that represents 'the funda-mental biopolitical paradigm of the West' (Agamben, 1998: 181) and to the warning about similarities between democracies and totalitarian states. Notwith-standing the importance of his intervention, it does suffer from a number of issues, the central being a collapsed distinction between sovereign power and biopower, which effectively turns all biopolitics into thanatopolitics (in an attempt to account for the death function in biopolitics, he seems to have gone too far, and, having prioritised sovereignty over biopolitics as the production site of the biopolitical body destined to be killed without being sacrificed, he deprives biopolitics of any distinctive logic of its own).

Like Agamben, Esposito is interested in interrogating the paradox of biopoli-tics, which, he believes, Foucault never fully explained, i.e. how can biopolitics turn into thanatopolitics. To do so, like Agamben, Esposito invites us to reinter-pret the relationship between biopolitics and sovereignty and attempts to restore 'the missing link of Foucault's argumentation' (Esposito, 2008: 9). He argues that only when it is linked to immunity and immunitary mechanisms does bio-politics reveal its modern genesis: 'sovereignty isn't before or after biopolitics, but cuts across the entire horizon, furnishing the most powerful response to the modern problem of self-preservation of life' (Esposito, 2008: 57). This suggests that, rather like for Agamben, sovereignty for Esposito is essentially biopolitical. He believes that it is in the immunitary paradigm that both constitutive elements of biopolitics, life and politics, emerge as an indivisible whole, as 'immunity is the power to preserve life', and politics, from this perspective, 'is nothing other than ... the instrument for keeping life alive' (Esposito, 2008: 46). Furthermore, the category of immunisation accommodates both poles of biopolitics – produc-tive and lethal – in the following way:

> immunisation is a negative [form] of the protection of life. It saves, insures, and preserves the organism, either individual or collective, to which it per-tains, but it does not do so directly, immediately, or frontally; on the con-trary, it subjects the organism to a condition that simultaneously negates or reduces its power to expand.
>
> (Esposito, 2008: 46)

Overall, while the immunisation paradigm does provide new insights regarding the nature of biopolitics and its relationship with sovereignty (parallels between Esposito's conceptualisation of immunity and Foucault's conceptualisation of racism are especially illuminating), situating biopolitics at a broader horizon of immunity deprives it of its specificity as a distinct technology of power and prevents us from appreciating multiple differences between its various manifestations.

Contrary to the above accounts, Foucault emphasised the transformation brought about by the rise of biopower, something that becomes even more pro-nounced when considered within a broader context of governmentality. In par-ticular, Foucault outlined important changes in terms of the overall orientation of power, as reflected in the reversal associated with biopower and its focus on care, with death becoming its limit 'to be hidden away' (Foucault, 2003: 247) and with any taking of life justified by overall preservation or improvement of it. Furthermore, he stressed the role of life sciences in carving out a new domain of governing – that of population – and the distinct mechanisms through which it is governed. Put differently, the rise of biopower takes place at a particular point in time, and this idea is central to Foucault's historico-genealogical account. As Blencowe (2012: 110) reiterates, '[t]he biological life that enters politics in the nineteenth century ... could not have been in play even a hundred years before'. Following Foucault, it can be argued that, before biopower, sovereignty found its legitimacy in force, not care. Given the limited knowledge of the body, access to it was mediated through the construct of a legal subject. One of the few occa-sions on which direct access was possible was during an execution; in other words, the power had a brief, but total and direct, hold over life only in the act of ending it. This is not to suggest, however, that sovereignty was nothing but murderous; rather I wish to highlight the difficulty power had accessing the living body. The ability of biopower, and of biopolitics in particular, to deliver its promise of care, which serves as a new basis of legitimacy, depends on knowing life. Such knowledge allows unmediated and more varied (albeit partial at any particular point) access to an individual or collective living body. Crucially, then, in Foucault's interpretation of what counts as life is simultaneously more complex and historically contingent.

At the same time, Foucault's double correction regarding the replacement of sovereignty with biopower and of discipline with biopolitics was very important, as it reinforced the idea of them working simultaneously, impacting on one another. Foucault also recognised the dangers resulting from combinations of different power technologies, terming some of such combinations a 'demonic project' (Foucault, in Prozorov, 2007: 57). As Prozorov (2007: 57) puts it, 'the demonic nature of the modern state [is produced by] the confluence of the murderous power of the sovereign's sword and the productive, vitalist power of biopolitics', the state thus becoming 'a monstrous unison of the executioner and the physician'. While I would argue that Foucault acknowledged the possibility of biopower allowing sovereignty new access to individual or collective bodies – e.g. through biopolitical norms, functioning as an operative condition of law, giving 'the law the access to the body in an unprecedented way' (Mills, 2007: 185) – the above interpretation seems to be overly deterministic, static and generalised. Instead, a more flexible understanding of the resulting power constellations is called for, whereby any of the technologies may dominate at any particular moment in any particular context, leading to different outcomes, something that the case studies of the specific assistance efforts in this book will also demonstrate. It follows, contra Esposito (2008), that genocide is always likely, but not inevitable (one of Foucault's most famous quotes is pertinent here: '[m]y point is not that everything is bad, but that everything is dangerous, which is not exactly the same as bad' (Foucault, 1983: 231)).

The relationship between sovereignty and biopolitics and the differences between the two were further elaborated in Foucault's discussion of the death function in biopolitics, operationalised through racism as a way of introducing a break into the domain of life. In line with that discussion, it can be suggested that with biopolitics the death function relies on sovereign violence, and the positive biopolitical concern of 'care' is used to justify it. Importantly, however, biopolitics has another death function, more specific to it, which has to do with letting die rather than direct killing, something that in the analysis of the case studies I term biopolitics of invisibility, endangerment and abandonment. Furthermore, as a 'caring' power, biopower is not as benign as it presents itself; it is also violent, as it

> allow[s] the individual to be 'cared to death' by the 'experts of life' who are capable of what no sovereign ever cared for: … restructuring the entire period of human existence in terms of a variable distribution of restrictions, sanctions and regimes.
>
> (Dillon, in Prozorov, 2007: 59).

The concepts of biopower and biopolitics never received sustained attention in Foucault's work. They were not the main focus even in his series of lectures (*Society Must be Defended; Security, Territory, Population* and, despite the title, *The Birth of Biopolitics*). However, there is no break in Foucault's work, and not only does 'the genealogy of bio-power remains the horizon' of his latest lectures, but it also 'ha[s] to be placed in a broader framework in order to become really operational' (Senellart, 2007: 370).

Three 'faces' of governmentality. Liberal and neoliberal governmentalities

Governmentality

Just as with the terms 'biopower' and 'biopolitics', there were ambiguities in the way Foucault used the term 'governmentality',[5] which resulted in debates about its interpretation (Kelly, 2010; Walters, 2012). Indeed, several different meanings, or 'faces', of governmentality can be considered. In *Security, Territory, Population* Foucault introduced the three sides of the concept of governmentality in the following way:

> By this word 'governmentality' I mean three things. First, by 'governmentality' I understand the ensemble formed by institutions, procedures, analyses and reflections, calculations, and tactics that allow the exercise of this very specific, albeit very complex, power that has the population as its target, political economy as its major form of knowledge, and apparatuses of security as its essential technical instruments. Second, by 'governmentality' I understand the tendency, the line of force, that for a long time, and throughout the West, has constantly led towards the pre-eminence over all other types of power – sovereignty, discipline and so on – of the type of power that we can call 'government' and which has led to the development of a series of specific governmental apparatuses ... on the one hand, [and, on the other] to the development of a series of knowledges.... Finally, by 'governmentality' I think we should understand the process, or rather, the result of the process by which the state of justice ... became the administrative state ... and was gradually 'governmentalized'.
>
> (Foucault, 2007: 108–109)

What this quote makes clear is that the term governmentality 'operates on several levels of meaning', and 'there are at the very least three ways in which ... it might be understood' (Walters and Haahr, 2005: 289; also Walters, 2012). First, governmentality can be seen as a specific understanding of government, which includes not just the government of others, but also self-government (Bröckling, Krasmann and Lemke, 2011; also Walters, 2012). It is this insight that gives governmentality its versatility and enables analysis of governing at all levels. In this respect, Senellart (2007: 389) argues that Foucault tried to distinguish between governmentality and government by interpreting the former as 'a strategic field of power relations in their mobility, transformability, and reversibility', within which the types of conduct, or 'conduct of conduct' that characterise 'government' are established. This points to governmentality as a perspective, or a form of political analysis, or a methodology that focuses on the relationship between rationalities and practices of governing and poses questions such as: 'who can govern; who is to be governed; what is to be governed, and how?' (Walters and Haahr, 2005: 290; also Dean, 1999; Weidner, 2011; Walters, 2012). Governmentality as a form of political analysis allows us to see 'important shifts in the territory of government – the emergence of new objects and subjects of governance, new techniques of governing, new ways of posing the problems of government' (Walters and Haahr, 2005: 291). In this way, governmentality reflects 'Foucault's working hypothesis on the reciprocal constitution of power techniques and forms of knowledge' (Lemke, 2001: 191). It is this insight that has been taken up by some of governmentality scholars in elaborating the so-called 'analytics of government' as a way of operationalising this theoretical framework and has also resulted in a proliferation of governmentality studies.

Importantly, this face of governmentality also points towards Foucault's overall understanding of power relations as de-centralised and dispersed in the social body. As Walters and Haahr (2005: 289–290) contend, Foucault 'sees government not in terms of the monopoly of the state but a plurality of practices that are conducted within and across countless social sites; practices that are often contradictory and only ever partially coordinated'. It is this understanding of government that, according to Bröckling, Krasmann and Lemke (2011: 1), signalled for Foucault 'a far-reaching correction and refinement of his analysis of power', which was also necessary for the critique of the more prevalent state-centric theories of power.

At the same time, it would be wrong to claim that Foucault's theorising on government ignores the state. In fact, it has been rightly suggested that we should understand the introduction of the concepts of government and governmentality as a way of generating a new approach to the state's nature and its role in broader power networks (e.g. Kelly, 2008; Walters, 2012), which reveals the second face of governmentality. In a similar vein, Jessop (2011) points out that Foucault's later work represents an attempt to complement his analysis of micro-practices with that of macro-level issues related to the state and political economy. What we see in this face of governmentality is its historicity, as it also represents the result of a process through which the administrative state was established and was gradually governmentalised, which, according to Foucault, was what 'allowed the state to survive' (Foucault, 2007: 109). Indeed, the third face of governmentality is 'a historically specific form of power' (Walters and Haahr, 2005: 292), which had 'population as its target, political economy as its major form of knowledge, and apparatuses of security as its essential technical instrument' (the main quote above). In this sense, governmentality represents a particular form of power that emerged in Europe at a particular point of time, and later came to dominate both the nature of the state and its relationship with the governed (Walters and Haahr, 2005). This face of governmentality also suggests that 'distinct historical epochs are characterised by particular ... governmentalities' (Nadesan, 2008: 1). Indeed, Foucault traced the genealogies of different governmentalities, which included Christian pastorate, *raison d'État* and the police state, liberalism and neoliberalism. According to Walters (2012: 29), this trajectory of Foucault's analysis allows us to: 'challenge the perception that governmentality is nothing more than liberalism'; 'better appreciate the unique features of liberal government'; and 'bring into clearer view the diversity of governmental forms that still surround us today'.

Liberal and neoliberal governmentalities

For Foucault, liberalism as a rationality of government is not an ideology or a doctrine, but rather a way of thinking about and approaching in practice the problem of government (Barry *et al.*, 1996; Burchell, 1996). In Foucault's (2008a: 318) words, liberalism is 'a "way of doing things" ... regulating itself by continuous reflection'. Liberalism represents one of the governmentalities developed around the population-economy-security nexus, and in this way it served as broader framework for biopolitics. As Foucault explained:

> With the emergence of political economy, with the introduction of the restrictive principle in governmental practice itself, an important substitution, or doubling rather, is carried out, since the subjects of right on which political sovereignty is exercised appear themselves as a population that a government must manage.
>
> This is the point of departure for the organizational line of a 'biopolitics'. But who does not see that this is only part of something much larger, which [is] this new governmental reason? ... liberalism as the general framework of biopolitics.
>
> (Foucault, 2008a: 22)

What we have here is more of a hint than a fully developed argument; however, it is clear enough that, for Foucault, 'liberalism constitutes the condition of intelligibility of biopolitics' (Senellart, 2007: 383), as it 'determine[s] the specific form that biopolitics assumed in Western societies' (Oksala, 2013: 329). The relationship between liberalism and biopolitics is not without problems and tensions, however, as biopolitical strategies are not the only strategies liberalism deploys, and bio-political imperatives are not the only imperatives it needs to comply with (Dean, 1999). Foucault (2008a: 317) expressed this difficulty in the following way:

> How can the phenomena of 'population', with its specific effects and problems, be taken into account in a system concerned about respect for legal subjects and individual free enterprise? In the name of what and according to what rules it can be managed?

The population appears as a problem for liberalism, and it simultaneously serves as an object to be managed and the limit of such management (Dean, 1999), in light of the need to respect its naturalness coupled with an inability to have a comprehensive knowledge of it (Foucault, 2008a). Political economy provided a 'solution' for this problem, as, according to Foucault (2008a: 13), it served as 'the intellectual instrument, the type of calculation ... that made possible the self-limitation of governmental reason'. In what way does political economy limit the government? It limits it by demanding that it respects the nature specific to its objects and operations with new economic experts supplying the necessary knowledge by 'tell[ing] the government what in truth the natural mechanisms are of what it is manipulating' (Foucault, 2008a: 16, 17). As Blencowe (2012: 111) argues:

> it is liberalism, with its naturalistic ideas about social and economic behaviour and autogenic, vital, natural processes of self-regulation that must be both respected (left alone) and protected (secured) that is the archetypical form of biopolitical governance.

Indeed, born with the understanding that one can govern too much – and in opposition to a previous rationality of government, the police state – liberalism represents a constant critique of, and striving for, getting the act of governing just right, which does not mean governing less, but governing 'cautiously, delicately, economically, modestly' (Rose, Osborne, in Barry *et al.*, 1996: 8). How does it know that it is governing just right? The market will supply the answer, as it is the market that becomes 'a site and a mechanism for the formation of truth', where exchange 'determines the true value of things' (Foucault, 2008a: 30, 46).

While with liberalism the market is understood as a naturally existing reality that needs to be respected, with neoliberalism the market economy becomes the model of all social relations. Therefore, what we have is 'a state under the supervision of the market rather than a market supervised by the state' (Foucault, 2008a: 116). Importantly, for neoliberals the essence of the market is not exchange but competition, and competition can only work if the right conditions are 'carefully and artificially constructed' (Foucault, 2008a: 120). Therefore, according to Foucault, it would a mistake to associate neoliberalism with *laissez-faire*, as what it is actually about is 'permanent vigilance, activity, and intervention' (Foucault, 2008a: 132). Intervention, however, targets not market mechanisms as such, but the conditions of the market; while it is light at the level of economic processes, it is heavy with regard to social factors. Indeed, for neoliberalism, society is a product of governmental intervention, and does not exist by itself (Foucault, 2008).

At the same time, the economy and the social policy are decoupled to prevent the disruption that can be caused by social mechanisms, which also become very limited, providing the lowest level of social security, sufficient only to prevent exclusion from the economy. Under these conditions, and with a move away from full employment, a mass of floating population emerges and is kept in a constant state of readiness for work should that be required by the market (Foucault, 2008a). At the same time, neoliberalism relies on the production of specific subjectivities by encouraging workers to be entrepreneurs of themselves, turning themselves into a kind of permanent and multiple enterprises, something that defines their existence and their relationship to themselves and others. In Foucault's (2008a: 148) words, '[t]he multiplication of the "enterprise" from within the social body is what is at stake in neoliberal policy'. Accordingly, the theory of human capital is central for neoliberalism. It is based on the assumption that for a worker the wage represents an income from a capital, which, as a combination of his abilities and skills, cannot be separated from the person who possesses it. The human capital is made of two groups of elements: innate and acquired, where the former are inborn physical-genetic predispositions and the latter are results of educational investments (broadly understood) and all health-related activities, as well as mobility (Foucault, 2008a). The theory of human capital renders workers governable in a new way, through their economic interests, as they become 'governmentalisable' to the extent that they are economic men. Indeed, for neoliberalism, improvement of the human capital is an important task, and it can be achieved not only through interventions focusing on education opportunities and health care, but also, in future, on genetic make-up, which makes such interventions biopolitical *par excellence*.

In promoting an enterprise culture, neoliberalism encourages individuals and groups to participate in activities that used to belong to the exclusive domain of government agencies. The consequence of such involvement is the transfer of responsibility for these activities and their outcomes, a new form of 'responsibilisation' (Burchell, 1996: 29). Hamann (2009: 43) suggests that interpreting one's social condition as a result of one's own choices and investments has far reaching implications, as it renders '[e]xploitation, domination, and every other form of social inequality ... invisible as social phenomena'. Indeed, the lives of those incapable of enterprising themselves, who do not have a role to play in the neoliberal order, not only are increasingly seen as disposable and redundant (Giroux, 2008), but are also punished in a number of ways (e.g. Hamann, 2009). One can see then how neoliberal logic, the logic of the market, informs the biopolitical imperative to divide populations, identifying sub-groups that can have a negative effect on the life of the population as a whole. Indeed, '[s]ocial death, disposability, and the creation of human waste represent more than exceptional moments' for the biopolitics of disposability that characterises neoliberalism (Giroux, 2008: 598). With globalising neoliberalism, these processes are also present at the international level, something that will be considered further.

Neoliberalism also establishes a different relationship with expertise to that of early liberalism as it

seeks to degovernmentalise the State and to de-estatise practices of government, to detach the substantive authority of expertise from the apparatuses

of political rule, relocating experts within a market governed by the rationalities of competition, accountability and consumer demand

(Rose, 1996: 4)

Indeed, for Foucault (2008a), neoliberalism leads to constant questioning of
actions of public authorities in terms of cost and efficiency. Importantly, expert
technologies carry the danger of depoliticisation, something that also fully
applies to humanitarian governing. With neoliberalism, the instruments of the
government critique are derived from budget disciplines, accountancy and audit,
the so-called 'grey sciences', which are 'simultaneously modest and omniscient,
limited yet apparently limitless in their application to [diverse] problems' (Rose,
1996: 54). In this way, neoliberalism emerges as the most 'rational' of all rationalities of government; however, according to Foucault (2008a), it is only one of
many rationalities, the interplay of which characterises the way we are governed
today.

Governmentality after Foucault

Foucault's theorising on governmentality has proved to be very influential in a
number of disciplines, resulting in the emergence of governmentality studies
(Bröckling *et al.*, 2011; Weidner, 2011; Walters, 2012). Governmentality studies
are very diverse, but the main focus here is on those using governmentality as a
perspective and/or focusing on neoliberal governmentality, as it is predominantly
these studies that engage with the international, therefore having the most relevance for the analysis of humanitarian governing.

As far as the reasons for the success of governmentality as a perspective are concerned, Larner and Walters (2004) argue that, first, it offers a promising line of
investigation to those dissatisfied with both positivism and excessive textualism of
some poststructuralist approaches. In their view, 'governmentality research has
been more historical and more avowedly empirical in its orientation', due to 'its
concern with power in its multifarious practical, technical manifestations' (Larner
and Walters, 2004: 3). Indeed, the empirical focus, or 'empirical mapping', as Rose
et al. (2006) call it, of rationalities and techniques of government is very important,
and will be elaborated further. Second, given that this perspective treats power as
dispersed and the state as just one of the many possible configurations of government, it is very well suited for analysing contemporary transformations of power;
the novel understanding of liberalism and neoliberalism it has offered is particularly
pertinent in this respect (Larner and Walters, 2004). What governmentality studies
have demonstrated is that, at certain historical moments, family resemblances of
programmes can be identified in that they share certain rationalities and technologies (Rose *et al.*, 2006). At the same time, the aim of any governmentality-inspired
analysis should not be a production of ideal types of some kind, or conclusions that
a certain regime or a programme of government is neoliberal; after all, elements of
neoliberal governmentality are omnipresent and, while calling certain regimes or
programmes neoliberal provides a useful indication of a family resemblance, it may

defeat the whole point of using governmentality as an approach (Rose *et al.*, 2006; also Walters, 2012). Instead, what this kind of analysis should be elucidating is the specifics of certain regimes of government. This is something that is attempted here in the analysis of humanitarian governing that characterises the post-Cold War 'new' humanitarianism and specific assistance efforts.

According to Bröckling, Krasmann and Lemke (2011: 11), most governmentality studies share a common analytical perspective that privileges the focus on the 'rationalities and technologies of government, modes of thinking and forms of intervention, [which] are inextricably connected and co-produce one another'. They also identify methodological principles suggested by governmentality studies,[6] which include appreciation of 'the significance of knowledge production and its connection with mechanisms of power' (Bröckling *et al.*, 2011: 12) and attention to what Foucault called 'politics of truth' and invites an investigation of various mechanisms, which make truth claims possible, along with the power effects of such claims. Investigations into the politics of truth allow for the appreciation of the necessary selectiveness of knowledge and its instrumental nature, in that knowledge used to define problems is also knowledge legitimising governmental intervention in 'solving' them. Nadesan considers this a feature that sets governmentality studies apart from other methodological approaches in that it takes 'problem-solution frames as its objects of analysis', thereby deconstructing 'social givens by exploring their historical constitution as objects of government' (Nadesan, 2008: 6). This is something that Foucault attempted to capture with his concept of problematisation discussed in more detail below. Other principles of the governmentality approach emphasise strategies and technologies of governing, and draw attention to the ways in which the political is produced and the inevitable divisions and exclusions that accompany them (Bröckling *et al.*, 2011).

In terms of the elements of analysis, several frameworks with the focus on the intimate connection between rationalities and technologies of power have been suggested (e.g. Dean, 1999; Miller and Rose, 2008). These frameworks are firmly rooted in Foucault's broader thinking on power and appear to follow his suggestion that any analysis of a regime of power requires the establishment of the following: (1) 'the system of differentiations', enabling one to act upon the actions of others; (2) 'the types of objectives' pursued in a particular power relation; (3) 'the means of bringing power relations into being'; (4) 'forms of institutionalisation', which can range from a closed apparatus with hierarchical structure to complex systems with multiple apparatuses; and (5) 'the degree of rationalisation', which allows for power relations to be framed as 'an action in the field of possibilities' (Foucault, 1987: 223–224).

Dean's (1999) approach is that of 'an analytics of government'. It is designed to challenge the established and taken-for-granted assumptions about a particular regime and open the space for possible alternatives by seeking to

> identify the emergence of that regime, examine the multiple sources of the
> elements that constitute it, and follow the diverse processes and relations by

which these elements are assembled into relatively stable forms of organization and institutional practice.

(Dean, 1999: 21)

This involves identification and consideration of both the particular types of knowledge on which the regime in question is dependant, and of its technical dimension. Therefore, an analytics of government should consider the following aspects of a regime: forms of visibility; procedures for the production of truth; specific interventions and their mechanisms and techniques; and ways of subject formation (Dean, 1999). This kind of analysis is capable of revealing an important disjuncture between programmes of government and their effects, which also means effects cannot be 'read off' the programmes themselves, but can only be understood within practices informed by them (Dean, 2002). Like Rose *et al.* (2006), Dean emphasises the importance of the empirical side of governmentality studies: 'governmentality is ... not simply about philosophies, mentalities or theories: it is about practices, regimes and effects' (Dean, 2002: 120). While governmentality studies do not evaluate the effectiveness of governmental interventions or ask how those can be improved, their contribution comes from studying the unfolding of their effects (Bröckling *et al.*, 2011).

Miller and Rose (2008) also focus on the two main aspects of a regime of governing: 'rationalities' or 'programmes', and 'technologies'. While rationalities are defined as 'styles of thinking, ways of rendering reality thinkable in such a way that it was amenable to calculating and programming', technologies represent 'assemblages of persons, techniques, institutions, instruments for the conducting of conduct' (Miller and Rose, 2008: 16). For their approach, the concept of problematisation is crucial, as it refers to the process through which a particular conduct is rendered 'visible' for governing through the use of language and existing formalised knowledge, and amenable to governing through deployment of governmental techniques and instruments (from the perspective of government, there is no point in identifying a problem that cannot be 'solved') (Miller and Rose, 2008: 14–15). This line of arguing supports Foucault's own insistence that the point of any problematisation is not only to develop a given into a question, but also to transform 'a group of obstacles and difficulties into problems to which diverse solutions will attempt to produce a response' (Foucault, 2000a: 118). His elaborations are pertinent here as

problematisation doesn't mean representation of a pre-existing object, nor the creation by discourse of an object that does not exist. It is the totality of discursive and non-discursive practices that introduce something into play of true and false and constitutes it as an object for thought.

(Foucault, 1990: 257)

Given a certain problematization, you can only understand why this kind of answer appears as a reply to some concrete and specific aspect of the world. There is a relation of thought and reality in the process of problematization.

(Foucault, 2001: 173)

It can be suggested that the process of problematising both establishes and activates a power-knowledge nexus, where 'power and knowledge directly imply one another' (Foucault, 1977: 27). This is a two-way relationship, where knowledge is never neutral or disinterested (Gordon, 1980; Smart, 1985). Importantly, such interrogation also opens up possibilities for alternative problematisations and, consequently, alternative actions. This points to another function of the process of problematisation: that of ethical transformation, involving responsiveness as a sustained focus on newly delineated problems, rather than an attempt to bring a closure by solving them once and for all (Gilson, 2014). The process of problematisation also places analysis within a broader Foucauldian methodological framework, that of genealogy; not surprisingly, Foucault himself emphasised the connection between governmentality and genealogy (Walters, 2012). Indeed, genealogical investigations allow us to identify dominant discourses and the practices they engender, along with their position with respect to other discourses and practices, which, in turn, makes it possible to identify and operationalise excluded alternatives (Howarth, 2002). Importantly, genealogy represents a method that can 'facilitate inquiries into the problematic aspects of contemporary condition that Foucault himself could hardly have anticipated' (Koopman, 2013: 7). Thus, in the genealogical investigations undertaken in this book, a modified version of Dean's analytics of government is used. This involves identification and critical interrogation of dominant problematisations of the situations in need of humanitarian response and their implications for specific assistance efforts, along with gesturing towards both existing and possible alternatives.

The analytics of government as an approach represents one of the significant strength of the governmentality studies. Amongst its advantages, according to Death (2013), are: the focus on specific practices; identification of 'homologies' between practices that traverse the domestic/international and public/private divides; and attention to the interdependence of different technologies of power and of their both violent and non-violent effects. These features make the analytics of government particularly well-suited for studying 'combinations and hybrids' (Walters, 2012: 41), or for performing what Collier (2009) terms a topological analysis of power relations. The focus of such analysis is an examination of how diverse technologies of power are 're-deployed and recombined in diverse assemblies' (Collier, 2009: 95). Consequently, the purpose of a topological analysis could be 'to show how styles of analysis, techniques or forms of reasoning associated with 'advanced liberal' government are being recombined with other forms, and to diagnose the governmental ensembles that emerge from these recombinations' (Collier, 2009: 99). Indeed, given that biopower does not displace sovereignty and that neoliberal governmentality is only one of the rationalities of government reliant on both of these power technologies, our empirical mapping should concern itself with 'a complex field of overlapping powers' (Dean, 2002: 123). At the same time, as Dean points out, there are contexts in which drawing clear boundaries between different technologies of power would mean missing 'zones of indistinction', where 'these heterogeneous powers act in such concert that it is difficult to know whether we are in the presence of biopolitical or sovereign powers' (Dean, 2002: 125). Indeed, this will be shown to be the case with respect to the conflict-related assistance effort in Afghanistan.

The above discussion helps us address the question of whether Foucault's theorising on biopolitics and governmentality can be applied to international concerns and to critically appraise the studies that have attempted to do so. The distinction between concepts (e.g. biopolitics, governmentality) and methods (e.g. analytics of government, genealogy) stressed by Koopman (2013), will be shown to be important in examining how Foucault-inspired approaches can help us in our attempts to understand international phenomena and developments.

Foucault and the international: 'global' biopolitics and international governmentality studies

'Global' biopolitics?

In the last two decades, Foucault's theorising on biopolitics has been actively engaged, resulting in a growing biopolitics scholarship in a number of disciplines[7] and signalling what some have called a 'biopolitical turn' (Campbell and Sitze, 2013: 4). Lemke (2011) suggests that one of the many lines of reception focuses on contemporary biopolitical processes and the systems of knowledge informing them. It is here that we are likely to find the appreciation of the significance of knowledge and knowledge production for biopolitical governing, combined with a focus on particular types of biopolitics, e.g. neoliberal. The second line of reception, according to Lemke (2011), positions the analysis of biopolitical processes within a broader framework of governmentality used as a perspective. These lines of reception do not result in a clear-cut divide, however, as many Foucault-inspired studies of the international have elements of both.

In what follows, some of the contributions belonging to the biopolitical scholarship within the studies of the international are selectively engaged.[8] What needs to be addressed first, however, is whether one can speak of international, or 'global', biopolitics. For Kelly (2010: 5), this question 'comes down to whether these two things exist: a global population, and a global apparatus that would allow its constitution and regulation'. He argues that a global population does not exist, as what we have internationally is a biopolitical border that not only divides different populations, but also serves as 'the point of suction of vitality from one side to the other' (Kelly, 2010: 8). This argument is in line with that expressed in Duffield's more recent work (from 2007 onwards) on the biopolitical divide, which informs the analysis of the post-Cold War humanitarian governing. However, as far as the term 'global' is concerned, there could be other ways to justify its use. For instance, we do not necessarily need both elements Kelly mentions, as existence of global apparatuses (in terms of their reach) managing a variety of populations could constitute what one may call global biopolitics. Collier and Lakoff (2005: 34) offer another take on the term global by suggesting that global biopolitical forms can be understood as global 'in the sense that they are not attached to a social or cultural context'. This suggestion points to the spread of the neoliberal rationality of governing, which carries with it specific biopolitical technologies. It is in this sense that the 'new' humanitarianism can be said to represent if not a global, then a globalising, regime of governing, one relying on a specific form of biopolitics.

Rather than an existing reality, a truly global biopolitics, according to Kelly, is a desired outcome: 'the protection and encouragement of life to all humanity' (Kelly, 2010: 22). This sentiment is shared by those attempting to envisage 'affirmative' biopolitics (e.g. Cooper, 2006: Hannah, 2011; Rutherford and Rutherford, 2013; Grove, 2014), which also implies resistance. Pertinently, certain forms of humanitarian action can be said to represent such affirmative biopolitics. What needs to be stressed, however, is that the existing neoliberal biopolitics does not represent a totality to be replaced with another totality of affirmative biopolitics. Moreover, it is impossible to step outside of power constellations that include biopolitics. Instead, resistances to the biopolitical governing, both local and transnational, both potential and already existing, present a challenge to specific biopolitical regimes of governing at their points of application, e.g. by subverting particular strategies or questioning the rationale behind the divisions they produce, or revealing and opposing the processes of drawing lines in the international domain between different populations and forms of life, the processes that often involve both biopolitical ('letting die') and sovereign violence. Indeed, what we see with the globalising neoliberal biopolitics is the continued focus on the presence of imperfect elements either inside or outside that need to be addressed, e.g. multiple illiberal populations beyond the state borders are often considered threatening. Kelly (2010: 18) himself recognises this when he states that '[w]ith biopolitics, the population owe their life to the state, and as such back the state against the biopolitical exterior'. And it is here that the continued role of the state and state borders becomes apparent, and it is here that the danger of biopolitics lies: the danger of wars waged using biopolitical justifications. Again, as Kelly (2010: 1) himself posits, 'analysis of the contemporary international through the lens of Foucauldian biopolitics ... shows us that our world system is marked by a parasitic imperialism of rich sovereign states over poor ones, carried at the level of populations'. This picture, however, is only partial, and obscures as much as it reveals. For instance, it ignores the role of non-state actors, and implies a unified rationality underlying the actions of all 'rich' states. Even more importantly, it ignores the existence of different types of biopolitics, informed by other rationalities, including illiberal biopolitics, which are pursued in different combination with other power technologies by many states, both 'rich' and 'poor'.

The continued relevance of the state and state borders also signals the continued and already emphasised relevance of sovereignty as a technology of power. Indeed, in the international domain 'the sovereign power is far from dead' (Edkins and Pin-Fat, 2004: 3). Thus, for Cairo, the complex interactions between biopolitics and sovereignty are reflected in the changing nature of current Western interventions, whose dual goal is to both 'eliminate some dangerous bodies' and 'reform the conduct of the population' (Cairo, 2006: 288). It can be argued that, more specifically, justifications are usually those of care and protection, and killing of some is presented as necessary to secure the population at large. However, what is often obscured is that the populations to be secured are predominantly those of the intervening states. When arguing that interventions informed by the new discourses of danger erode the sovereignty of the targeted states, Cairo (2006) also tends to overemphasise the role of the hegemonic state, and does not seem to address the reality of biopolitical technologies being applied by many actors, for a variety of purposes, and often not in concert with one another.

The interventions Cairo (2006) refers to were characteristic of the wars on terrorism, which has direct relevance for the analysis of the 2001 US-led intervention in Afghanistan as the context within which the international assistance effort has been taking place. In terms of understanding the biopolitics of the Global War on Terror, Dauphinee and Masters (2007: xiii) suggest reading Foucault and Agamben simultaneously, and this kind of reading has indeed informed other accounts of the wars on terrorism, especially in terms of examining processes of depoliticisation and biologisation of life of populations subject to intervention, which turns them into a form of 'bare life', and in terms of sovereignty and biopolitics entering into a zone of indistinction. Crucially though, for biopolitical justifications to work, 'death needs to be made invisible', and so '[b]iopolitics hides its death-producing activities under the rhetoric of making live' (Dauphinee and Masters, 2007: xii, xiii). In addition to this, what needs to be stressed is the reliance of biopolitics on sovereign violence. Masters (2007) draws our attention to the depoliticisation of death during the Iraq war, as reflected in body counts, with bodies of American soldiers at least being counted, although still hidden, while those of Iraqis going unnoticed or their deaths being justified as necessary. She also stresses the de-individualising effects of body counts and the way they obscure individual suffering, an insight which will prove to be useful in a completely different setting (i.e. while examining the Chernobyl-related assistance effort in Belarus).

A significant contribution to our understanding of the wars on terrorism as biopolitical is made by Dillon and Reid. In their 2009 *Liberal way of war: Killing to make life live* they take the discussion of the biopolitical nature of the wars on terrorism to a high level of theoretical abstraction and stress the importance of war as an instrument for liberal rule. They argue that, '[i]n [an] attempt to instrumentalize, indeed universalize, war in pursuit of its own global project of emancipation, the practice of liberal rule itself has become profoundly shaped by war' (Dillon and Reid, 2009: 5). It should be stressed that their use of the concept of 'liberal' in the discussion of the liberal rule is not unproblematic, as, unlike Foucault's understanding of liberalism, theirs is too totalising in that it suggests the existence of just one rationality of governing, which has 'life itself' as 'the referent object'. Furthermore, they do not specify either the 'who' or the 'what' of governing: what kind of life is it? Through what dividing and boundary-drawing practices is it produced? Is all life governed uniformly and to the same ends? For instance, they argue that as we have entered the 'age of life as information', all governing of life will, in effect, be governing of information, as 'information as code come to replace function in defining what a living thing is currently said to be' (Dillon and Reid, 2009: 21). While this is certainly true of some biopolitical technologies of governing populations by some advanced liberal states in certain contexts, this is not true of all of them at all times and in all contexts; in other words, while what they call 'recombinant biopolitics' may be seen as *a* liberal biopolitics, it is not *the* liberal biopolitics. They further argue that the referent object of contemporary biopolitics is biohumanity, that is, the species as a whole, with life posing threat to life: '[f]or just war has constantly to be waged for biohumanity against the continuous becoming-dangerous of life itself' (Dillon and Reid, 2009: 32). This argument implies the existence of a global population, all elements of which are equally available for governing, which is rather problematic.

While Dillon and Reid's (2009) continued emphasis on the role of life sciences and on the processes of auditing and sorting life, which inform the killing of threatening life, is both significant and helpful, they do not seem to explain on what kinds of criteria such processes of auditing and sorting are based. It can be argued that, instead of talking about generic 'productivity' of life, it would be more illuminating to explore, for instance, how productivity of life, understood in economic terms and measured by the markets and marked-inspired mechanisms, serves as such a criterion. The same criticism can be applied to their discussion of the threats to life, which the liberal way of war addresses, i.e. 'the threats to species existence which arise within the very processes of life itself' (Dillon and Reid, 2009: 44). Overall, when attempted at this level of abstraction, their line of argument seems to smooth over important analytical distinctions and loses some of its interpretive power.

Moving away from considering the relationship between sovereignty and biopolitics in the wars on terrorism, Bell and Evans (2010) interpret the shift from counter-terrorism to counterinsurgency (COIN) as a shift from sovereignty to biopolitics, from exterminating enemies to transforming societies. This shift, for them, 'deepens the division of humanity into qualitatively distinct forms of life, contributing to the dramatic materialization of global civil war at the level of life itself' (Bell and Evans, 2010: 371). While their appreciation of the existence of distinct forms of life is helpful, as is the appreciation of the dual goal of the Global War on Terror interventions, the shift from counter-terrorism to COIN cannot be said to be complete and the claim about a global civil war seems to be overly totalising. Like Dillon and Reid (2009), Bell and Evans talk about conflicts at the level of life itself, which seems to flatten many differences and ignore the context. Furthermore, they also seem to collapse the distinction between biopolitics and liberalism and to treat all neoliberal biopolitics as negative. Biopolitical liberalism, according to Bell and Evans (2010: 375), has 'planetary ambitions' and is implicated in the construction of spaces, posing a danger to the West and to the spaces themselves, which is used to justify current interventions. They also argue that 'the resurfacing of the insurgent as the challenge to the expansion of liberal order generates not a tyranny of closure but an intensification of the spatial regulation of circulation' (Bell and Evans, 2010: 383). What this line of arguing misses, however, are the related processes of exclusion and disengagement, as reflected in strengthening borders and containing threatening populations *in situ*, with only minimal intervention to ensure threat reduction, to establish minimal order and promote self-sufficiency, as examined by Duffield (2007 onwards). In their account, however, such processes are subsumed by the claim that liberalism's planetary mission is humanitarian, which consists in the 'management of disenfranchised populations' (Bell and Evans, 2010: 385). Given that such management is mostly outsourced to humanitarian agencies, one can see what kind of impact the coupling with liberal interventionism has for the humanitarian action, with the latter being complicit in the production of negative biopolitical effects.

Perhaps unsurprisingly, exploration of the shifting boundaries between geopolitics and biopolitics often focuses on limit spaces, such as borders (e.g. Amoore, 2006; Salter, 2006; Doty, 2007, 2011; Muller, 2008; Walters, 2011a, 2011b) and limit figures, such as internally displaced persons, refugees, asylum seekers and detainees (e.g. Diken, 2004; Isin and Rygiel, 2007; Sheshadri, 2008). For example, Doty's (2007) empirically rich analysis of the complex nature of the border between Mexico and the USA accounts for both sovereign and biopolitical violence to which would-be border-crossers are subject. She shows that the visibility/invisibility interplay is important for understanding the border regime, with the enforcement operations being visible and the bodies of the border-crossers being rendered invisible (Doty, 2007). This rendering invisible is not accidental, and, as has been discussed already, any death, even resulting from a 'letting die' rather than direct killing, represents a biopolitical limit, challenges the biopolitical promise of care and protection, and, therefore, needs to be hidden or otherwise made invisible. Isin and Rygiel also explore abject spaces, which they define as 'those in and around which increasingly distressed, displaced, and dispossessed peoples are condemned to the status of strangers, outsiders, and aliens ... and stripped of their ... citizenship (rights of becoming political)' (Isin and Rygiel, 2007: 181). Importantly, they do not find Agamben's ahistorical concept of the camp analytically helpful, as it obscures important differences among diverse forms of camps. They further argue that, if we appreciate different strategies used in these spaces 'to reduce people to abject inexistence', we will be able to appreciate different 'logics and acts of resistance' (Isin and Rygiel, 2007: 185).

Continuing with the theme of abjection, in his influential piece on governing HIV/AIDS, Elbe (2008) considers three different conceptions of risk, and argues that HIV/AIDS risk is best understood as a biopolitical technology. Attentive to the processes of the erasure of the individual body, necessary for biopolitical governing of the population, Elbe refers to Castel's insight with respect to discourses of risk that 'dissolve the notion of a subject or concrete individual, and put it in its place a combinatory of factors, the factors of risk' (Castel, 1991, in Elbe, 2008: 193). These discourses of risk dominate more and more areas, outside those of insurance, signalling the expansion of biopolitical governing

(Elbe, 2008). A number of his observations with respect to HIV/AIDS interventions are equally applicable to other humanitarian interventions, including the suggestion that the language of risk facilitates the reduction/removal of sovereign obstacles – such as the consent of states where interventions take place – while allowing international institution to govern through risk factors as opposed to concrete threats/dangers. What such interventions demonstrate is not the replacing of sovereign or disciplinary powers, but their appropriation and use towards biopolitical ends (Elbe, 2008).

Despite any limitations of some of the above interventions, cumulatively they offer a good illustration of the diversity and significance of biopolitical scholarship in examining the international, and they clearly represent much more than what Koopman (2013) terms 'biopower-hunting', as not only do they tend to use Foucault's concepts, but also some of his methodological insights.

International governmentality studies: promises and limitations

For some time, the predominantly domestic orientation has been regarded as one of the major limitations of governmentality studies, and, while such an orientation may be understandable, due to the disciplinary location of scholars and well-founded scepticism about the claims of grand theories, it still seemed counter-intuitive, given that governmentality studies proliferated at the time when ideas about globalisation were receiving increased attention (Larner and Walters, 2004). From the early 2000s, the situation has changed with the proliferation of what Walters (2012)[9] terms 'international governmentality studies'.[10]

Unsurprisingly, many international governmentality scholars have considered neoliberal forms of governmentality (Weidner, 2011), but not all of them are attentive to the need to distinguish between governmentality as a perspective and neoliberal governmentality as a specific type of rationality of government, which, as has been discussed above, is crucial. This lack of distinction has resulted in a number of debates, both within the international governmentality studies themselves, where some have used the either/or argument to privilege the use of the governmentality as a perspective (e.g. Death, 2013; Zanotti, 2013) and to criticise studies of international neoliberal governing (e.g. Joseph and Corry, 2014), and outside of it, with some scholars challenging the applicability of governmentality to the study of international/global concerns (e.g. Selby, 2007). In order to make sense of some of these disagreements, both real and perceived, and to establish what is required for a meaningful engagement with Foucault's theorising, examples from the now rather varied international governmentality studies need to be considered.

In his early analysis, Dillon (1995) referred to governmentality as a historically specific regime of power and suggested that the international domain could be best understood through the Foucauldian triangle of 'sovereignty-discipline-government', where states could be seen as 'an ensemble of governmental practices more or less suspended within and between (inter)national juridical and territorial boundaries' (Dillon, 1995: 339). Following Foucault, he argued that governmentalisation of the state was constitutive of the state system. For him, as for Lui-Bright (1997), the state system was as much a product of governmentality as it was of sovereignty. This is a crucial insight; however, it is still important to appreciate the historical specificity of both modalities of power, and the antecedent nature of sovereignty. As far as the post-Cold War order is concerned, Dillon argued that it was characterised by the spread of governmentality to all regions, but did not specify whether this was due to the overall governmentalisation of the international or to the spread of a particular rationality of governing. For Dillon (1995), migration was the issue that best illustrated the intersection between sovereignty and governmentality, with assigning value to life being crucial in the process of managing populations.

Nadesan (2008) applies Foucault's conceptual framework of discipline, sovereignty and government to explore a variety of spheres of neoliberal governing: markets, public health, mind and brain, and security. In her analysis, she examines a variety of technologies of governing and the intersections between them, including the role of biopolitics in serving interests 'of capitalist accumulation and market forces by eliciting and optimizing the life forces of a state's population, maximizing their capacity as human resources and their utility for market capitalization' (Nadesan, 2008: 3). She talks about globalising, rather than global neoliberalism, which more accurately reflects the dominance of neoliberal governmentality, without suggesting the existence of an all-encompassing, truly global and uncontested rationality of government. In terms of economic governing, Nadesan stresses the complex role of inequality for neoliberal policies: as a condition of existence, an opportunity for expansion and as a source of risks, which need to be managed by a variety of actors, often requiring the use of discipline and sovereign violence.

Giroux (2008) draws attention to new modes of individual and collective suffering under neoliberalism that he terms the 'biopolitics of disposability'. In his analysis, he is attentive to the fact that neoliberalism is first and foremost an economic rationality that strives to extend market forces into the social, as well as to its operation at the collective and the individual levels. Thus, with the state functioning more and more like a market, there is pressure to produce neoliberal subjects, which inevitably results in the production of what he calls 'human waste', where 'some lives, if not whole groups, are seen as disposable and redundant' (Giroux, 2008: 594). He argues that, under neoliberal governmentality, it is the market rationality that decides 'who matters and who doesn't, who lives and who dies' (Giroux, 2008: 594). This is a very important insight, as it allows us to see how biopolitical governing, when informed by a specific rationality, is anything but an inclusive and progressive system of care and protection. As this rationality and the forces it promotes are successful internationally, it is possible to draw parallels between the domestic and the international and to see how Foucault's ideas can be applied to understand developments in the latter.

Similar to Dean (2002) and Nadesan (2008), Giroux draws our attention to the repressive side of neoliberalism, which, for him, is operationalised not only through sovereign violence, but also through the violence of the market:

the unleashing of a powerfully regressive symbolic and corporeal violence against all those individuals and groups who have been 'othered' because their very presence undermines the engines of wealth and inequality that drive neoliberal dreams of consumption, power, and profitability.

(Giroux, 2008: 601)

As another scholar attentive to the fact that neoliberal governmentality is an economic rationality of governing, Kiersey (2011: 3) emphasises the importance of Foucault's 'concern with the manner in which contemporary capitalism relies on the market as a potential vector for the solicitation of specific norms of individual responsibility'. It is in this way that neoliberalism answers the question about the purpose of securing life. Kiersey (2011: 24) suggests that, as an indirect form of power, neoliberal governmentality targets states, communities and individuals alike, and, in so doing, it both 'idealise[s] a global population as [economic men] and develop[s] strategies to recruit that population in its own self-government'. Weidner (2011) makes a similar point regarding simultaneous idealisation as, and transformation into, neoliberal subjects, but what seems to be somewhat problematic with Kiersey's statement is the reference to the 'global population', which assumes that there is one unitary object of governing, rather than multiple populations, governed differently according to different logic.

In his analysis of neoliberal governmentality, Joseph (2009) appreciates the important difference between, on the one hand, governmentality as a theoretical approach used to understand local constellations of power and, on the other hand, claims about the existence of global governmentality, but he remains sceptical about the latter being neoliberal governmentality. His scepticism is based on the assumption that it is difficult to imagine techniques of neoliberal governmentality working effectively outside of the advanced liberal societies where they have emerged, and, as a result, there will always be a need to resort to coercive forms of power to regulate illiberal populations. While the idea that different technologies of power often function simultaneously has already been discussed and supported, there is no need to see a failure of neoliberal governing as problematic in and of itself. Instead, we should try to understand why, important differences between social and economic conditions notwithstanding, neoliberal governmentality promotes and relies upon the same or very similar strategies and technologies to govern both liberal and illiberal populations. It is possible to identify a number of ways in which this has happened: as parallel application to both liberal and illiberal populations, with minor adjustments; as experimentation on illiberal populations with a view to later applying tested techniques to liberal populations (think of colonial times (e.g. Reiss, 2004; Venn, 2009; Walters, 2012), as well as numerous contemporary examples), and, finally, as an export of techniques applied to liberal populations to govern illiberal ones, often in combination with other, more coercive, technologies of power. As for possible reasons for this cross-over, one could point towards the demands of the markets and their reliance on the existence/production of certain types of subjectivities. What also needs to be remembered is that, biopolitically, there will always be a divide between liberal and illiberal populations, which is necessary and has to be sustained, not only for economic reasons (i.e. inequality as a necessary condition for capitalist expansion), but also to maintain the legitimacy of the rule based on care (i.e. the need for an outside against which to protect). Seen this way, the failure Joseph (2009) talks about might not actually be a failure, but more of a desired strategic outcome. Indeed, as Vrasti (2013: 64) argues, '[i]t is precisely because liberalism functions as a universal measure of truth that we can understand the exclusion or failure of certain communities and spaces'. Furthermore, while Joseph's (2010: 204) contention that neoliberal governmentality does not work outside advanced liberal societies (where it is met with different conditions) may imply a commitment to development with a view to establishing the necessary conditions in all parts of the world, the absence of such a commitment is becoming more and more evident, as Duffield has consistently argued.

While Joseph (2009) uses the term 'global governmentality', he does not interrogate the 'global' aspect of it sufficiently. While 'global' in the case of governmentality may imply the existence of a global population (which is evidently not the case, given the continued importance of borders, both sovereign and biopolitical, and the existence of different social and economic conditions in different parts of the world), it could also imply a drive to apply to the same way of governing used in advanced liberal societies outside them, in which case, Nadesan's (2008) 'globalising governmentality' or Vrasti's (2013) 'universal, but not truly global' terms provide a more accurate description. Joseph's understanding of the workings of global governmentality suggests that, while governmentality 'should always mean governmentality of populations', the global governmentality of today focuses 'on states rather than populations as the target entities' (Joseph, 2009: 425, 423). To reconcile these two claims, he concludes that 'the regulation of states takes place through the targeting of populations' (Joseph, 2009: 427). Instead, this argument should be reversed, as what we are witnessing is both direct governing of populations and governing of populations through states (as it is not states as such that are the ultimate objective of governmental interventions, but rather states are used instrumentally to ensure that their populations are governed in a particular way). Crucially, it is increasingly difficult to identify the 'who' of such interventions, in light of the formation of what Duffield (2001) called 'complexes', consisting of a variety of actors, often including the states where the target populations reside. Sending and Neumann (2006), who use the governmentality perspective to analyse the role of various actors in two issue-areas – the international campaign to ban landmines and international population policy – also argue that it enabled them to appreciate that, as far as non-state actors are concerned, their role in fulfilling the function of global governance had less to do with the diminished role of the state and more to do with the way in which 'civil society is redefined from a passive object of government to be acted upon into an entity that is both an object and a subject of government' (Sending and Neumann, 2006: 651).

Elsewhere, Joseph (2010) puts forward a number of suggestions which are largely in line with the general methodological principles of governmentality studies discussed in the previous section. Thus, he advises to combine macro- and micro-level analysis to 'look at the relationship between the dominant dynamics in the international system and the specific conditions in different places' (Joseph, 2010: 203). He also suggests: to distinguish between governmentality in a generic sense and specific governmentalities; to analyse the triangle of sovereignty, discipline and government; and to appreciate the relationship between governmentality and biopower (biopolitics). While Joseph (2009, 2010) is correct in pointing out that biopower (biopolitics) should be distinguished from governmentality and that these terms should not be used interchangeably, he does not propose how one should view their relationship as far as the international is concerned.

Rosenow, in turn, sets out to challenge 'the idea that contemporary (global) power relations can be depicted solely through the lens of neoliberalism, sovereignty, or biopolitics' or, in other words, 'the problematic impression that the 'international' is determined by a single overarching project' (Rosenow, 2009: 497). In line with Foucault's wider thinking on power, she argues that 'global power is located in complex and flexible constellations of diverse and contradictory, mutually constituting and mutually destabilising strategies and tactics at particular sites' (Rosenow, 2009: 497). For her, the concept of 'dispositif, understood as the "arrest" and integration of a heterogenous set of power relations at a multiplicity of sites and a variety of scales', is helpful in operationalising Foucault's thinking with respect to the international (Rosenow, 2009: 501). It is for this reason that she advocates working with the Foucauldian triangle of neoliberal governmentality, sovereignty, and discipline. One may add to this suggestion the need to distinguish between the three different 'faces' of governmentality, which can allow application of the analytics of government to examine a particular instance of the governmentalisation of the international, informed by different rationalities of government and reliant on specific sovereign, disciplinary and biopoltical instruments.

Conclusion

This chapter has introduced Foucault's theorising on biopower and biopolitics. His approach, unlike those of Agamben (1998) and Esposito (2008), is historical and genealogical. For Foucault, biopower represents a new technology of power that has evolved in two forms: discipline, focused on an individual body; and biopolitics, focused on the collective body of the population. Biopower did not replace sovereignty, and is distinct in its overall orientation and mechanism, as it is more concerned with care over living beings and relies on the improved knowledge of the body, both individual and collective. Indeed, knowledge of the population in its 'naturalness' and its relationship with its environment is essential for biopolitical governing. Importantly, if we follow Foucault, biopolitics appears to have a death function reliant on sovereign violence, with the positive biopolitical concern of 'care' used for its justification, and a death function, which has to do with letting die rather than direct killing.

The concept of biopolitics is better understood in a broader context of governmentality. In this respect, three different 'faces' of governmentality (Foucault, 2007; also, Walters and Haahr, 2005; Walters, 2012) have been discussed and the importance of distinguishing between them has been stressed. With respect to the relationship between liberal and neoliberal governmentalities and biopolitics, it has been argued, in line with Dean (1999) and Senellart (2007), that while liberalism and neoliberalism utilise biopolitical strategies to govern, the focus on the population presents these rationalities of governing with a number of challenges, as it is not just biopolitical imperatives that they take into account and not just biopolitical tools that they use. As a rationality of government, neoliberalism is characterised, first and foremost, by its prioritisation of the market as the principle of government and self-government, with competition being its essence (Foucault, 2008a). This results both in questioning of actions of public authorities in terms of cost and efficiency and circumscription of social support mechanisms, and in pressures on individuals to become entrepreneurs of themselves. Neoliberal policies and practices produce biopolitical divides between those capable of enterprising themselves and those incapable of it, with the latter often subject to disciplining measures or treated as disposable.

In turn, productive use of governmentality as a perspective involves placing it within a broader context of Foucault's thinking on power and, in particular, reconnecting it with such concepts as power/knowledge and problematisation (e.g. Miller and Rose, 2008; Bröckling et al., 2011) and such methodologies as genealogy (e.g. Walters, 2012; Koopman, 2013). In terms of operationalising governmentality as a perspective, following Rose et al. (2006), as well as Dean (2002), an argument in favour of empirical investigations has been made. Such investigations would benefit from productively combining topological analysis (Collier, 2009), which is attentive to different technologies of power, including sovereignty, discipline and biopolitics, and rationalities of governing, and analytics of government (Foucault, 1987; Dean, 1999; Miller and Rose, 2008), which focuses on the relationship between rationalities and technologies of power. By so doing, we can effectively map out and understand different regimes of governing.

In the last decade, Foucault's theorising on biopolitics and governmentality has informed investigations of the international domain, contributing to the development of biopolitics scholarship and of governmentality studies. As for the former, accounts focusing on the sovereignty-biopolitics nexus and contexts and conditions that produce negative biopolitical effects, which include studies of the biopolitics of the war on terror (e.g. Dauphinee and Masters, 2007; Dillon and Reid, 2009; Bell and Evans, 2010) and studies of limit spaces, such as borders and limit figures (e.g. Amoore, 2006; Cairo, 2006; Salter, 2006; Doty, 2007; Isin and Rygiel, 2007), are of particular significance to the analysis of humanitarian governing. International governmentality studies, in turn, provide important insights and productive ways of using governmentality for the study of the international (global) domain, such as the need to be attentive to the different rationalities and technologies of governing that characterise specific regimes of governing (e.g. Rosenow, 2009; Walters, 2012), which often traverse domestic/international boundaries.

Notes

1 This expression is used here in a way signalled by Massumi (2009: 158, in Lemke, 2014: 3), i.e. to refer to a critical engagement with Foucault's conceptual and methodological tool-box and its extension to explore issues he did not consider.
2 See Esposito (2008) and the *Generation Online* for the versions of the origin of the term itself.
3 See also Altamirano (2014) for an insightful discussion of the genealogy of this concept and its significance for understanding and challenging the nature/artifice divide.
4 Agamben's account and his attempt to 'correct' and 'complete' Foucault has been widely engaged: Fitzpatrick (2005); Lemke (2005); Ojakangas (2005); Dillon (2005); Mills (2007); Patton (2007); Connolly (2007); Vaughan-Williams (2009a, 2009b); Campbell (2011); Blencowe (2012). Esposito's contribution is yet to receive the full attention it deserves: for some exceptions see Campbell (2008); Campbell (2011); Revel (2009); and Cooter and Stein (2010).
5 See Lemke (2010) for the discussion of the origins of the term.
6 Nadesan (2008), in turn, identifies six methodological assumptions on which the governmentality approach rests, including: extending analysis beyond the state; appreciating interplays of multiple systems of power and strategies of resistance, including the continued importance of sovereignty; conducting analysis at multiple levels; and incorporating alternative histories.
7 See Campbell (2011) for an overview of some of the key conceptualisations of biopolitics; Lemke (2011) for a general overview; and Rutherford and Rutherford (2013) for the overview of biopolitics scholarship in a specific disciplinary setting, that of Geography.
8 I draw on the scholarship on biopolitics of development and humanitarianism in the next chapter.
9 Walters (2012) also provides his own excellent overview of the field.
10 In his recent overview of the field, Weidner (2011) emphasises the importance of governmentality as a conceptual framework for analysis of the international/global domain and outlines some crucial differences between governmentality studies and other approaches. Thus, with reference to Larner and Walters (2004), Weidner points out that even globalisation itself is problematised in governmentality studies in that it is understood as one possibility among many, and its discourses are viewed as making possible certain policies and practices, while foreclosing others.

References

Agamben, G. 1998. *Homo Sacer: sovereign power and bare life*. Stanford: Stanford University Press.

Agamben, G. 2002. *Remnants of Auschwitz: the witness and the archive*. New York: Zone Books.

Altamirano, M. 2014. Three Concepts for Crossing the Nature – Artifice Divide: Technology, Milieu, and Machine. *Foucault Studies*, **17**: 11–35.

Amoore, L. 2006. Biometric borders: governing mobilities in the War on Terror. *Political Geography*, **25**(2): 336–351.

Barry, A. *et al.* 1996. Introduction. *In*: A. Barry, T. Osborn and N. Rose (eds). *Foucault and political reason: liberalism, neoliberalism and rationalities of government*. London: The University of Chicago Press, pp. 1–17.

Bell, C. and B. Evans. 2010. Terrorism to insurgency: mapping the post-intervention security terrain. *Journal of Intervention and Statebuilding*, **4**(4): 371–390.

Blencowe, C. 2012. *Biopolitical experience: Foucault, power and positive critique*. Basingstoke: Palgrave Macmillan.

Bröckling, U., S. Krasmann and T. Lemke. 2011. From Foucault's lectures at the *Collège de France* to studies of governmentality: an introduction. *In*: U. Bröckling, S. Krasmann and T. Lemke (eds). *Governmentality: current issues and future challenges*. London: Routledge, pp. 1–33.

Burchell, G. 1996. Liberal government and techniques of the self. *In*: A. Barry, T. Osborne and N. Rose (eds). *Foucault and political reason: liberalism, neo-liberalism and rationalities of government*. Chicago: University of Chicago Press, pp. 19–36.

Cairo, H. 2006. The duty of the benevolent master: from sovereignty to suzerainty and the biopolitics of intervention. *Alternatives: Global, Local, Political*, **31**: 285–311.

Campbell, T. 2008. Bíos, immunity, life: the thought of Roberto Esposito. Translator's introduction. *In*: R. Esposito. *Bíos: biopolitics and philosophy*. Minneapolis: University of Minnesota Press, pp. vii–xlii.

Campbell, T. 2011. *Improper life: technology and biopolitics from Heidegger to Agamben*. London: University of Minnesota Press.

Campbell, T. and A. Sitze. 2013. Introduction. Biopolitics: an encounter. *In*: T. Campbell and A. Sitze (eds). *Biopolitics: a reader*. London: Duke University Press, pp. 1–40.

Collier, S.J. 2009. Topologies of power: Foucault's analysis of political government beyond 'governmenatlity'. *Theory, Culture & Society*, **26**(6): 78–108.

Collier, S.J. and A. Lakoff. 2005. On regimes of living. *In*: A. Ong and S.J. Collier (eds). *Global assemblages: technology, politics, and ethics anthropological problems*. Oxford: Blackwell, pp. 22–39.

Connolly, W.E. 2007. Complexities of sovereignty. *In*: M. Calarco and S. DeCaroli (eds). *Giorgio Agamben: sovereignty and life*. Stanford: Stanford University Press, pp. 23–42.

Cooper, M. 2006. Pre-empting emergence: the biological turn in the war on terror. *Theory, Culture & society*, **23**(4): 113–135.

Cooter, R. and C. Stein. 2010. 'Cracking' biopower. *History of Human Sciences*, **23**(2): 109–128.

Dauphinee, E. and C. Masters. 2007. Introduction: living, dying, surviving. *In*: Dauphinee, E. and C. Masters (eds). *The logics of biopower and the War on Terror: living, dying, surviving*. Basingstoke: Palgrave Macmillan, pp. vii–xix.

Dean, M. 1999. *Governmentality: power and rule in modern society*. London: SAGE.

Dean, M. 2002. Powers of life and death beyond governmentality. *Journal for Cultural Research*, **6**(1): 119–138.

Death, C. 2013. Governmentality at the limit of the international: African politics and Foucauldian theory. *Review of International Studies*, **39**(3): 763–787.

Diken, B. 2004. From refugee camps to gated communities: biopolitics and the end of the city. *Citizenship Studies*, **8**(1): 83–106.

Dillon, M. 1995. Sovereignty and governmentality: from the problematic of the 'New World Order' to the ethical problematic of the world order. *Alternatives: Global, Local, Political*, **20**(3): 323–368.

Dillon, M. 2005. Cared to death: the biopoliticised time of your life. *Foucault Studies*, **2**: 37–46.

Dillon, M. 2008. Security, race and war. *In*: M. Dillon and A.W. Neal (eds). *Foucault on politics, security and war*. Basingstoke: Palgrave Macmillan, pp. 166–196.

46   'Working with Foucault after Foucault'

Dillon, M. and L. Lobo-Guerrero. 2008. Biopolitics of security in the 21st century: an introduction. *Review of International Studies*, **34**: 265–292.
Dillon, M. and A.W. Neal. 2008. Introduction. *In*: M. Dillon and A.W. Neal (eds). *Foucault on politics, security and war*. Basingstoke: Palgrave Macmillan, pp. 1–18.
Dillon, M. and J. Reid. 2009. *The liberal way of war: killing to make life live*. Abingdon: Routledge.
Doty, R.L. 2007. Crossroads of death. *In*: Dauphinee, E. and C. Masters (eds). *The logics of biopower and the War on Terror: living, dying, surviving*. Basingstoke: Palgrave Macmillan, pp. 3–24.
Doty, R.L. 2011. Bare life, border-crossing deaths and spaces of moral alibi. *Environment and Planning D: Society and Space*, **29**(4): 599–612.
Duffield, M. 2001. *Global governance and the new wars: the merging of development and security*. London: Zed Books.
Duffield, M. 2007. *Development, security and the unending war: governing the world of peoples*. Cambridge: Polity Press.
Edkins, J. and V. Pin-Fat. 2004. Introduction: life, power, resistance. *In*: J. Edkins, V. Pin-Fat and M.J. Shapiro (eds). *Sovereign lives: power in global politics*. Abingdon: Routledge, pp. 1–22.
Elbe, S. 2008. Risking lives: AIDS, security and there concepts of risk. *Security Dialogue*, **39**(2–3): 177–198.
Enoch, S. 2004. The contagion of difference: identity, bio-politics and National Socialism. *Foucault Studies*, **1**: 53–70.
Esposito, R. 2008. *Bíos: biopolitics and philosophy*. Minneapolis: University of Minnesota Press.
Fitzpatrick, P. 2005. Bare sovereignty: Homo Sacer and the insistence of law. *In*: A. Norris (ed.). *Essays on Giorgio Agamben's Homo Sacer*. Durham and London: Duke University Press, pp. 49–73.
Foucault, M. 1977. *Discipline and punish: the birth of the prison*. London: Allen Lane.
Foucault, M. 1983. On the genealogy of ethics: an overview of work in progress. *In*: H. L. Dreyfus and P. Rabinow. *Michel Foucault: Beyond Structuralism and Hermeneutics*. Chicago: The University of Chicago Press, pp. 231–232.
Foucault, M. 1987. Nietzsche, genealogy, history. *In*: M. T. Gibbons (ed.). *Interpreting politics*. Oxford: Basil Blackwell, pp. 221–240.
Foucault, M. 1990. *Politics, philosophy, culture: interviews and other writings, 1977–1984*. L.D. Kritzman (ed.). London: Routledge.
Foucault, M. 1998. *The history of sexuality. Volume 1: The will to knowledge*. Harmondsworth: Penguin Books.
Foucault, M. 2000a. Polemics, politics and problematizations: an interview with Michel Foucault. *In*: P. Rabinow (ed.). *Essential works of Michel Foucault 1954–1984. Volume 1. Ethics: Subjectivity and Truth*. London: Penguin, pp. 113–119.
Foucault, M. 2000b. The political technology of individuals. *In*: J.D. Faubion (ed.). *Power: essential works of Foucault 1954–1984. Volume 3*. London: Penguin Books, pp. 403–417.
Foucault, M. 2001. *Fearless speech*. J. Pearson (ed.). Los-Angeles, CA: Semiotext(e).
Foucault, M. 2002. *The order of things: An archaeology of the human sciences*. London: Routledge.
Foucault, M. 2003. *Society must be defended: Lectures at the Collége de France, 1975–76*. London: Penguin Books.
Foucault, M. 2007. *Security, territory, population. Lectures at the Collége de France, 1977–78*. Basingstoke: Palgrave Macmillan.

Foucault, M. 2008a. *The birth of biopolitics: Lectures at the Collège de France, 1978–1979*. Basingstoke: Palgrave Macmillan.

Foucault, M. 2008b. The incorporation of the hospital into modern technology. *In*: J. W. Crampton and S. Elden (eds). *Space, knowledge and power: Foucault and geography*. Aldershot: Ashgate, pp. 141–151.

Foucault, M. 2008c. The meshes of power. *In*: J. W. Crampton and S. Elden (eds). *Space, knowledge and power: Foucault and geography*. Aldershot: Ashgate, pp. 153–162.

Generation Online (no date). *The first use of biopolitics.* [online]. [Accessed 11 June 2014]. www.generation-online.org/c/fc_biopolitics1.htm.

Gilson, E.C. 2014. Ethics and the ontology of freedom: problematization and responsiveness in Foucault and Deleuze. *Foucault Studies*, **17**: 76–98.

Giroux, H.A. 2008. Beyond biopolitics of disposability: rethinking neoliberalism in the New Gilded Age. *Social Identities*, **14**(5): 587–620.

Gordon, C. 1980. Afterword. *In*: C. Gordon (ed.). *Power/knowledge: selected interviews and other writings 1972–1977. Michel Foucault.* Harvester Press Limited, pp. 229–259.

Grove, K. 2014. Biopolitics and adaptation: governing socio-ecological contingency through climate change and disaster studies. *Geography Compass*, **8**(3): 198–210.

Hamann, T.H. 2009. Neoliberalism, governmentality, and ethics. *Foucault Studies*, **6**: 37–59.

Hannah, M.G. 2011. *Biopower, life and left politics. Antipode*, **43**(4): 1034–1055.

Hardt, M. and A. Negri. 2000. *Empire*. London: Harvard University Press.

Howarth, D. 2002. An archaeology of political discourse? Evaluating Michel Foucault's explanation and critique of ideology. *Political Studies*, **50**: 117–135.

Isin, E.F. and K. Rygiel. 2007. Abject spaces: frontiers, zones, camps. *In*: Dauphinee, E. and C. Masters (eds). *The logics of biopower and the War on Terror: living, dying, surviving*. Basingstoke: Palgrave Macmillan, pp. 181–203.

Jessop, B. 2011. Constituting another Foucault's effect: Foucault on states and statecraft. *In*: U. Bröckling, S. Krasmann and T. Lemke (eds). *Governmentality: current issues and future challenges*. London: Routledge, pp. 56–73.

Joseph, J. 2009. Governmentality of what? Populations, states and international organisations. *Global Society*, **23**(4): 413–427.

Joseph, J. 2010. What can governmentality do for IR? *International Political Sociology*, **4**(2): 202–205.

Joseph, J. and O. Corry. 2014. Jonathan Joseph and Olaf Corry review each other's books on governmentality and global politics and then respond to each other's reviews. *European Political Science*, **13**: 124–130.

Kelly, M.G.E. 2008. *The political philosophy of Michel Foucault*. London: Routledge.

Kelly, M.G.E. 2010. International biopolitics: Foucault, globalisation and imperialism. *Theoria*, **57**(123): 1–26.

Kiersey, N.J. 2011. Neoliberal political economy and the subjectivity of crisis: why governmentality is not hollow. *In*: N.J. Kiersey and D. Stokes (eds). *Foucault and International Relation: new critical engagements*. Abingdon: Routledge, pp. 1–24.

Koopman, C. 2013. *Genealogy as critique: Foucault and the problems of modernity*. Bloomington, IN: Indiana University Press.

Larner, W. and W. Walters. 2004. Introduction. *In*: W. Larner and W. Walters (eds). *Global governmentality: governing international spaces*. London: Routledge, pp. 1–20.

Lemke, T. 2001. 'The birth of bio-politics': Michel Foucault's lecture at the Collège de France on neo-liberal governmentality. *Economy and Society*, **30**(2): 190–207.

Lemke, T. 2005. A zone of indistinction: a critique of Giorgio Agamben's concept of bio-politics. [online]. [Accessed 17 March 2009]. www.thomaslemkeweb.de/engl.%20 texte/A%20Zone3.pdf.

Lemke, T. 2007. *Biopolitics: an introduction.* [online]. [Accessed 5 November 2008]. www.thomaslemkeweb.de/engl.%20texte/Introductionfinal.pdf.

Lemke, T. 2010. Foucault's hypothesis: from the critique of the juridico-discursive concept of power to an analytics of government. *Parrhesia*, **9**: 31–43.

Lemke, T. 2011. *Biopolitics: an advanced introduction.* Albany: New York University Press.

Lemke, T. 2014. New materialisms: Foucault and the 'Government of Things'. *Theory, Culture & Society*, **0**(0): 1–23.

Lui-Bright, R. 1997. International/national: sovereignty, governmentality and International Relations. *Australasian Political Studies*, **2**: 581–597.

Masters, C. 2007. Body counts: the biopolitics of death. *In*: Dauphinee, E. and C. Masters (eds). *The logics of biopower and the War on Terror: living, dying, surviving.* Basingstoke: Palgrave Macmillan, pp. 43–57.

Miller, P. and N. Rose. 2008. *Governing the present: administering economic, social and personal life.* Cambridge: Polity Press.

Mills, K. 2007. Biopolitics, liberal eugenics, and nihilism. *In*: M. Calarco and S. DeCaroli (eds). *Giorgio Agamben: sovereignty and life.* Stanford: Stanford University Press, pp. 180–202.

Muller, B.J. 2008. Securing the political imagination: popular culture, the security dispositive and the biometric state. *Security Dialogue*, **39**(2–3): 199–220.

Nadesan, M.H. 2008. *Governmentality, biopower, and everyday life.* London: Routledge.

Ojakangas, M. 2005. Impossible dialogue on bio-power: Agamben and Foucault. *Foucault Studies*, **2**: 5–28.

Oksala, J. 2013. From biopower to governmentality. *In*: C. Falzon, T. O'Leary and J. Sawicki (eds). *A Companion to Foucault.* Chichester: Wiley-Blackwell, pp. 320–336.

Pasha, M.K. 2010. Disciplining Foucault. *International Political Sociology*, **4**(2): 213–215.

Patton, P. 2007. Agamben and Foucault on biopower and biopolitics. *In*: M. Calarco and S. DeCaroli (eds). *Giorgio Agamben: sovereignty and life.* Stanford: Stanford University Press, pp. 203–218.

Picket, B. 2005. *On the use and abuse of Foucault for politics.* Oxford: Lexington Books (Rowman & Littlefield).

Prozorov, S. 2007. The unrequited love of power: biopolitical investment and the refusal of care. *Foucault Studies*, **4**: 53–77.

Reid, J. 2008. Life struggles: war, discipline and biopolitics in the thought of Michel Foucault. *In*: S. Morton and S. Bygrave (eds). *Foucault in an age of terror: essays on biopolitics and the defence of society.* Basingstoke: Palgrave Macmillan, pp. 14–42.

Reiss, T. 2004. Calculating humans: mathematics, war, and the colonial calculus. *In*: D. Glimp and M.R. Warren (eds). *Arts of calculation: quantifying thought in early modern Europe.* Basingstoke: Palgrave Macmillan, pp. 137–163.

Revel, J. 2009. Identity, nature, life: three biopolitical deconstructions. *Theory, Culture & Society*, **26**(6): 45–54.

Richmond, O.P. 2010. Foucault and the paradox of peace-as-governance versus everyday agency. *International Political Sociology*, **4**(2): 199–202.

Rose, N. 1996. Governing 'advanced' liberal democracies. *In*: A. Barry, T. Osborne and N. Rose (eds). *Foucault and political reason: liberalism, neoliberalism and rationalities of government.* London: The University of Chicago Press, pp. 37–64.

Rose, N., O'Malley, P. and M. Valverde. 2006. Governmentality. *Annual Review of Law & Social Sciences*, **2**: 83–104.

Rosenow, D. 2009. Decentring global power: the merits of a Foucauldian approach to International Relations. *Global Society*, **23**(4): 497–517.

Rutherford, S. and P. Rutherford. 2013. Geography and biopolitics. *Geography Compass*, **7**(6): 423–434.

Salter, M.B. 2006. The global visa regime and the political technologies of international self: borders, bodies, biopolitics. *Alternatives: Global, Local, Political*, **31**: 167–189.

Selby. J. 2007. Engaging Foucault: discourse, global governance and the limits of Foucauldian IR. *International Relations*, **21**(3): 324–345.

Sending, O.J. and I.B. Neumann. 2006. Governance to governmentality: analyzing NGOs, states, and power. *International Studies Quarterly*, **50**: 651–672.

Senellart, M. 2007. Course context. *In*: M. Foucault. *Security, territory, population. Lectures at the Collége de France, 1977–78*. Basingstoke: Palgrave Macmillan, pp. 369–401.

Senellart, M. 2008. Course context. *In*: M. Foucault. *The birth of biopolitics: Lectures at the Collège de France, 1978–1979*. Basingstoke: Palgrave Macmillan, pp. 327–330.

Sheshadri, K. R. 2008. When home is a camp: global sovereignty, bio-Politics and internally displaced persons. *Social Text*, **26**(1): 29–58.

Smart, B. 1985. *Michel Foucault*. London: Routledge.

Vaughan-Williams, N. 2009a. Giorgio Agamben. *In*: J. Edkins and N. Vaughan-Williams (eds). *Critical theorists and international relations*. London: Routledge, pp. 19–30.

Vaughan-Williams, N. 2009b. The Generalised Biopolitical Border? Re-conceptualising the Limits of Sovereign Power', *Review of International Studies*, **35**(4): 729–749.

Venn, C. 2009. Neoliberal political economy, biopolitics and colonialism a transcolonial genealogy of inequality. *Theory, Culture & Society*, **26**(2): 206–233.

Vrasti, W. 2013. Universal but not truly 'global': governmentality, economic liberalism, and the international. *Review of International Studies*, **39**(1): 49–69.

Walters, W. 2011a. Foucault and frontiers: notes on the birth of the humanitarian border. *In*: U. Bröckling, S. Krasmann and T. Lemke (eds). *Governmentality: current issues and future challenges*. London: Routledge, pp. 138–164.

Walters, W. 2011b. Rezoning the global: technological zones, technological work and the (un-)making of biometric borders. *In*: V. Squire (ed.). *The contested politics of mobility: borderzones and irregularity.* New York: Routledge, pp. 51–73.

Walters, W. 2012. *Governmentality: critical encounters*. London: Routledge.

Walters, W. and J.H. Haahr. 2005. *Governmentality and political studies*. *European Political Science*, **4**: 288–300.

Weidner, J.R. 2011. Governmentality, capitalism, and subjectivity. *In*: N.J. Kiersey and D. Stokes (eds). *Foucault and International Relation: new critical engagements*. Abingdon: Routledge, pp. 25–49.

Zanotti, L. 2013. Governmentality, ontology, methodology: re-thinking political agency in the global world. *Alternatives: Global, Local, Political*, **38**(4): 288–304.

2 'New' humanitarianism as a regime of governing

Context, agendas, actors and technologies

> Humanitarianism is an act of people helping people. It is a service, a calling, an expression of human solidarity ... humanitarianism is also a business driven by market forces and by agencies seeking to maintain and expand market share.
>
> (Smillie and Minear, 2004: 11)

> Technical knowledge and expertise – the nutritionist, the camp manager, the protection officer – are never neutral. Nor is the technology they bring.
>
> (Donini, 2010: 226)

Introduction

The term 'new humanitarianism' is said to have been coined by Duffield (Smillie and Minear, 2004: 159). Duffield is undoubtedly one of the first and most influential scholars to engage with the issue of the changing nature of humanitarian action and to use this term. In his *Global Governance and the New Wars: the Merging of Development and Security* (2001), Duffield uses it to refer to the global humanitarian action of the late 1990s. Although he does not provide a definition, he identifies and considers some of the important developments in the nature of global humanitarian action, many of which are also examined here.

The term 'new humanitarianism'[1] has also been widely used by others (e.g. Fox, 2001; Macrae, 2002; Smillie and Minear, 2004; Hoffman and Weiss, 2006), but, in some instances, with respect to humanitarian action in conflict environments only. For Allen and Styan (2000), 'new' humanitarianism is associated with practices of humanitarian intervention, while for Bah (2013: 5) it is 'a collaborative and holistic human development action and the broader policy and moral shift in the way the international community approached human security and sovereignty in Sierra Leone'. Here, the term is used to denote a post-Cold War evolutionary stage of the development of global humanitarian action, with a particular focus on what has been aptly termed an 'inter-war' period (Kahn and Cunningham, 2013: S142), i.e. between the end of the Cold War and the start of the War on Terror.

In particular, I demonstrate that while 'new' humanitarianism is 'new' in a number of important ways,[2] it is also about continuity; however, the changes that have been occurring in the nature of humanitarian action since the end of the Cold War are pervasive and significant enough to warrant the label, as well as special attention. This implies that 'new' humanitarianism represents a particular historical incarnation of humanitarianism. It is an evolving outcome of a number of shifts towards the increased prominence, broadening agenda and scope and increased intrusiveness of humanitarian action, along with its increased instrumentalisation in terms of the use of humanitarian rhetoric and humanitarian action for purposes other than those dictated by the humanitarian imperative. Furthermore, this kind of humanitarian action is better resourced and more institutionalised than before, and is carried out by a considerable number of different actors.

One of the first attempts to use Michel Foucault's theorising to produce an understanding of humanitarian issues was undertaken by Barbara Hendrie (1997), who operationalised Foucault's concept of power-knowledge to examine a particular relief operation, the one carried out to assist Tigrayan refugees in Eastern Sudan in 1984–1985. She argued that '[i]t is in the understanding of which practices and knowledges are dominant in a relief operation, and which subordinate, that an analysis of the real power effects that relief interventions produce should be grounded' (Hendrie, 1997: 7). Although in her analysis Hendrie did not follow all the steps of the analytics of government,[3] she emphasised the importance of problematisations (of famine) and the types of knowledge they were based on for producing uniform, decontextualised responses, while marginalising alternatives. According to Hendrie, while Tigrayans were portrayed as passive victims, it was their bodies that became the privileged site of intervention, made knowable through the data collected by aid workers. The focus of this data generation was very partial, as it was limited to questions of morbidity and mortality, with bodies stripped of their social functions and meaning (Hendrie, 1997), which points to processes of biologisation and aggregation characteristic of biopolitical governing and resulting in 'erasure' of individual bodies and individual stories. Given the focus on the quantifiable aspects of the bodies, famine was understood in a particularly decontextualised way, with the responses aimed at preventing mass mortality, i.e. at reducing death rates by keeping people alive (Hendrie, 1997). This is undoubtedly characteristic of biopolitical governing, for which death represents a limit. Overall, Hendrie (1997: 61) concluded that, 'despite the wide diversity of situations in which famine occur[ed], relief interventions exhibit[ed] a remarkable uniformity of approach, in terms of timing and orientation of the response', which points towards an emergence of a particular regime of governing.

Any analysis of an international regime of governing using Foucault's theorising on biopolitics and governmentality presents a number of challenges, and, to be productive, it needs to go further than simply suggesting that it represents an instance of neoliberal governing. It would be equally insufficient to simply claim that a regime is biopolitical, as it is necessary to demonstrate what specific biopolitical imperatives, strategies and technologies are characteristic to it. Therefore, using the logical steps of the analytics of government to critically examine 'new' humanitarianism, in this chapter I consider the ways in which situations in need of humanitarian response were problematised post-Cold War, the strategies and technologies of governing used during humanitarian interventions (broadly conceived), the actors carrying out these interventions and their networks, and the ways in which those to be assisted were constructed.

I argue that 'new' humanitarianism represents a project of neoliberal governmentality, reliant on sovereignty, discipline and biopolitics, and that interpreting it in such a way can provide important insights into the changing nature of humanitarian action post-Cold War. In particular, while biopolitical imperatives and technologies had previously characterised the humanitarian enterprise, it was only following the end of the Cold War, when the conditions were set for the unhindered spread of neoliberal governmentality, that 'new' humanitarianism emerged. In the process, some of the more 'positive' biopolitical imperatives of humanitarianism were substituted with 'negative' ones, deepening existing dilemmas, as well as creating new ones, while transforming the overall nature of humanitarian action.

Conditions of possibility I: changes in the post-Cold War environment

The principle of state sovereignty, a central pillar of Public International Law in general, and the UN Charter in particular, enjoyed unconditional respect and served as the main organising principle of international relations during the Cold War. However, post-Cold War, the perceived illegitimacy of certain governments and their inability to govern effectively, on one hand, and changing rules of intrastate relations, particularly between North and South, on the other hand, resulted in a considerable 'erosion' of the value of the principle of state sovereignty (Macrae, 2001). Already in 1992 the then UN Secretary General Boutros Boutros-Ghali famously proclaimed in his *Agenda for Peace* that '[t]he time of absolute and exclusive sovereignty ... ha[d] passed' (Boutrous-Ghali, 1992).

Increasingly, sovereignty began to be viewed in biopolitical terms, i.e. as a measure of the ability of a state to govern its own population. This shift, reflected in the new rhetoric of limited or conditional sovereignty, or sovereignty as responsibility (e.g. *The Responsibility to Protect*), was extremely selective to the extent that the question of sovereignty became a question of unequal sovereignties, at least de facto, if not de jure. Indeed, the language of 'weak' and 'failed' states was never meant to be applied to major Northern powers, and served, instead, to justify 'new' interventionism. This 'new' interventionism was made possible by the selective reinterpretation of the sovereignty-based principles of state equality and inviolability of sovereign borders previously guaranteed by non-intervention into domestic affairs and prohibition of a threat or use of force (Macrae, 2002). At the same time as Southern borders were increasingly becoming more porous, facilitating outside intervention, the Northern bloc was strengthening its borders, relying on tighter immigration rules and policies of containment adopted in response to the instability caused by the new generation of conflicts. Such policies made it increasingly difficult 'for people to get out of, or stay out of, their home countries' (Macrae, 2002: 6).

The Cold War dynamics ensured enduring Northern interest in the South. The division of the world by superpowers into the spheres of geostrategic influence informed the distribution of considerable resources and determined the rules under which they could be provided. The collapse of this bipolarity led to the increased disengagement of the North (Macrae, 2001: 1). Although the superpowers' disengagement facilitated the end of some conflicts, it also contributed to the emergence of new ones (Macrae, 2002), as the end of the bipolar system and the relative order and discipline associated with it, and the drying up of both political and economic support, led to mounting civil strife and intensification of latent rivalries in the former peripheral areas (Delorenzi, 1999). Most of these conflicts were occurring within, rather than between, states, and were therefore considered fundamentally different from those in the past, i.e. 'new wars' (Kaldor, 1999). Even if not radically new, these conflicts, according to Hoffman and Weiss (2006: 58), differed from those of the Cold War period in several important respects,[4] such as: locus (areas of fragmented political authority); agents (an increased role of non-state actors); economies (a growing role of illegal activities and aid); targets and victims (a prevalence of civilian casualties); technologies (new technologies); and media coverage (a greater media coverage). Importantly, these developments were interconnected, as, for instance, changes in the composition of the agents had an impact on the means and methods of warfare, and on the main targets. Thus, while during the Cold War conflicts a government was usually opposed by one or two identifiable and well-organised forces, which made the application of International Humanitarian Law (IHL) possible, including the principle of non-combatant immunity, post-Cold War conflicts occurred against the backdrop of disintegrating state structures and involved various non-state actors, rendering both IHL and a traditional humanitarian approach inadequate (Bugnion, in Delorenzi, 1999: 36).

The diminishing respect for IHL made post-Cold War conflicts appear especially brutal and barbaric; however, as Kalyvas (2001: 116) argues, 'both the perception that violence in old civil wars [was] limited, disciplined, or understandable and the view that violence in new civil wars [was] senseless, gratuitous, and uncontrolled fail[ed] to find support in the available evidence'. Extending the critique of the 'new' wars thesis, Berdal (2003) suggests it to be too simplistic, as well as uncritical and ahistorical. He stresses the importance of a more balanced approach, one that would appreciate continuity and change, material and nonmaterial incentives, and unique and common characteristics of a particular conflict. In particular, he points out that civil wars were not unique to the post-Cold War period, that international conflict was alive and well, and that 'the very distinction between "civil" and "international" ... [is] less than clear-cut' (Berdal, 2003: 483). While it is important to appreciate that internal conflicts inflicting suffering on civilian populations were not new (UNHCR, 1998), and to not view their violent practices as totally irrational or unprecedented, thus ignoring their context and driving forces (Delorenzi, 1999; Berdal, 2003), other differences highlighted above are arguably too significant to be disregarded. Indeed, it is clear that the changing nature of war had profound implications for humanitarian action, so much so that, for some, 'new' humanitarianism can be seen as a 'response to the complexity of the new wars' (Duffield, 2001: 80).

Duffield's reference to the complexity of the 'new' wars invites a discussion of another set of problematisations of post-Cold War instability, which includes 'complex emergency', 'complex political emergency', or 'complex humanitarian emergency'. The term 'complex emergency' itself was introduced in the late 1980s, initially in relation to conflicts in Africa and the Gulf, and was defined by the UN as 'a major humanitarian crisis of a multi-causal nature that requires a system-wide response' (as interpreted by Duffield, 1994a). As the definition suggests, we are confronted with two types of complexities – that of the cause and that of the response. Importantly, as Duffield (1994b: 50) points out, 'the difficulties in resolving such emergencies and relieving the suffering they cause[d] ha[d] increasingly highlighted the limitations of the ... international humanitarian system'.

The wide (and persistent) use of the term 'complex emergency' has important implications. Thus, Edkins (2000) argues that by calling a conflict a complex emergency, we obscure any possible political connotations, blaming instead the complexity of the causal picture and excusing the absence of solutions. In this respect, the use of the term 'complex humanitarian emergency' (e.g. Natsios, 2001) can result in further depoliticisation and decontextualisation. As Rieff (2002: 75) notes, 'all wars have causes. They are not humanitarian emergencies, and to describe them in this way is to distort both their reality and their significance.' Indeed, the complexity of emergencies refers not to the perception of those who suffer the wars, but rather to the experience of outsiders seeking to respond to such wars (Slim, 1997). Moreover, complex, or multi-faceted responses to complex emergencies, are not necessarily right (Roberts, 1996). At the same time, in the UN definition the stress was placed on the complex response, which had important implications for humanitarian action, as 'the objectives of aid, diplomacy, military and trade policies [began to be seen as] necessarily compatible' (Macrae and Leader, 2001: 295). It can be argued that problematisations like 'complex emergency' are not really suggestive of an increasingly complex world, but rather of a biopolitical will to grasp and govern collective life of suffering populations in all its complexity, to govern it through its immediate milieu.[5]

The change in the way in which the situations requiring humanitarian responses were framed post-Cold War, i.e. as emergencies, humanitarian or complex, with depoliticising effects, was instrumental in the rise of 'new' humanitarianism. Another problematisation, that of catastrophisation, applied to situations in which 'natural and man-made forces and factors work together to create devastating effects on a large population' (Ophir, 2010: 60). The catastrophisation discourse was also one through which exception could be created and which brought together humanitarian and state agents (Ophir, 2010). As the presence and involvement of humanitarian actors often presented an implied challenge to states, 'the urgent needs of people caught up in crises' became 'the contested ground on which states and humanitarian actors clash[ed]' (Kahn and Cunningham, 2013: S140, 139).

This new protracted instability associated with 'new' wars and complex emergencies presented a serious threat of large-scale population flows that had to be contained. For instance, the prevention of refugee flows from the former Yugoslavia in 1991–1995 is widely considered to have been an explicit strategy of the West (e.g. Borton, 1998; Rieff, 2002; Braem, 2008), a strategy 'tested' for the first time during the Gulf War (1991 *Operation Safe Heaven*):

> The international reaction to the Kurdish exodus is perhaps the most clear-cut example of the new containment policy ... based on the triad of repatriation, security zones and humanitarian assistance. It was as though this policy was designed to force refugee camps back into countries in crisis, in zones theoretically protected by an international presence and, in principle, supplied by aid convoys.
>
> (Jean, 1997: 52)

This containment required not only the strengthening of borders through imposing restrictions on the numbers of asylum-seekers and refugees and the increased use of *refoulement* (involuntary return to the country where security of refugees could be jeopardised) and even expulsion, but also re-engagement with the violent conflict. Such re-engagement was operationalised, *inter alia*, through the 'new' interventionism, which included supporting and protecting conflict-affected populations *in situ* (Duffield, 1997a; Borton, 1998; Macrae, 2002) and therefore called for new roles for humanitarian aid and humanitarians. Seen in this way, what may seem as a genuine paradox in fact was not, as closure of borders and new interventionism represented two sides of the same coin. Thus, according to Bennet (in Dubernet, 2001: 19), '[i]ntervention is disengagement, for it is associated with containment which supports populations in war zones, discourages refugee flows and internalises causes and consequences'. For Duffield (1997a: 338), humanitarian interventionism was 'part of a wider trend towards separate development within the global economy and the containment of the associated instability'. He argues (1997a; also 2008) that such interventions served to ensure containment and to prevent people in crisis from crossing international borders, thus further sustaining the biopolitical divide. Indeed, with humanitarian assistance being the response of choice to any crisis or instability beyond Western borders, the absence of a commitment to bridging the gap between the developed and the under-developed became even more apparent (Duffield, 1997b).

One of the serious implications of the prevention of refugee flows was the creation of large numbers of internally displaced persons (IDPs), who did not enjoy the legal protection of refugees. Thus, according to the 2006 *State of the World Refugees Report*, while the number of refugees halved from 18 million in 1992 to just over nine million in 2004, the number of IDPs had been steadily increasing from 1997 (UNHCR, 2006). In a powerful account of international policies regarding IDPs, which draws on the cases of Iraq, Bosnia, Rwanda and Somalia, Dubernet (2001: 30) contends that protection of IDPs serves as a tool of containment policies, as 'promises of safety for IDPs are contingent on fears of mass exodus', while 'safety for IDPs is subordinated to containment objectives'. Importantly, the restrictive policies towards refugees employed by the West were mirrored by the developing countries in their relationships with each other, which began to be characterised by a shift from an 'open door' policy to policies of containment, the *refoulement* of refugees, disregard for their rights, and abandonment of any durable solutions apart from repatriation (e.g. Rutinwa, 2002). Thus, according to the UN High Commissioner for Refugees, in Africa '[p]eople who would otherwise seek safety in neighbouring states [were] more frequently compelled to remain within the borders of their own country, most often in similar conditions as refugees' (UNHCR, 2006: xi).

Conditions of possibility II: new agendas for humanitarian action

The so-called 'coherence' agenda was born within the UN in the early 1990s and was driven by the convergence of geopolitical (e.g. reinterpretation of state sovereignty, widening the definition of security, and a search for new conflict management tools), aid-specific (declining aid-flows and mounting critique of aid) and domestic factors in donor countries (e.g. calls for 'joined-up' government) (Macrae and Leader, 2000, 2001). Having entered a veto-free era of international consensus (Slim, 1995), the UN wanted to seize the opportunity to fulfil its goal of saving 'succeeding generations from the scourge of war' (UN Charter preamble), or at least to re-establish its central role in this process, which was reflected in the 1992 *Agenda for Peace*. This report delivered a vision in which all the various tools that the UN had at its disposal – preventive diplomacy, peacemaking, peacekeeping and post-conflict peacebuilding – 'taken together' were to 'offer a coherent contribution towards securing peace' (para. 22), thereby providing a conceptual framework for a coherent approach to conflict management (Macrae and Leader, 2000). Coherence in that context can be defined as:

> the attempt to bring together, cohere or join up political action in peace operations with other actions including humanitarian and human rights ... it is the attempt to bring together all elements of a multi-dimensional peace operation to serve the UN's central objective to make, maintain or build peace and security in [a particular] country.
>
> (The Henry Dunant Centre for Humanitarian Dialogue, 2003: 24)

The *Agenda for Peace* closely followed the 1991 General Assembly Resolution 46/182 '*Strengthening the coordination of humanitarian emergency assistance of the United Nations*' that already established a link between emergency relief, rehabilitation and development. Even though *Agenda for Peace* did not specifically focus on humanitarian action, it had important implications for it, both conceptual and practical. Thus, Macrae and Leader (2000: 12) suggest that the Report presented significant steps in: redefining security to embrace new threats and paving the way for the concept of human security and, therefore, bridging the traditionally separate domains of the Security Council and humanitarian enterprise; rationalising the idea of limited state sovereignty, thereby justifying interventions, including those by humanitarian actors, on the grounds of 'human rights, peace and prosperity'; and eliminating divisions between aid instruments and political and military instruments in addressing the root causes of conflicts. The coherence agenda was instrumental in governmentalising the international by encouraging the rise of new complex networks of actors, including states, international intergovernmental organisations and NGOs, with a view to addressing the post-Cold War instability and disorder.

Importantly, not only did *Agenda* influence a number of Security Council resolutions, but it also informed a series of what Slim (1995) calls 'humanitarian experiments', e.g. UN operations in countries like Somalia, the former Yugoslavia and Rwanda. Overall, in the 1990s multilateral peacekeeping operations proliferated in number and saw their mandates radically expanded (Kahn and Cunningham, 2013; for more details see Zanotti, 2011). However, out of all the crises in the 1990s, it was the genocide in Rwanda that marked a turning point in the UN approaches to conflict (The Henry Dunant Centre for Humanitarian Dialogue, 2003: 3). The 1996 *Joint Evaluation of Emergency Assistance in Rwanda* stressed 'a lack of coherence in policy and strategy formulation' and concluded that 'humanitarian action [could not] substitute for political action'. It was recommended to the Secretary General and the Security Council to form a team of core advisors for each such crisis with a view to formulating

> [t]he essential framework for an integrated UN line of command between headquarters and the field, and within the field, for political action, peacekeeping and humanitarian assistance to ensure that the system [spoke] with one voice and that there [was] mutual reinforcement among the three types of action.
>
> (Eriksson *et al.*, in The Henry Dunant Centre for Humanitarian Dialogue, 2003: 3)

The evaluation was important in providing support for the coherence agenda, and it also informed the further pursuit of the integrated approach to peace, which culminated in the concept of the 'integrated mission', introduced in 2000 by *The Brahimi Report* (the *Report of the Panel on United Nations Peace Operations*). The UN Office for the Coordination of Humanitarian Affairs (UN OCHA) defined integrated mission as an

> instrument with which the UN seeks to help countries in transition from war to lasting peace, or address a similarly complex situation that requires a

system-wide UN response, through subsuming various actors and approaches within an overall political-strategic crisis management framework.

(Reindorp and Wiles, in Weir, 2006: 12)

This definition, rather like that of complex emergency, invoked the idea of a system-wide response – based on the assumption that development assistance and humanitarian relief were compatible with all other conflict management tools – and that, used together, they could actually form a kind of synergy in bringing about peace and security. What remained unclear, however, was which priorities, humanitarian or those of peacemaking, would prevail if in conflict. This was not just a theoretical question – i.e. one of a tension between the deontology of the humanitarian imperative and the teleology of peacemaking – but also a practical one, as the experience of Liberia and Sierra Leone showed. In practice, on a number of occasions humanitarian agencies were subjugated to the UN political mandate (Macrae and Leader, 2000), which led to the argument that 'coherence and integration [became] euphemisms for the subordination of principles to political objectives' (Donini *et al.*, 2006: 23). Therefore, an integrated mission[6] might be better understood as 'one where the management structure [was] such as to ensure that varied actions [were] coordinated through a clear chain of command to serve a single or coherent policy objective of peace and security' (The Henry Dunant Centre for Humanitarian Dialogue, 2003: 24). It is in this way that '[h]umanitarian aid [became] an integral part of donors' comprehensive strategy to transform conflicts, decrease violence and set the stage for liberal development' (Curtis, 2001: 3). Indeed, as Thede (2013) convincingly demonstrates, the coherence agenda was a major conduit through which neoliberal rationality was promoted internationally. Thus, DAC policy documents were clear in stressing a free market economy as the basis for development, the latter redefined as economic growth, leaving little space for any alternatives. The coherence agenda also informed related changes in donor countries themselves, as reflected in 'whole-of-government' or 3D (defence-diplomacy-development) approaches (Thede, 2013).

The 1990s saw many concepts and policies redefined, including that of security, which was broadened to encompass human security, and it was *An Agenda for Peace*, together with the 1994 *UNDP Human Development Report*, that played an important role in introducing and promoting human security. As far as the latter is concerned, Duffield and Waddell (2006: 7) believe that it represented 'one of the first systematic elaborations of the idea that the post-Cold War period was defined by threats to people's well-being rather than inter-state conflict'. The main focus of the UNDP document was on development, and it interpreted human security not just as 'freedom from fear', but also as 'freedom from want', thereby encompassing a broad range of insecurities associated with poverty, unemployment and disease (Reindorp, 2002: 30). This conceptualisation firmly established the focus on populations as both affected by, and generative of, threats and insecurities (e.g. Zanotti, 2011). In terms of responses to these threats and insecurities, human security was one of the key problematisations that made possible the coming together of military and civilian actors (Makaremi, 2010). Like other problematisations already considered, it had depoliticising effects, but also reflected 'the long-standing dream of liberal political economy: to secure life, choices, and opportunities, through an adequate management of risks and contingencies' (Makaremi, 2010: 109). In this way, human security discourse could be seen as bringing together the two 'faces' of biopolitics: elimination of threats to life and care provision, with the former often reliant on sovereign violence and the latter predominantly focused on survival. Indeed, human security is widely held to be a biopolitical approach *par excellence* (e.g. Duffield and Waddell, 2006; Grayson, 2008; de Larrinaga and Doucet, 2008).

At the same time, with the establishment of the link between development and security, aid was increasingly seen as 'a strategic tool of conflict resolution and social reconstruction' (Duffield, 2002: 1049), and was used to govern chaotic and disorderly global borderlands. Importantly, the inhabitants of the global borderlands were perceived as essentially different, and the divide between them and populations of the developed countries was informed by a new sociocultural racism (Duffield, 1996, 2006). All these developments revealed the essentially biopolitical nature of the divide between developed and under-developed, or 'insured' and 'non-insured', populations (Duffield, 2005, 2007, 2008). While the former 'exist[ed] in relation to massified and pluralistic welfare regimes that, in addition [to] private insurance cover, include[d] comprehensive state-based or regulated safety-nets covering health care, education, employment protection and pensions', the latter were 'distinguished by the absence of such massive life-support mechanisms; they [were], essentially, non-insured' (Duffield, 2005: 145). In the absence of commitment to genuine development and with assistance interventions focusing on self-reliance, the responsibility for the non-insured did not lie with anybody but themselves (Duffield, 2006; Kelly, 2010), which can be seen as a stark example of neoliberal responsibilisation. Kelly suggests seeing minimalist humanitarian and development aid as inferior biopolitics, which only resembles that available to the developed populations 'insofar as it involves monitoring and intervention' (Kelly, 2010: 11). The 'development' that constitutes the core of this biopolitics 'is non-material' and 'is more an exercise in reducing expectations rather than in providing significant material gains' (Pupavac, 2005, in Duffield, 2010a: 56).

Both the *Agenda for Peace* and the UNDP Report not only signalled a shift of emphasis from state sovereignty to that of people, but also established the right of the international community to consider a whole range of issues as security threats and to address them accordingly (Reindorp, 2002: 30). This right, later interpreted as a responsibility in the 2001 *Responsibility to Protect* (R2P) produced by the International Commission on Intervention and State Sovereignty (ICISS), was crucial in legitimising military humanitarianism in the form of humanitarian interventions. Military interventions were common in the pre-Charter, force-based world order. The prohibition of the threat or use of force made them less frequent, but failed to eradicate them completely (MacFarlane, 2005). The Cold War period witnessed interventions by superpowers, great powers, regional powers (e.g. Egypt in Yemen, Tanzania in Uganda) and multilateral organisations. In general, however, 'intervention during the Cold War was mainly unilateral, state-based and self-centred' (MacFarlane, 2005: 20). Even though some of the interventions had humanitarian outcomes, the attempts to justify them on humanitarian grounds were rare. The post-Cold War changes in the global context, such as the previously considered erosion of state sovereignty, coupled with the UN's desire to engage with violent conflict, and reinterpretation of gross human rights violations (often associated with civil strife within a state, as in case of Somalia, Rwanda and former Yugoslavia), as posing a threat to international peace and security, led to the revival of the concept of 'humanitarian intervention' (MacFarlane, 2005). This concept, although arguably one of the most controversial, quickly gained support and prominence, which meant a dramatic transformation of the humanitarian project, as it no longer was one which just mitigated violence, but also one that justified it (Slim, 2001: 327), thus signalling the use of biopolitical concerns to justify sovereign violence.

Neither of the elements of the concept of 'humanitarian intervention' (i.e. 'humanitarian' and 'intervention'), nor their combination, easily lends itself to a definition; however, overall it can be understood as a 'coercive action by one or more states involving the use of armed force in another state, [mainly] without the consent of its authorities, and with the purpose of preventing widespread suffering or death among the inhabitants' (Roberts, 2000: 4). The UN operation in Somalia was to become not only the first intervention in a civil war (the Gulf War was unambiguously an international armed conflict) with the humanitarian mandate, but also an instance of multidimensional peace-keeping (UN, 1996: 3–4). With respect to the first feature, Breau (2005: 192) believes that the intervention in Somalia presented an important development in UN practice, where 'a civil war was declared to be a threat to international peace and security and the use of force was authorised in the delivery of humanitarian supplies'. Given the widespread acceptance of the legality of the intervention by the international community, Somalia was precedent-setting with respect to the Security Council authorisation for humanitarian intervention (Breau, 2005). As far as multidimensional peace-keeping was concerned, although the ambitious and ever-shifting mandate was widely recognised as one of the major reasons for the Somalia debacle, the UN evaluation not only put the blame on the complexity of the situation and obstructions created by the warring factions, but rather uncritically called for even more coherence and integration:

> For peace-keeping operations ... in a failed State, no issue can be considered purely military or purely humanitarian.... It is necessary to enunciate a coherent vision, strategy and plan of action which integrate all the relevant dimensions of the problem, including humanitarian, political and security.
>
> (UN, 1996: 85)

Intervention in Somalia had important implications for humanitarian action, as humanitarian organisations found themselves working amidst an on-going conflict and under military protection. Significantly, working amidst on-going hostilities was something that previously had been done almost exclusively by the ICRC (Morris, 2008). As Slim (1997), '[w]ith increasing international commitment to humanitarian action in the midst of war, UN agencies and international NGOs ... found themselves pulled in from the periphery of war to much nearer its epicentre'. Duffield (1996) suggests that this new ability to work within ongoing wars and civil conflicts could be regarded as one of the major developments in humanitarian action. For him, it was this development that presented an opportunity for NGO expansion (Duffield, 1997b).

Soon after Somalia, humanitarian actors were made an indispensable part of a 'humanitarian counteroffensive' (Ogata, in Breau, 2005: 195) in the Kosovo 'humanitarian war', a war in which, for Rieff (2002: 197), 'the battle for independent humanitarianism was probably lost'. Significantly, unlike the UN operation in Somalia, the NATO bombing campaign of 1999 against the Federal Republic of Yugoslavia in response to the events in Kosovo was not authorised by the UN Security Council (for a detailed discussion see Wheeler, 2000, 2001; Breau, 2005; Head, 2012). With respect to the Kosovo intervention, it is also important to emphasise the great extent to which: humanitarian justifications were utilised; humanitarian action was co-opted into interveners' political agendas; and distinctions between military and humanitarian actors were blurred, as '[n]ational militaries were acting as humanitarians, and NGOs were reporting to NATO officials' (Rieff, 2002: 225). Finally, although neither the 2001 intervention in Afghanistan, nor the 2003 intervention in Iraq was presented as humanitarian per se, humanitarian considerations featured prominently during both campaigns (e.g. Macrae and Harmer, 2003; Suhrke and Klusmeyer, 2004; Breau, 2005; also Chapter 3).

Overall, although this does not constitute the main focus of the analysis here, the importance of considering the War on Terror in terms of implications for humanitarian action is informed by the fact that it 'constitute[d] not only a series of actual and potential armed conflicts, but also a framework within which international and national policy, including humanitarian aid policy, [were] implemented' (Macrae and Harmer, 2003: 1). Thus, the damage to the UN and multilateralism in general was reflected not just in the absence of the UN Security Council authorisation in Iraq (not unprecedented, as we have established), but also in the way the UN was treated by the Occupying Power (e.g. de Torrente, 2004; Donini *et al.*, 2004). By working through bilateral relationships, the US Administration managed to overcome existing constraints on international decision-making, and the coalition it created was effectively used as a vehicle for promoting US foreign policy agendas (Macrae and Harmer, 2003). Within the framework of the War on Terror, any alternative, non-military, counter-terrorist approaches were not seriously considered (Jackson, 2005), and humanitarian action was seen as an essential part of the war effort, its second front or force-multiplier (e.g. Minear, 2002; de Torrente, 2004; Vaux, 2006;

Hoffman and Weiss, 2006), something that will be examined in more detail with respect to Afghanistan. While humanitarian biopolitics can be considered inferior (Kelly, 2010), with the War on Terror interventions it was further transformed towards the production of predominantly negative biopolitical effects. Thus, in these interventions the humanitarian imperative was abandoned in favour of drawing lines between different forms of life, of achieving security policy objectives, and the assistance was used as an instrument of violent pacification, containment and management of threatening illiberal populations (Reid, 2010). Although not as uniform and universal as Reid (2010) suggests, this transformation of the role of humanitarian assistance was significant, and revealed the continued threat of sovereign violence being unleashed under the biopolitical pretext of care and protection. Sovereign violence also complemented what I term the biopolitical violence of invisibility, endangerment and abandonment.

Furthermore,[7] the disrespect for International Law in general (e.g. the so-called doctrine of pre-emptive self-defence), and IHL in particular (e.g. Beyani, 2003), including blurring of the lines between humanitarian agencies and military forces, contributed to the overall vulnerability of civilians caught in the counter-terrorism campaigns and to the worsening of security of humanitarian workers[8] (e.g. Donini, 2004; Donini *et al.*, 2004; also Chapter 3). The War on Terror also blurred the lines between aid and security, while shifting the priorities in favour of homeland security, and contributed to further reinforcement of containment policies. This was very much the case with the asylum and refugee protection regime, the purpose of which was 'severely misunderstood, misrepresented, or even stood upside-down' (Okoth-Obbo, 2007, in Druke, UNHCR, 2011: 13). Finally, the War on Terror affected humanitarian funding mechanisms through increased securitisation and through criminalisation of humanitarian transfers which are considered to have a nexus to terrorism (e.g. Pantuliano *et al.*, 2011; de Goede, 2012).

A 'new' humanitarian enterprise: growth, institutionalisation and consolidation

The bipolar system of the Cold War placed a number of constraints on humanitarian action, and a very small and precarious humanitarian space had very few inhabitants apart from the superpowers themselves, usually presented by the UN and/or the ICRC (Delorenzi, 1999; West, 2001; Collinson and Elhawary, 2012; Kahn and Cunningham, 2013). The end of the Cold War created both new opportunities for, and new challenges to, humanitarians, with some of the developments clearly presenting both. That said, none of the new challenges prevented humanitarian action from expanding. Opportunities for expansion were created by the new post-Cold War instability coupled with a desire and a rediscovered capacity to address it, informed by globalising neoliberal governmentality. The international community was determined to act, to 'do something', and it was humanitarian action that quickly became an instrument of choice in the absence of other policy alternatives, later becoming the 'primary form of international policy at the geopolitical periphery' (Macrae, 1998, in Macrae and Leader, 2000: 4). Indeed, having acquired the status of a conflict-management tool, humanitarian action seemed to have gained an importance and prominence previously denied to it. Humanitarian presence was now required everywhere, funds were provided to enable humanitarians to do the job, and unnecessary obstacles, such as the consent of the affected state, were removed. The consent of the recipient state, previously sacrosanct, was still formally recognised in early policy documents, such as UN Resolution 46/182, but was overridden in later practices of the new interventionism, further signalling the strengthening role of humanitarian biopolitics.

The growth in the number of humanitarian NGOs following the end of the Cold War is well-recognised and well-documented (e.g. Duffield, 2001; West, 2001; Kahn and Cunningham, 2013). This is not to deny the gradual, evolutionary increase in their numbers, or that many of the major international players, like Oxfam, CARE, World Vision or MSF, were established well before 1990s. However, although it has been suggested otherwise (e.g. West, 2001), it seems that newly available opportunities and the dominant rationality of governing that informed the convergence of agendas and resources, provide a better insight into the reasons for the growth in NGO numbers and influence. Importantly, humanitarian NGOs became not just numerous, but also very diverse in terms of their size, structure, geographical coverage and content of programmes, operational principles, sources of income, and relationship with donors. The post-Cold War period also saw expansion of international networks or confederations of INGOs, with Oxfam, World Vision or CARE International as primary examples. Both trends in the evolution of humanitarian INGOs evident immediately after post-Cold War – growth and consolidation – continued during 2000s (Feinstein International Famine Center, 2004).

The notion of 'humanitarian' activities also expanded to include: material relief and assistance; emergency food aid; relief coordination; protection and support services; reconstruction and rehabilitation, provided both in conflict and non-conflict environments (for instance, in response to natural and technological disasters); along with disaster prevention and preparedness (e.g. Development Initiatives, 2011). The resulting conglomerate of entities evolved into a 'humanitarian enterprise', i.e. 'the global network of organisations involved in assistance and protection' (Smillie and Minear, 2004: 11). The core of the enterprise was, and still is, comprised of the four main groups of organisations: the UN family; the Red Cross Movement (to include ICRC itself, the International Federation of the Red Cross and Red Crescent Societies (IFRC) and national Red Cross and Red Crescent societies)); international non-governmental organisations (INGOs); and local non-governmental organisations (NGOs).[9] While sometimes referred to as the 'humanitarian system', the humanitarian enterprise did not have the implied cohesion of objectives and the ordered nature of relationships between the elements and can be better understood as 'networked assemblages of donor governments, multilateral organizations, UN agencies and

NGOs, both national and international, that are formally responsible for disbursing international humanitarian and development assistance' (Duffield, 2010b: 454).

The growth of NGO numbers combined with the introduction of subcontracting led to aid privatisation (Duffield, 1997b). While the idea of subcontracting was not new in the 1990s, having been tried and tested before on domestic fronts, its import into the humanitarian assistance sector had profound implications (de Waal, 1997). Such implications included a gradual reduction of the role of humanitarian agencies to that of service providers, and fierce competition for funds among all players of what essentially became the humanitarian marketplace, including for-profit private sector agencies, commercial contractors, and even international peacekeeping troops and international military forces in unstable environments. In terms of funds available to the humanitarian enterprise, the 1990s witnessed a doubling in official humanitarian funding (up to US$4.5 billion in 1998), followed by another doubling in the 2000s, reaching US$11.8 billion in 2008 (Development Initiatives, 2000 and 2010). This rate of growth is impressive, especially if compared to just under US$2 billion a year in the 1980s. As the overall amount of humanitarian aid increased, so did its share in Official Development Assistance (ODA), which reached over 10 per cent in 2000 and 11 per cent in 2008 (Development Initiatives, 2006 and 2010). Humanitarian aid from OECD DAC (Development Assistance Committee of the Organisation for Economic Co-operation and Development) donors was rarely channelled directly to recipient governments, and, instead, flowed through a multitude of agencies and organisations. Importantly, post-Cold War spending through non-governmental channels increased, and '[b]y the end of the 1990s, most donors were channelling at least a quarter of their humanitarian assistance through NGOs' (Buchanan-Smith and Randel, 2002: 3). While at the end of the 1980s the UN agencies received around 4 per cent of humanitarian funds, in 1991 their share fell to around 2 per cent and remained at that level until the end of the decade (Development Initiatives, 2000: ix). However, in the 2000s multilateral organisations (mostly UN agencies) were again the largest recipients, accounting for approximately 60 per cent of humanitarian aid from DAC donors (Development Initiatives, 2010). In 2008, the biggest recipients of funds within the UN system were World Food Programme (WFP) (US$2.9 billion) and UNHCR (US$1.3 billion), which reflected donors' overall priorities in terms of crisis response, such as containing population flows. Also, while NGOs registered in donor countries received US$1.6billion (13 per cent of the total), those in developing countries received only US$47million (0.4 per cent) (Development Initiatives, 2010).

Unlike the UN family organisations, which are heavily reliant on donor governments, humanitarian NGOs receive their funds from a variety of sources – donor governments, the UN and other international organisations, subcontracts or grants from other NGOs, money or gifts from businesses and private contributions – which means that they can be donors, recipients and implementers at the same time (Development Initiatives, 2006: 40–41; 2010). The share of voluntary income differs significantly between various NGOs. Thus, for instance, while in the period between 2006 and 2008 MSF received 87 per cent to 90 per cent of its humanitarian income from private sources, for the Norwegian Refugee Council this figure for the same period was only 2.4 per cent (Development Initiatives, 2010: 61–62). Some NGOs contributed more humanitarian assistance than donors, with MSF contributions in 2009 being higher than those of 20 out of 23 DAC members (Development Initiatives, 2010: 62). In 2010, MSF received US$1.1 billion for humanitarian activities from private contributions (Development Initiatives, 2011: 7). This serves as a reflection of the oligopolisation of humanitarian aid, i.e. its concentration in the hands of a small group of large NGO networks/federations. Thus, in 2008 CARE, Catholic Relief Services (CRS), MSF, Oxfam, Save the Children and World Vision International had US$1.7 billion worth of humanitarian programming (Harvey *et al.*, 2010: 20).

In addition to the impact of the number of NGOs, post-Cold War competition for funds was further exacerbated by trends in funding such as increased earmarking. Earmarking (also known as 'cherry-picking') is a system through which donors allocate resources for specific regions, countries or operations; it represents one of the elements of increased bilateralisation of humanitarian assistance post-Cold War (Randel and Germain, 2002). While beneficial for donors (in terms of, for instance, satisfying their own agendas and providing more control), earmarking can have serous negative implications for humanitarian action, such as the inequitable distribution of resources resulting in: greater selectivity and diminishing ability to provide the response according to needs; reduced flexibility, damaging for the ability to respond quickly; and an inability to fund core costs, threatening the very existence of humanitarian organisations (Randel and Germain, 2002).

From the perspective of nation states, in the post-Cold War decades humanitarian assistance was heavily concentrated. The top ten recipients of humanitarian aid from DAC donors since 1999 – Sudan, Palestine/OPT, Iraq, Afghanistan, Ethiopia, DRC, Bosnia-Herzegovina, Serbia, Ex-Yugoslavia States and Somalia (in order) – accounted for 57.7 per cent (US$41.5 billion) of the total humanitarian aid disbursed by DAC donors over the ten-year period (Development Initiatives, 2010: 27). In 2008, the ten largest recipients (Sudan, Palestine/OPT, Afghanistan, Ethiopia, Somalia, DRC, Myanmar, Iraq, Zimbabwe and Kenya) received 62.5 per cent of the total DAC humanitarian funding, while the remaining 37.5 per cent was shared by 138 countries (Development Initiatives, 2010: 27), signalling wide-spread biopolitical abandonment of those in need. In 2009, over 65 per cent of all humanitarian assistance was given to conflict-affected and post-conflict countries (Development Initiatives, 2010: 7). In the 1998–2008 decade, humanitarian funding to Sudan and Afghanistan increased six and eight times respectively (Development Initiatives, 2010: 86).

Unfortunately, far too often such differentiation of response, representing a trend in itself (Macrae, 2002), was not needs-based. For example, while only US$58 was spent per person in DRC, US$993 per person was spent in Haiti after the earthquake (Development Initiatives, 2010: 14). In 2003 and 2004, Iraq received a larger share of DAC humanitarian assistance than any other single country over the past ten years (Development Initiatives, 2006: 14–15), in spite of the fact the humanitarian needs were not great (Smillie and Minear, 2004; Donini *et al.*, 2004). The Iraq experience also demonstrated how the dependence on funds trumped all other operational considerations of humanitarians, as even those agencies whose services were not essential chose to stay engaged, even in the face of an increased threat of instrumentalisation. What happened was that

> [g]iven the choice between cooptation and irrelevance, many humanitarian actors were willing to risk cooptation in order to ensure relevance. Afraid of losing funds and contracts, many agencies found reasons to stay on, regardless of their particular mandate.
>
> (Donini *et al.*, 2004: 196)

Inevitably, and understandably, many humanitarian actors follow the funds, and Iraq was not by any means the first, or the most illustrative example, in this respect. One can be reminded of what Rieff (2002) called a 'humanitarian circus' in Goma, in the Democratic Republic of Congo, where from 1994 to 1996 more than 200 NGOs were competing for more than US$1 billion worth of relief-related contracts to aid Rwandan refugees (Cooley and Ron, 2002). What made Iraq (and also Afghanistan) special in terms of competition, however, was the unprecedented presence of other players. As a result, some NGOs found themselves competing with other NGOs, while others were competing with the UN agencies, military and/or commercial contractors. While this trend is much less pronounced in 'forgotten' emergencies, its significance should not be underestimated.

Finally, the INGO explosion and increased competition resulted not only in crowding out of local NGOs (Smillie and Minear, 2004), but also in 'copy-cat' humanitarianism, whereby 'indigenous NGOs, many struggling to survive, [were pressed] to mimic the structures and behavior of their Northern counterparts' (Donini *et al.*, 2006: 15). This development carried on from early experiences in places like Bosnia, where many Bosnian groups, originally focused on helping war victims overcome psychological trauma, shifted their attention to reconstruction and public infrastructure following the changes in donor priorities (Cooley and Ron, 2002). In addition, international NGOs and UN agencies, who all needed local staff and were capable of paying good salaries, were often guilty of depopulating local agencies and even governments (Smillie and Minear, 2004).

Overall, the situation in which many humanitarian NGOs found themselves post-Cold War can be summarised as follows:

> Increased reliance on state funding challenge[d] their independence. Being drawn into the *modus operandi* of the commercial market place challenge[d] the role of ideals and advocacy, while competition from the military challenge[d] their sense of worthiness and self-value.
>
> (Feinstein International Famine Center, 2004: 60)

Given the myriad of different actors involved in humanitarian action, the issue of coordination became key for the humanitarian enterprise. In this respect, it can be argued that although different from coherence and integration as such, the pressure towards more coordination could be seen as an extension of these agendas, a process driven by both donors and the UN, and as cementing of a new regime of humanitarian governing.

Perhaps not surprisingly, one of the first attempts in the 1990s to address the perceived organisational disarray of the humanitarian system was made within the UN, which itself housed at least six key humanitarian actors – UNHCR, WFP, Food and Agriculture Organisation (FAO), World Health Organisation (WHO) and UNDP. Dissatisfaction with ad-hoc coordination bodies and the lack of coordination during the crisis in Iraq in 1990–1991 resulted in the adoption of UN Resolution 46/182, which followed a number of previous resolutions and decisions to strengthen disaster response. The Resolution established the Inter-Agency Standing Committee (IASC), created the post of Emergency Relief Coordinator (ERC) to lead the new Department of Humanitarian Affairs (DHA), established the Consolidated Appeal Process (CAP) and set up Central Emergency Revolving Fund (CERF).

The DHA was not a big success, as the experience in Rwanda demonstrated (Minear, 2002). In 1997, as a result of a reform, DHA was replaced by UN OCHA, with the status of its head upgraded to the Under-Secretary-General, but with reduced staff and budget (Minear, 2002). The reform was supposed, *inter alia*, to strengthen the ERC in three core functions: policy development and coordination; advocacy on humanitarian issues; and the coordination of emergency response. From the start, OCHA was in a difficult position, with a big mandate for coordination, but undermined by a lack of authority, resistance from other agencies, and uncertain funding (Reindorp, 2002). Other challenges for OCHA included dealing with the issue of protecting and assisting IDPs, as well as battling with the Department of Political Affairs (DPA) and the Department of Peacekeeping Operations (DPKO) (Reindorp, 2002). The latter relationship was influenced by the previously considered 'coherence' agenda and integrated approach to peace.

The UN also had considerable difficulties in producing effective coordination structures in the field (Minear, 2002). In different emergencies it tried out three different models of coordination: the Resident Coordinator as Humanitarian Coordinator (reporting to a Special Representative of the Secretary General (SRSG) for a given crisis)), the Humanitarian Coordinator appointed separately (but also reporting to SRSG), and the 'lead' agency (Macrae *et al.*, 2002; Minear, 2002). The success rate of the 'lead' agency model, built on the assumption that a major UN operational institution, chosen according to the nature of the problem and the agency's relevant strength on the ground, would be playing the leading role, proved to be uneven (Minear 2002). Coordination efforts on the ground were even more complicated when a mission had both civilian and military elements, as was the case in the post-2001 Afghanistan (see Chapter 3).

To address coordination issues, the UN initiated a number of reviews, culminating in the *2004–2005 Global Humanitarian Response Review* (UN OCHA, 2004–2006) and the 2006 Report *Delivering as One* (UN GA, 2006) with the former calling for greater coordination both within and outside the UN system and the latter focusing on different elements of the UN system (Walker and Maxwell, 2009). In response to difficulties of coordinating in the field, the positions of Humanitarian Coordinators or Resident Coordinators were established, and the cluster approach, based on the lead agency model, was introduced (UN OCHA, no date). Global clusters were designated in the following areas: agriculture (FAO); camp coordination and management (UNHCR for conflict IDPs and IOM for disasters); early recovery (UNDP); education (UNICEF and Save the Children); emergency shelter (UNHCR and IFRC); emergency telecommunications (WFP); health (WHO); logistics (WFP); nutrition (UNICEF); protection (UNHCR for conflict IDPs and UNHCR/OHCHR/UNICEF for disasters and civilians affected by conflict other than IDPs) (UN OCHA, no date). So far, the results of the cluster approach have been mixed (e.g. Harvey *et al.*, 2010), and it has been rightly criticised by the ICRC Director General as being a 'one-size-fits-all' solution which cannot work in all contexts (Daccord, 2012). More importantly, the cluster approach also serves as an instrument of closure, of preventing, or at least restricting, alternative and more context-specific ways of responding to humanitarian needs.

Further consolidation of the post-Cold War humanitarian regime of governing was signalled by the development of specific financial coordination mechanisms, such as the Consolidated Appeal Process (CAP). CAP is defined as 'a tool developed by aid organisations in a country or region to raise funds for humanitarian action as well as to plan, implement and monitor their activities together' (UN OCHA, no date). CAP is put together annually by UN agencies, NGOs and other humanitarian actors, and then presented to the international community and donors. CAP stakeholders include NGOs, IFRC, International Organisation for Migration (IOM) and UN agencies. CAP was supposed to be a breakthrough in terms of ensuring that needs were met and inter-agency competition was minimised, but it never lived up to expectations. In terms of needs, analysis of donor response showed, for instance, that slow onset and chronic disasters tended to attract much lower levels of funds than quick onset ones, complex emergencies were better funded than natural disasters, and programmes addressing more chronic issues of health, water, sanitation and economic recovery were neglected compared to emergency food aid (Development Initiatives, 2006). Sadly, the most poorly funded appeals were those with modest requirements, which suggests that 'low political priority – rather than resources per se – [were] behind many neglected emergencies' (Development Initiatives, 2006: 33). Overall, a modest positive trend notwithstanding, approximately 40 per cent of needs identified through CAP remained underfunded almost every year in the last decade (OCHA, 2013), which is suggestive of a biopolitical triage that is not informed by the humanitarian imperative.

'Quantifying disasters[10]:' knowledges, technologies, divides

In terms of the knowledges informing humanitarian governing post-Cold War, one should stress the increased reliance on the advances in life sciences (Reid, 2010), with the language of international crisis interventions extensively relying on the use of medical metaphors (McFalls, 2010). This is not surprising, as life-saving and related technologies, or 'technologies of disaster' have become the specialisation of this new regime. These technologies include 'more or less coordinated physical instruments, spatial arrangements, means of communication, means of data collecting and processing, organizational procedures, and discursive practices' (Ophir, 2007: 163) and are applied to a biologised collective life. Their aim is 'to improve the biological attributes of a statistically-defined population' and 'to maximise survival' (Branch, 2009: 489). Due to the technical nature of the technologies of disaster, they can only be applied by experts, and only relief agencies possess this kind of expertise. The biologised conception of life and the technical nature of the interventions allows for universal application of a uniform set of responses. This, in turn, allows for the expansion of the humanitarian industry, which is becoming more and more reliant on technically sophisticated surveillance tools and early warning systems (Branch, 2009). The increased reliance on technology is characteristic of what has been termed 'digital humanitarianism' (Burns, 2014), which in itself can be seen as one of many evolving strands of 'new' humanitarianism.

The pressures to use quantification and managerial tools are often donor-driven, and the tools themselves – such as LogFrames – are often those originally designed to be used by military organisations (Calhoun, 2010), which, again, facilitates not just the coming together of civil and military actors, but also the military involvement in humanitarian response. Humanitarians respond to donor pressures by developing standards and manuals of best practice (Calhoun, 2010). These developments result in further professionalisation of humanitarian action, and also serve as an indication of a regime being established (with new areas of expertise such as humanitarian logistics and humanitarian robotics), a regime that is profoundly influenced by neoliberal logic and imperatives. In addition, 'standards, professionalisation, institutionalisation and the increasing oligopolisation of the [humanitarian] enterprise are functioning as barriers for entry for other players' (interview, 18 May 2010). As McFalls (2010: 318) argues, 'the benevolent dictatorship of humanitarian government based on scientific expertise and relying on the institutional form of the nongovernmental organization has become the uncontested and uncontestable radical biopower of our age'.

This managerial orientation also points to a certain continuity with colonial projects. The development of many biopolitical instruments and techniques was closely associated with colonialism, including the art of calculation itself. Reiss (2004: 137–138; original emphasis) has traced the process of how 'mathematics could become such a constructive, manipulating, and instrumentalist knowledge – notably *of people*'. Thus, in the sixteenth century Europe the idea that the world could be known in its materiality was still new. In particular, what was new was precisely 'the idea that calculation ... gave *true understanding* of the physical world and human actions' (Reiss, 2004: 144; original emphasis). Not surprisingly (and in line with Foucault's argument), calculation of people was first put into practice in the military, where '[a]t issue was ... distribution of human bodies on the battlefield, in camp, or on the march by a strict calculus' (Reiss, 2004: 145). These techniques were soon applied in the New World, where the colonisers 'sought to know the Americas and its inhabitants by count and geometrical order' (Reiss, 2004: 153). The lists they produced required data types alien to the indigenous populations, as 'the colonising gaze' always represented a clash between the will to ownership and the people to be bent before it (Reiss, 2004). In many important ways, colonies served as experimental grounds at the times when links between governing different populations were forged and tested; the imposition of alien, decontextualised requirements is as characteristic of 'new' humanitarianism as it is of colonial projects.

The counting of the bodies – political arithmetic – both persisted and expanded (Reiss, 2004: 157). According to Hacking, the whole story of biopolitics can be seen 'as the transition from the counting of hearths to the counting of bodies' (Hacking, 1982: 281). This exercise required the establishment of the categories people could fall in, which, in turn, resulted in new conceptualisations of the human: '[e]numeration demands kinds of things or people to count. Counting is hungry for categories. Many of the categories we now use to describe people are byproducts of the needs of enumeration' (Hacking, 1982: 280). In its attempt to quantify a disaster, humanitarian 'counting' captures suffering in the following objectifying way: '[o]f the 110,415 shelters, 8.6 percent are experiencing mild suffering, 50.2 percent are experiencing moderate suffering, and 41.1 percent are experiencing severe suffering' (Zeid and Cochran, no date). This description comes from a survey of health status of IDPs in a region of Somalia, whose authors also stress that '[l]ack of population estimates hinders the attempts of the humanitarian community to generate meaningful estimates of important rates such as a prevalence of various diseases'. With estimates used to generate estimates, there is double remove from the suffering, which will be addressed on the basis of an instrument of inferior biopolitics, that of minimal humanitarian standards. Thus, the Sphere Project's Standards, which are among the most widely used and wide-ranging, cover the following issue areas: 'water supply, sanitation and hygiene promotion'; 'food security and nutrition'; 'shelter, settlement and non-food items'; and 'health action'. This discussion is not meant to either criticise the specific standards or suggest that provision of assistance should not be based on data, but rather draw attention to specific biopolitical techniques and their effects, including the radical limiting of resources and the focus on keeping alive. Importantly, once certain technologies and techniques have been tried and tested, it becomes increasingly difficult to do without them (Hoskin and Macve, 1986: 134).

Links between 'new' humanitarianism and colonialism extend beyond a reliance on calculation techniques. Indeed, '[h]umanitarianism was often part of the "civilization that colonial powers sought to bring to the peoples they conquered"'

(Calhoun, 2010: 39). Colonial policies and practices, just as those of the 'new' humanitarianism, were biopolitical (Sylvester, 2006; Kelly, 2010); it could be argued that this similarity eventually facilitated the absorption of humanitarianism into a new neoliberal regime of biopolitical governing, which is very comprehensive and detailed, as the discussion of the minimum humanitarian standards has shown.

Despite important continuities with its previous reincarnations, the purpose of 'new' humanitarianism is arguably very different in that, unlike previous long-term projects, it is divorced from long-term agendas, which, to an extent, is an outcome of the donor pressures and budget pressures (Calhoun, 2010). However, this short-termism is also an outcome of other kinds of pressures, informed by the advancing neoliberalism and the associated rise of so-called 'disaster capitalism'. The notion of 'disaster capitalism', introduced by Klein, is designed 'to illustrate how assistance strategies rooted in neoliberal policy frameworks channel recovery through private-corporate interests and entities ... more interested in profiteering than purely humanitarian motives' (Gunewardena, 2008: 4). Disaster capitalism will be expanding for as long as there are profits to be made from rehabilitation and reconstruction projects (de Waal, 2008). In so doing, not only will it be promoting particular interests, but it will also be producing tensions between the short-term interests of corporate entities and the long-term interests of affected communities (Gunewardena, 2008). Importantly, combined with neoliberal economic reforms, disaster capitalism often results in a gradual dismantling of positive state biopolitics (Kelly, 2010), with devastating consequences for affected populations.

Managerial and other neoliberal pressures conflict with the moral core that many would argue 'new' humanitarianism still retains (Ophir, 2007; Calhoun, 2010), while others tend to overlook it (e.g. Branch, 2009; Dillon and Reid, 2009). While 'new' humanitarianism can be seen as an outcome of the process of co-optation of humanitarian action into specific interventionist agendas, this does not mean that their relationship is free from conflict or that all humanitarians have completely departed from the humanitarian imperative. Indeed, such co-optation is always partial (Ophir, 2007), and there is always room for resistance.

This, however, does not change the fact that a key rationality behind the 'new' humanitarian regime is that of sustaining and policing the biopolitical divide between different populations. Thus, Duffield (2007) argues that international biopolitics of the global population does not exist, as development's new biopolitical function is to maintain the biopolitical divide between developed (insured) and underdeveloped (non-insured). Notwithstanding the differences between the biopolitical governing of these two kinds of populations, there are important connections, many of which are driven by and realised through markets. As Duffield (2007: 11) argues, '[a] superfluous and potentially dangerous waste-life is continuously thrown off as markets are relentlessly made and remade in the endless search for progress'. And just as markets engage in a constant search for progress, so do aid programmes influenced by the neoliberal rationality of governing, whose self-critical nature produces the perpetual cycle of failing and improvement. Thus, with humanitarian assistance serving as 'insurance of the last resort' (Duffield, 2008: 151) for the non-insured populations in the absence of a genuine commitment to development, relapses into humanitarian emergencies become inevitable, which, in turn, require interventions to pacify and contain threatening, underdeveloped populations. As a result, what we have internationally is an 'expanding zone of international pacification', where 'a post-interventionary society has emerged in the global borderland' (Duffield, 2008: 159). A post-interventionary society may be a totalising concept, but it reflects very well the cyclical nature of the process of disengagement followed by a necessary minimal engagement (promotion of self-reliance – crisis – intervention – pacification and consolidation – promotion of self-reliance, and so on), or, in other words, 'while a given situation may be temporally stabilized, since self-reliance is in permanent crisis, interventionism appears cyclical, ongoing and expansive' (Duffield, 2010a: 56). It is in this way that development as a neoliberal technology of governing answers the question of how to govern underdeveloped populations effectively, which also means with minimal resources and suggests the existence of a time-specific regime of humanitarian governing, informed by the neoliberal rationality. The end of the Cold War allowed for this rationality to expand unopposed, which was reflected in a number of developments we associate with 'new' humanitarianism.

The developed states also intervene to address disasters affecting their own populations; in doing so, they also rely on biopolitical technologies of disaster that serve not only to predict, avoid or alleviate disasters, but also to expand and to strengthen the control of the governed populations (Ophir, 2007: 173). However, developed and under-developed populations are never treated in the same way. The biopolitical divide simultaneously produces and relies upon a particular construction of those to be assisted. Importantly, the traditional language of humanitarianism implies the absence of such a divide, which reflects its original logic of unity and solidarity. According to Fassin (2007: 518), this idea of the indivisibility of humanity opposes other positions that 'either imply distinctions among human beings ... or promote indifference to distant others'. However, when used within the framework of 'new' humanitarianism, this language, while still implying unity and solidarity, serves as a convenient way to conceal both the existence of the divide[11] and the role of a variety of actors and institutions in maintaining it. Indeed, with 'new' humanitarianism, '[d]istinctions among different forms of life ... led to disastrous distinction between life worth living and life whose abandonment and even elimination is permitted' (Ophir, 2007: 166).

Fassin (2007) points to a particular distinction: that of the lives to be saved and lives to be risked. While the former are merely physical, the latter are political (this distinction clearly echoes Agamben's concept of 'bare life'). As the decision between these two types of life is a political one, so humanitarianism for Fassin should be understood as 'politics of life'. The decision as to whether to sacrifice their lives saving others is made by the interveners; the populations in need do not have any choice. Furthermore, one can argue that, at times, it is the lives of those to be assisted that are sacrificed in favour of saving the lives of the interveners (for instance, when assistance is used for force protection). Thus, Fassin himself speaks of

> the unequal value accorded to lives on the battlefield: the sacred life of the Western armies of intervention, in which each life lost is counted and honored, versus the expendable life of not only the enemy troops but also their civilian populations, whose losses are only roughly numbered and whose corpses end up in mass graves.
>
> (Fassin, 2007: 519)

What is missing from Fassin's picture is the presence of the populations to be secured, as it is these populations of the intervening countries who are prioritised over the other two (interveners themselves and assisted populations) through processes of the securitisation of assistance. Given that biopolitics implies the constant process of creating divisions between different groups and sacrificing (or abandoning) some to secure others, it is more appropriate to speak of multiple biopolitical divides of a varied nature. For instance, Fassin himself considers another distinction, that between the expatriates and local staff of humanitarian agencies, with neither being a biologised reduction of life. In fact, Fassin (2007: 519) concludes that humanitarianism has 'a series of dimensions of what may be called a complex ontology of inequality ... that differentiates in a hierarchical manner the values of human lives', which reveals its biopolitical nature. The varied nature of biopolitical choices is discussed by Fassin elsewhere (2009: 53), and he argues that these are 'implicit or sometimes explicit choices over who shall live what sort of life and for how long'. Life expectancy statistics can serve as a reflection of the outcome of such choices:

> Disparity in mortality rates are not only statistical data, they mean differences in value attached to life.... Statistics about life expectancy ... tell us about how much life is worth depending on the social environment into which one was born.
>
> (Fassin, 2009: 53)

As Calhoun (2010: 34) argues, 'the category [of the human] is not self-evident': while it can imply ethical universalism, its decontextualised nature can also pave the way for seeing (and governing) people as populations. It is also possible to argue that the perceived humanitarian/political divide produces similar outcomes by inviting technical responses to essentially political problems. Indeed, as has been stressed already, relief operations in response to humanitarian emergencies rely on a particular conception of those to be assisted – that of the population – a conception which is a product of processes of decontextualisation, biologisation, quantification and de-individuation through aggregation. Indeed, the population as a biopolitical category can only be visible through statistics, and visible only as an aggregate (Branch, 2009). This limited visibility obscures many types of suffering (Calhoun, 2010), so these are the people who are counted, but who do not count. This limited visibility also results in the erasure of the individual (Selmeczi, 2011), as well as potentially making individuals more vulnerable to biopolitical, disciplinary and/or sovereign violence. Indeed, the issue of invisibility will be shown to be crucial to the biopolitical governing that characterises two very different assistance efforts in Afghanistan and Belarus.

'New' humanitarianism relies on intrusive and varied technologies of the administration of life. Its wide reach and improved ability to access and govern collective life through interventions, both forceful and not, means that it is increasingly implicated in deciding how those under its care and protection should live (think, for example, of the countries like Somalia or Afghanistan, where large numbers of people rely on humanitarian interventions, broadly conceived, in order to survive). While, contra Branch (2009: 488), not all those assisted are steered 'towards becoming helpless victims', and, contra Agamben (1998), not all of them are reduced to 'bare life', the ways in which they are constructed are profoundly different from the ways in which both interveners and developed populations are viewed, and so is the value assigned to their lives. And while biopolitics is always about creating divisions and prioritising some lives over others, it is not sufficient to say that 'new' humanitarianism is biopolitical, especially as it does not realise any positive potential that biopolitical governing can have. Consequently, it may be more appropriate to see 'new' humanitarianism as a regime producing predominantly negative biopolitical effects. After all, it arose from a common ground between 'those who are preoccupied with superfluous, preventable human suffering and those who are preoccupied with superfluous human beings who, under certain circumstances, may be eliminated' (Ophir, 2007: 166), a common ground, which arguably should not have existed.

Conclusion

This chapter has considered a number of important post-Cold War developments in the international environment, such as the unequal erosion of state sovereignty, increased disengagement of the North from the South accompanied by the policies of containment, 'new' interventionism and the War on Terror, and outlined the implication they had for the humanitarian action in terms of both challenges and opportunities. In particular, convergences between the opportunities and specific agendas, such as the 'coherence' agenda and the integrated approach to peace, have been emphasised. It has been shown that the emergent humanitarian enterprise was an outcome of a set of shifts and convergences, which included: the proliferation of humanitarian actors; aid privatisation and an increased competition for funds; further institutionalisation of humanitarian action through the establishment of coordination structures; a shift towards increased standardisation and professionalisation and increasingly technological nature; and increased bilateralisation of humanitarian assistance.

In arguing that 'new' humanitarianism is best understood as a biopolitical regime of neoliberal governmentality, the focus has been placed, in particular, on: the importance of dominant problematisations of humanitarian situations and their implications; the role of 'new' humanitarianism in sustaining the biopolitical divide between the developed (insured) and the underdeveloped (non-insured) populations; and the ways in which the latter are constructed as targets of interventions. While humanitarian action is essentially biopolitical, with 'new' humanitarianism positive imperatives are often substituted by negative ones, overriding its original logic of equality, unity and solidarity.

Importantly, the changes in the nature of humanitarian action associated with 'new' humanitarianism informed the ways in which particular assistance efforts were carried out in a variety of conflict and non-conflict environments by establishing the conditions for the possibility of particular problematisations, policies and practices, as a detailed analysis of the post-2001 assistance effort in Afghanistan and the post-2000 Chernobyl-related assistance effort in Belarus demonstrates.

Notes

1 A number of alternative terms, such as 'neo-humanitarianism' (Mills, 2005), 'state humanitarianism' (Rieff, 2002) and 'military humanitarianism' (Slim, 1995) have also been suggested. While not being much different to the prefix 'new' and suffering from the same problem of implied discontinuity, 'neo' can also mean 'revived' (*Concise Oxford English Dictionary*, 2002), which is not the case. In turn, the term 'state humanitarianism' appears to construe humanitarianism very narrowly, implying that the action is carried out only by the states. It also makes distinguishing it from the colonial humanitarianism of the nineteenth century difficult. Finally, 'military humanitarianism' seems to be far too narrow, as it only refers to militarised humanitarian action in conflict environments. In addition, some of the ways of defining the 'new' humanitarianism have been unhelpful, for instance, using the label 'principled' (Fox, 2001). This creates confusion with the ICRC (International Committee of the Red Cross) principles of humanity, impartiality, neutrality and independence, which are commonly associated with traditional humanitarian action.

2 It should also be noted that term 'the new humanitarianisms' has also been used to refer to post-Cold War trends in global humanitarian action, albeit without an explicit explanation of the plural form (Macrae *et al.*, 2002). The same term is used by Hoffman and Weiss (2006: 6) with respect to 'the multiple developments in the international humanitarian system', but invoking the issue of temporality rather than heterogeneity. While in this chapter I use the term in the singular, it is not meant to suggest that there exists only one universal and totalising regime of humanitarian governing, but rather to identify dominant convergences in relevant rationalities, strategies and technologies. This appreciation of the diversity of co-existing forms of humanitarian action would justify the use of the plural form in this book.

3 In a similar vein, Edkins (2000: 41) explored the 'role of power/knowledge in the constitution of the subjects of food aid and practices of famine relief'.

4 Duffield (2001) identifies a similar set of distinctive features of 'new' wars.

5 I am grateful to Louise Amoore for pointing out a possible link between the declared complexity of emergencies and governing populations through milieu.

6 See Metcalfe, Giffen and Elhawary (2011) for a comprehensive overview of the UN integration and its impact on humanitarian space.

7 See Howell and Lind (2009) and Pantuliano *et al.* (2011) for a more comprehensive analysis of the impact of the War on Terror on aid policies and practices.
8 Collinson and Elhawary (2012) challenge this conclusion.
9 See Development Initiatives (2010: 128; 2011: 36) for helpful maps of the existing aid players.
10 I take inspiration from the title of an article by Zeid and Cochran (no date) *'Quantifying a humanitarian disaster: survey of the health status of internally displaced populations in South Central Somalia'.*
11 For similar reasons, transcendental terms such as 'biohuman' and 'biohumanity', suggested by Dillon and Reid (2009; also Reid, 2010), are too totalising, being inattentive to the existence of the divide.

References

Agamben, G. 1998. *Homo Sacer: sovereign power and bare life.* Stanford: Stanford University Press.
Allen, T. and D. Styan. 2000. A right to interfere? Bernard Kouchner and the new humanitarianism. *Journal of International Development,* **12**: 825–842.
Bah, A.B. 2013. The contours of new humanitarianism: war and peacebuilding in Sierra Leone. *Africa Today,* **60**(1): 2–26.
Berdal, M. 2003. How 'new' are 'new wars'? Global economic change and the study of civil war. *Global Governance,* **9**: 477–502.
Beyani, C. 2003. International law and the 'war on terror'. *In*: J. Macrae and A. Harmer (eds). *Humanitarian action and the 'global war on terror': a review of trends and issues.* HPG Report 14. London: Overseas Development Institute, pp. 13–24.
Borton, J. 1998. The state of the international humanitarian system. *Refugee Survey Quarterly,* **17**(1): 16–23.
Boutros-Ghali, B. 1992. *An Agenda for Peace: Preventive diplomacy, peacemaking and peace-keeping. Report of the Secretary General pursuant to the statement adopted by the Summit meeting of the Security Council on 31 January 1992.* New York: United Nations.
Braem, Y. 2008. Managing territories with rival brothers: the geopolitical stakes of military-humanitarian relations. *In*: C. Ankersen (ed.). *Civil-military cooperation in post-conflict operations: emerging theory and practice.* London: Routledge, pp. 31–51.
Branch, A. 2009. Humanitarianism, violence, and the camp in Northern Uganda. *Civil Wars,* **11**(4): 477–501.
Breau, S. 2005. *Humanitarian intervention: the United Nations and collective responsibility.* London: Cameron May.
Buchanan-Smith, M. and J. Randel. 2002. *Financing international humanitarian action: a review of key trends. HPG Briefing* [online]. [Accessed 10 June 2014]. www.odi.org.uk/sites/odi.org.uk/files/odi-assets/publications-opinion-files/365.pdf.
Burns, R. 2014. Moments of closure in the knowledge politics of digital humanitarianism. *Geoforum,* **53**: 51–62.
Calhoun, C. 2010. The idea of emergency: humanitarian action and global (dis)order. *In*: D. Fassin and M. Pandolfi (eds). *Contemporary states of emergency: the politics of military and humanitarian intervention.* New York: Zone Books, pp. 29–58.
Collinson, S. and S. Elhawary. 2012. *Humanitarian space: a review of trends and issues* [online]. [Accessed 7 June 2014]. www.odi.org.uk/sites/odi.org.uk/files/odi-assets/publications-opinion-files/7643.pdf.

Cooley, A. and J. Ron. 2002. The NGO scramble: organizational insecurity and the political economy of transnational action. *International Security*, **27**(1): 5–39.

Curtis, D. 2001. *Politics and humanitarian aid: debates, dilemmas and dissention.* HPG
Report 10. London: Overseas Development Institute.

Daccord, Y. (ICRC). 2012. *The changing humanitarian landscape: obstacles and opportunities. Lecture at the Overseas Development Institute* [online]. [Accessed 10 June 2014].
www.odi.org.uk/events/3052-hpg-lecture-icrc-yves-daccord-changing-humanitarian-
landscape.

De Goede, M. 2012. *Speculative security: the politics of pursuing terrorist monies.* Minneapolis: University of Minnesota Press.

De Larrinaga, M. and M.G. Doucet. 2008. Sovereign power and the biopolitics of human
security. *Security Dialogue*, **39**(5): 517–537.

De Torrente, N. 2004. Humanitarian action under attack: reflections on the Iraq War.
Harvard Human Rights Journal, **17**: 1–29.

De Waal, A. 1997. *Famine crimes: politics and the disaster relief industry in Africa.*
Oxford: African Rights and the International African Institute in association with James
Currey.

Delorenzi, S. 1999. *Contending with the impasse in international humanitarian action:
ICRC policy since the end of the Cold War.* Geneva: ICRC.

Development Initiatives. 2000. *Global Humanitarian Assistance 2000* [online]. [Accessed
10 June 2014]. www.globalhumanitarianassistance.org/wp-content/uploads/2010/07/2000-
GHA-report.pdf.

Development Initiatives. 2006. *Global Humanitarian Assistance 2006* [online]. [Accessed
20 February 2008]. www.globalhumanitarianassistance.org/gha2006.htm.

Development Initiatives. 2010. *Global Humanitarian Assistance Report 2010* [online].
[Accessed 10 May 2011]. www.globalhumanitarianassistance.org/reports.

Development Initiatives. 2011. *GHA Report 2011* [online]. [Accessed 23 January 2012].
www.globalhumanitarianassistance.org/wp-content/uploads/2011/07/gha-report-2011.pdf.

Dillon, M. and J. Reid. 2009. *The liberal way of war: killing to make life live.* Abingdon:
Routledge.

Donini, A. 2004. Taking sides: the Iraq crisis and the future of humanitarianism. *Forced
Migration Review*, **19**: 38–40.

Donini, A. 2010. The far side: the meta functions of humanitarianism in a globalised
world. *Disasters*, **34**(S2): 220–237.

Donini, A. *et al.* 2006. *Humanitarian agenda 2015: Afghanistan country study*
[online]. [Accessed 11 March 2011]. https://wikis.uit.tufts.edu/confluence/display/
FIC/Humanitarian+Agenda+2015+-+Afghanistan+Country+Study.

Donini, A., L. Minear and P. Walker. 2004. The future of humanitarian action: mapping
the implications of Iraq and other recent crises. *Disasters*, 2004, **28**(2): 190–204.

Druke, L. (UNHCR). 2011. *Mobilizing for refugee protection: reflections on the 60th anniversary of UNHCR and the 1951 Refugee Convention* [online]. [Accessed 12 June 2014].
http://acuns.org/wp-content/uploads/2012/06/MobilizingforRefugeeProtection.pdf.

Dubernet, C. 2001. *The international containment of displaced persons: humanitarian
spaces without exit.* Aldershot: Ashgate.

Duffield, M. 1994a. Complex emergencies and the crisis of developmentalism. *In*: S.
Maxwell and M. Buchanan-Smith (eds). Linking relief and development. *IDS Bulletin*,
25(4): 37–45.

Duffield, M. 1994b. The political economy of internal war: asset transfer, complex emergencies and international aid. *In*: J. Macrae, A. Zwi, M.R. Duffield and H. Slim (eds).

War and hunger: rethinking international responses to complex emergencies, London: Zed Books, pp. 50–69.

Duffield, M. 1996. The symphony of the damned: racial discourse, complex political emergencies and humanitarian aid. *Disasters*, **20**(3): 173–193.

Duffield, M. 1997a. Humanitarian intervention, the new aid paradigm and separate development. *New Political Economy*, **2**(2): 336–340.

Duffield, M. 1997b. NGO relief in war zones: towards an analysis of the new aid paradigm. *Third World Quarterly*, **18**(3): 527–542.

Duffield, M. 2001. *Global governance and the new wars: the merging of development and security*. London: Zed Books.

Duffield, M. 2002. Social reconstruction and the radicalization of development: aid as a relation of global liberal governance. *Development and Change*, **33**(5): 1049–1071.

Duffield, M. 2005. Getting savages to fight barbarians: development, security and the colonial present. *Conflict, Security and Development*, **5**(2): 141–160.

Duffield, M. 2006. Racism, migration and development: the foundations of planetary order. *Progress in Development Studies*, **6**(1): 68–79.

Duffield, M. 2007. *Development, security and the unending war: governing the world of peoples*. Cambridge: Polity Press.

Duffield, M. 2008. Global civil war: the non-insured, international containment and post-interventionary society. *Journal of Refugee Studies*, **21**(2): 145–165.

Duffield, M. 2010a. The liberal way of development and the development-security impasse: exploring the global life-chance divide. *Security Dialogue*, **41**(1): 53–76.

Duffield, M. 2010b. Risk management and the fortified aid compound: everyday life in post-interventionary society. *Journal of Intervention and Statebuilding*, **4**(4): 453–474.

Duffield, M. and N. Waddell. 2006. Securing humans in a dangerous world. *International Politics*, **43**: 1–23.

Edkins, J. 2000. *Whose hunger?: concepts of famine, practices of aid*. Minneapolis: University of Minnesota Press.

Fassin, D. 2007. Humanitarianism as a politics of life. *Public Culture*, **19**(3): 499–520.

Fassin, D. 2009. Another politics of life is possible. *Theory, Culture & Society*, **26**(5): 44–60.

Fox, F. 2001. New humanitarianism: does it provide a moral banner for the 21st century? *Disasters*, **25**(4): 275–289.

Grayson, K. 2008. Human security as power/knowledge: the biopolitics of a definitional debate. *Cambridge Review of International Affairs*, **21**(3): 383–401.

Gunewardena, N. 2008. Human security versus neoliberal approaches to disaster recovery. *In*: N. Gunewardena and M. Schuller (eds). *Capitalizing on catastrophe: neoliberal strategies in disaster reconstruction*. Plymouth: Altamira (Rowman & Littlefield), pp. 3–16.

Hacking, I. 1982. Biopower and the avalanche of printed numbers. *Humanities in Society*, **5**: 279–295.

Harvey, P. *et al.* 2010. *The state of humanitarian system: assessing performance and progress. A pilot study* [online]. London: ODI. [Accessed 8 February 2010]. www.alnap.org.

Head, N. 2012. *Justifying violence: communicative ethics and the use of force in Kosovo*. Manchester: Manchester University Press.

Hendrie, B. 1997. Knowledge and power: a critique of an international relief operation. *Disasters*, **21**(1): 57–76.

Hoffman, P.J and T.G. Weiss. 2006. *Sword and salve: new wars and humanitarians crises*. Maryland: Rowman & Littlefield.

Hoskin, K.W. and R.H. Macve. 1986. Accounting and examination: a genealogy of disciplinary power. *Accounting, Organizations, and Society*, **11**(2): 105–136.

Howell, J. and J. Lind. 2009. *Counter-terrorism, aid and civil society*. Basingstoke: Palgrave Macmillan.

ICISS (International Commission on Intervention and State Sovereignty). 2001. *The Responsibility to Protect: Report of the International Commission on Intervention and State Sovereignty*. Ottawa: International Development Research Centre.

Interview with a former high-level UN official, with extensive experience of coordinating the assistance effort in Afghanistan, 18 May 2010.

Jackson, R. 2005. *Writing the war on terrorism: language, politics and counter-terrorism*. Manchester: Manchester University Press.

Jean, F. 1997. The plight of the world refugees. *In*: *Médecins Sans Frontières* (eds). *World in crisis: the politics of survival at the end of the twentieth century*. London: Routledge.

Kahn, C. and A. Cunningham. 2013. Introduction to the issue of state sovereignty and humanitarian action. *Disasters*, **37**(S2): S139–150.

Kaldor, M. 1999. *New and old wars: organised violence in a global era*. Cambridge: Polity Press.

Kalyvas, S.N. 2001. 'New' and 'old' civil wars: a valid distinction? *World Politics*, **54**: 99–118.

Kelly, M.G.E. 2010. International biopolitics: Foucault, globalisation and imperialism. *Theoria*, **57**(123): 1–26.

MacFarlane, N.S. 2005. International politics, local conflicts and intervention. *In*: N. Mychajlyszyn and T.M. Shaw (eds). *Twisting arms and flexing muscles: humanitarian intervention and peacebuilding in perspective*. Aldershot: Ashgate, pp. 11–34.

Macrae, J. 2001. *Aiding recovery?: The crisis of aid in chronic political emergencies*. London: Zed Books.

Macrae, J. (ed.). 2002. *The new humanitarianisms: a review of trends in global humanitarian action*. HPG Report 11. London: Overseas Development Institute.

Macrae, J., *et al.* 2002. *Uncertain power: the changing role of official donors in humanitarian action*. HPG Report 12. London: Overseas Development Institute.

Macrae, J. and A. Harmer. 2003. Humanitarian action and the 'war on terror': a review of issues. *In*: J. Macrae and A. Harmer (eds). *Humanitarian action and the 'global war on terror': a review of trends and issues*. HPG Report 14. London: Overseas Development Institute, pp. 1–11.

Macrae, J. and N. Leader. 2000. *Shifting sands: the theory and practice of 'coherence' between political and humanitarian responses to complex political emergencies*. HPG Report 8. London: Overseas Development Institute.

Macrae, J. and N. Leader. 2001. Apples, pears and porridge: the origins and impact of the search for 'coherence' between humanitarian and political responses to chronic political emergencies. *Disasters*, **25**(4): 290–307.

Makaremi, C. 2010. Utopias of power: from human security to the Responsibility to Protect. *In*: D. Fassin and M. Pandolfi (eds). *Contemporary states of emergency: the politics of military and humanitarian intervention*. New York: Zone Books, pp. 107–128.

McFalls, L. 2010. Benevolent dictatorship: the formal logic of humanitarian government. *In*: D. Fassin and M. Pandolfi (eds). *Contemporary states of emergency: the politics of military and humanitarian intervention*. New York: Zone Books, pp. 317–334.

Metcalfe, V., A. Giffin and S. Elhawary. 2011. *UN Integration and Humanitarian Space: An Independent Study Commissioned by the UN Integration Steering Group* [online].

[Accessed 9 June 2014]. www.odi.org.uk/sites/odi.org.uk/files/odi-assets/publications-opinion-files/7526.pdf.

Mills, K. 2005. Neo-humanitarianism: the role of international humanitarian norms and organisations in contemporary conflict. *Global Governance*, **11**: 161–183.

Minear, L. 2002. *The humanitarian enterprise: dilemmas and discoveries*. Bloomfield: Kumarian.

Morris, N. 2008. The evolution of humanitarian action. *Refugee Survey Quarterly*, **27**(1): 24–29.

Natsios, A.S. 2001. NGOs and the UN system in complex humanitarian emergencies: conflict or cooperation? *In*: P.F. Diehl (ed.). *The politics of global governance: international organisations in an interdependent world*. London: Lynne Rienner Publishers, pp. 388–405.

Ophir, A. 2007. The sovereign, the humanitarian, and the terrorist. *In*: M. Feher with G. Krikorian and Y. McKee (eds). *Nongovernmental politics*. New York: Zone Books, pp. 161–181.

Ophir, A. 2010. The politics of catastrophization: emergency and exception. *In*: D. Fassin and M. Pandolfi (eds). *Contemporary states of emergency: the politics of military and humanitarian intervention*. New York: Zone Books, pp. 59–88.

Oxford University Press. 2002. *Concise Oxford English Dictionary*. Tenth edition reissued with new title and jacket. Oxford: Oxford University Press.

Pantuliano, S. *et al.* 2011. *Counter-terrorism and humanitarian action: Tensions, impact and ways forward. HPG Policy Brief 43* [online]. [Accessed 5 June 2014]. www.odi.org.uk/sites/odi.org.uk/files/odi-assets/publications-opinion-files/7347.pdf.

Randel, J. and T. Germain. 2002. Trends in the financing of humanitarian assistance. *In*: J. Macrae (ed.). *The new humanitarianisms: a review of trends in global humanitarian action*. HPG Report 11. London: Overseas Development Institute.

Reid, J. 2010. The biopoliticization of humanitarianism: from saving bare life to securing the biohuman in the post-interventionary societies. *Journal of Intervention and State-building*, **4**(4): 391–411.

Reindorp, N. 2002. Trends and challenges in the UN humanitarian system. *In*: J. Macrae (ed.). *The new humanitarianisms: a review of trends in global humanitarian action*. HPG Report 11. London: Overseas Development Institute, pp. 29–38.

Reiss, T. 2004. Calculating humans: mathematics, war, and the colonial calculus. *In*: D. Glimp and M.R. Warren (eds). *Arts of calculation: quantifying thought in early modern Europe*. Basingstoke: Palgrave Macmillan, pp. 137–163.

Rieff, D. 2002. *A bed for the night: humanitarianism in crisis*. London: Vintage.

Roberts, A. 1996. *Humanitarian action in war*. Adelphi Paper 305. New York: Oxford University Press.

Roberts, A. 2000. *The so-called right of humanitarian intervention*. Trinity Papers [online]. No. 13, [Accessed 11 November 2005], pp. 4–23. www.trinity.unimelb.edu.au/publications/trinity_papers/TrinityPaper13.pdf.

Rutinwa, B. 2002. The end of asylum? The changing nature of refugee policies in Africa. *Refugee Survey Quarterly*, **21**(1&2): 12–41.

Selmeczi, A. 2011. '... we are being left to burn because we do not count': biopolitics, abandonment, and resistance. *In*: N.J. Kiersey and D. Stokes (eds). *Foucault and International Relation: new critical engagements*. Abingdon: Routledge, pp. 157–176.

Slim, H. 1995. Military humanitarianism and the new peacekeeping: an agenda for peace? *Journal of Humanitarian Assistance* [online]. [Accessed 19 December 2007]. www.jha.ac/articles/a003.htm.

Slim, H. 1997. International humanitarianism's engagement with civil war in the 1990s: a glance at evolving practice and theory. *Journal of Humanitarian Assistance* [online]. [Accessed 10 January 2008]. http://jha.ac/articles/a033.htm.

Slim, H. 2001. Violence and humanitarianism: moral paradox and the protection of civilians. *Security Dialogue*, **32**(3): 325–339.

Smillie, I. and L. Minear. 2004. *The charity of nations: humanitarian action in a calculating world*. Bloomfield: Kumarian.

Suhrke, A. and D. Klusmeyer. 2004. Between principles and politics: lessons from Iraq for humanitarian action. *Journal of Refugee Studies*, **17**(3): 273–285.

Sylvester, C. 2006. Bare life as a development/postcolonial problematic. *The Geographical Journal*, **172**(1): 66–77.

The Feinstein International Famine Center. 2004. *Ambiguity and change: humanitarian NGOs prepare for the future* [online]. [Accessed 8 December 2007]. http://nutrition.tufts.edu/docs/pdf/famine/ambiguity_and_change.pdf.

The Henry Dunant Centre for Humanitarian Dialogue. 2003. *Politics and humanitarianism: coherence in crisis?* [online]. [Accessed 10 December 2007]. www.hdcentre.org/publications?page=15.

The Sphere Project (no date). *Humanitarian Charter and Minimum Standards in Humanitarian Response* [online]. [Accessed 12 June 2014]. www.spherehandbook.org/.

Thede, N. 2013. Policy coherence for development and securitization: competing paradigms or stabilizing North-South hierarchies? *Third World Quarterly*, **34**(5): 784–799.

UN. 1996. *The United Nations and Somalia 1992–1996*. New York: United Nations.

UN. 2000. *Report of the Panel on United Nations Peace Operations (A/55/305-S/2000/809)* [the Brahimi Report] [online]. [Accessed 10 December 2007]. www.un.org/peace/reports/peace_operations/.

UNDP (United Nations Development Programme). 1994. *Human Development Report 1994* [online]. [Accessed 12 June 2014]. http://hdr.undp.org/sites/default/files/reports/255/hdr_1994_en_complete_nostats.pdf.

UN GA (United Nations General Assembly). 1991. Resolution No. 46/182 of 19 December 1991 *Strengthening of coordination of humanitarian emergency assistance of the United Nations* (A/RES/46/182) [online]. [Accessed 10 May 2011]. www.un.org/documents/ga/res/46/a46r182.htm

UN GA. 2006. *Report of the Secretary-General's High-level Panel on System-wide Coherence: 'Delivering As One' (A/61/583)* [online]. [Accessed 12 June 2014]. http://daccess-dds-ny.un.org/doc/UNDOC/GEN/N06/621/41/PDF/N0662141.pdf?OpenElement.

UNHCR (United Nations High Commissioner for Refugees). 1998. Introduction. The humanitarian debate: context and content. *Refugees Survey Quarterly*, **17**(1): vi–xvi.

UNHCR. 2006. *The State of the World Refugees: Human Displacement in the New Millennium* [online]. [Accessed 16 December 2007]. www.unhcr.org/cgi-bin/texis/vtx/template?page=publ&src=static/sowr2006/toceng.htm.

UN OCHA (United Nations Office for the Coordination of Humanitarian Assistance). 2004–2006. *Global Humanitarian Response Review 2004–2005* [online]. [Accessed 12 June 2014]. https://icvanetwork.org/doc00001369.html.

UN OCHA. 2013. *An Overview of Global Humanitarian Action at Mid-Year* [online]. [Accessed 10 June 2014]. https://docs.unocha.org/sites/dms/CAP/MYR_2013_Overview_of_GHA.pdf.

UN OCHA (no date). *Consolidated Appeal Process: about the Process* [online]. [Accessed 10 June 2014]. www.unocha.org/cap/about-the-cap/about-process.

Vaux, T. 2006. Humanitarian trends and dilemmas. *Development in Practice*, **16**(3): 240–254.

Walker, P. and D. Maxwell. 2009. *Shaping the humanitarian world*. London: Routledge.

Wheeler, N.J. 2000. *Saving strangers: humanitarian intervention in international society*. New York: Oxford University Press.

Wheeler, N.J. 2001. Humanitarian intervention after Kosovo: emergent norm, moral duty or the coming anarchy? *International Affairs*, 77(1): 113–128.

Weir, E.A. 2006. *Conflict and compromise: UN integrated missions and the humanitarian imperative*. KAIPTC Monograph No. 4 [online]. [Accessed 7 December 2007]. www. reliefweb.int/rw/lib.nsf/db900SID/OCHA-6SSFEA?OpenDocument.

West, K. 2001. *Agents of altruism: the expansion of humanitarian NGOs in Rwanda and Afghanistan*. Aldershot: Ashgate.

Zanotti, L. 2011. *Governing disorder: UN peace operations, international security, and democratization in the post-Cold War era*. Pennsylvania: The Pennsylvania State University Press.

Zeid, A.A. and J.J. Cochran (no date). *Quantifying a humanitarian disaster: survey of the health status of internally displaced population in South Central Somalia* [online]. [Accessed 5 June 2014]. www.informs.org/ORMS-Today/Public-Articles/August-Volume-40-Number-4/Quantifying-a-humanitarian-disaster.

3 'Caring' for the population of Afghanistan

The biopolitics of aid securitisation and militarisation

Aid ha[d] long been part of the strategy by which outside nations ... gained influence in Afghanistan.

(Johnson and Leslie, 2004: 147)

the provision of assistance ... in Afghanistan [was] a means of prosecuting a war ... rather than saving peoples' lives.

(interview, 21 June 2010)

Introduction

Affected by conflict and other crises, Afghanistan had been a recipient of various forms of assistance for decades (see Johnson and Leslie, 2004: Donini, 2009; Marsden, 2009). As an operational environment in which the post-2001 assistance effort was taking place, Afghanistan 'present[ed] a number of unique and unenviable characteristics', including 'the world's longest running armed conflict' (Donini, 2010: 4). The on-going conflict featured prominently among the factors that had given rise to humanitarian needs. Thus, according to the 2009 *Opinion Survey and In-depth Research*, '[v]ery few people ha[d] been unaffected by the armed conflict', with 60 per cent of the population having had direct personal experience of it (ICRC/IPSOS, 2009: 6). The violent conflict in Afghanistan unfolded against a backdrop of natural disasters, including 'floods, epidemics and pandemics, earthquakes, landslides, windstorms, sandstorms, avalanches, drought, rockslides, and extreme weather patterns' (UN OCHA, 2011: 7). Given limited infrastructure, this combination made effective recovery and development extremely challenging (UN OCHA, 2011: 1).

Following the 2001 US-led intervention and the overthrow of the Taliban regime, an unprecedented amount of resources was poured into the country. In 2008 and 2009, Afghanistan was the largest recipient of official development assistance (ODA), and received around US$27 billion during the 2002–2009 period, with the US providing almost 41 per cent of the total (Poole, 2011). ODA represented only part of the total international resource flows to Afghanistan and was 'dwarfed by security-related funding and military spending', with the US Department of Defense (DoD) itself being a major donor (Development Initiatives, 2010: 100).

A decade and billions of dollars on, Afghans still suffered from a significant number of deficits, reflected in some of the world's worst social indicators. In the 2011 *UNDP Human Development Index* (HDI), Afghanistan was ranked 172 out of 187 countries. It was also one of the worst places in the world in terms of life chances for children (Save the Children, 2010: 1). In 2011, around three million children in Afghanistan suffered from chronic malnutrition (UNICEF, in UN OCHA, 2011: 35). By the end of the decade, the humanitarian needs in Afghanistan were as enormous as they were diverse, and, according to the 2011 UN OCHA assessment, included 'food and nutrition security, forced displacement, access to water, sanitation and hygiene, livelihood assistance, and social protection, in particular for women and children' (1).

This evident disconnect between the needs and the amount of resources suggests that the post-2001 assistance effort in Afghanistan was informed and driven by considerations other than those of need and opportunity. In an attempt to account for this disconnect and to advance our understanding of the post-2001 (2001–2011) assistance effort in Afghanistan, the chapter will deploy the analytics of government to consider: conflicting ways in which the post-2001 situation in Afghanistan was problematised (first as counter-terrorism in a post-conflict context, then as counter-insurgency (COIN) and stabilisation)); systems of knowledge underpinning these problematisations (e.g. intelligence and Human Terrain Mapping (HTM), as opposed to needs assessments); strategies and technologies of governing used during assistance interventions (broadly conceived) and the role of the actors carrying out these interventions; and ways in which people in need of assistance were constructed (e.g. as a social base for insurgency, whose loyalty could be 'bought' through 'hearts and minds' campaigns, and whose deaths could be dismissed as 'collateral' damage).

With the focus on aid securitisation and militarisation, the chapter considers conditions of possibility and the nature of specific policies and practices, along with their implications for assistance providers and recipients. For the purposes of this analysis, securitisation is understood as the 'absorption of global and national security interests into the framing, structuring and implementation of development and aid' (Howell and Lind, 2009: 4). Militarisation is understood as:

> a significant up-turn in involvement of military actors in traditionally civilian fields of engagement[,] including direct delivery of relief supplies, emergency health, water and sanitation[,] as well as funding and implementation of early recovery activities, as an adjunct to military activities.
>
> (Development Initiatives, 2010: 98)

Policies and practices of aid securitisation and militarisation are understood as interrelated; in a way, militarisation can be simultaneously seen as a condition of possibility (e.g. military involvement in assistance provision facilitates securitisation) and as an instance and a consequence of broader processes of aid securitisation (e.g. military involvement is made possible by linking development and security, and conceptualising aid as a conflict-resolution and stabilisation tool).

The main argument advanced here is that both the reinforcement of the earlier trends associated with 'new' humanitarianism by the wars on terrorism, and the ways in which the situation in Afghanistan post-2001 was problematised, created the conditions of possibility for further securitisation and militarisation of aid. Although not new, policies and practices of aid securitisation and militarisation in post-2001 Afghanistan were unprecedented in terms of their scale, variety and the range of actors involved, and signalled further instrumentalisation of the assistance effort and its incorporation into the war effort, which combined bio-political concerns with sovereign violence. Not only did these developments create a deeper biopolitical divide between 'developed' and 'underdeveloped' populations (e.g. Duffield, 2008), but they were also indicative of a further trans-formation of the role of assistance in terms of the displacement of the human-itarian imperative with imperatives informed by counter-terrorism or COIN and stabilisation, and the use of the biopolitical rhetoric of care and protection to legitimise killings, justify civilian casualties and obscure the abandonment of those in need of assistance.

The chapter begins by critically examining the dominant problematisations of the situation in Afghanistan post-2001. The central parts of the chapter are devoted to the analysis of the policies and practices of securitisation and milita-risation of the post-2001 assistance effort in Afghanistan, and their implications for assistance providers and recipients. It concludes by reflecting on the import-ance of the developments that characterised the assistance effort in Afghanistan during the decade of intense international military involvement.

Problematising Afghanistan post-2001: from counter-terrorism and a post-conflict context to counter-insurgency and stabilisation

As has already been discussed, identifying problematisations, understood as ways of both framing a problem and simultaneously informing solutions to it, represents an important first step for an analytics of government. As Leader and Atmar (2004: 174) remind us, '[t]he way in which a problem is defined, and thus a solution implied, is a reflection of institutional and political power'. Indeed, as a former high-level UN official argued, the ways in which issues were framed in the post-2001 Afghanistan had very dramatic consequences (interview, 18 May 2010). Consequently, a closer consideration of the dominant problematisations of the situation in Afghanistan post-2011 can aid our understanding of the nature of the related assistance effort in general, and policies and practices of securiti-sation and militarisation of assistance in particular.

This section offers a critical account of the ways in which the post-2001 situ-ation in Afghanistan was problematised by external actors, including by donor governments, international military forces, IGOs, INGOs and NGOs. The purpose of this account is to demonstrate that dominant problematisations do matter, and, in the case of Afghanistan, they contributed to the creation of the conditions of possibility for securitisation and militarisation of the assistance effort. This is not to suggest that all humanitarian actors in Afghanistan, let alone all external actors, were the same in terms of their values, agendas, mandates, principles, approaches, programmes/projects, etc., or that they all supported or resisted dominant problematisations. But what is of the most interest here are the developments and the underlying logic behind them that led to a considerable convergence of positions of different actors regarding what role the international assistance effort in Afghanistan should play and how, by whom, and to whom assistance should be provided.

Counter-terrorism and its overall implications for the assistance effort

The fact that the 2001 US-led international military intervention in Afghanistan *(Operation Enduring Freedom* (OEF)) was carried out within the then emerging framework of the Global War on Terror was crucial in terms of informing the priorities and modalities of the international presence in the country for the years to come. Thus, the counter-terrorist focus is believed to have led to the use of means that contributed to the insecurity that followed, including bargaining with warlords, which not only resulted in their empowerment, but also compromised disarmament and demilitarisation activities, exacerbated regional tensions and undermined the legitimacy of the state through increased factionalisation (Barakat *et al.*, 2008; also Sedra, 2013). In fact, the initial narrow counter-terrorist focus mitigated against any form of reconciliation, failing to exploit the advantage that existed after the overthrow of the Taliban (Greentree, 2013), and prevented the US troops from engaging in any broader peacebuilding or security functions (Suhrke, 2011, in Paris, 2013: 539). This focus also meant that neither humanitarian or development assistance, nor state-building, were among the engagement priorities (Donini, 2006; Barakat *et al.*, 2008), following George W. Bush's 'we are not into nation-building' mantra (Suhrke, 2011, in Paris, 2013: 539). This was particularly regrettable, given that opportunities for such activities did exist at the time (Cornish, 2007; Paris, 2013).

The counter-terrorist priorities also informed the Bonn talks and the post-Taliban transition (Goodhand and Sedra, 2009). Short-term stability was prioritised (Goodhand and Sedra, 2007; also Howell and Lind, 2009), and the situation was problematised by the interveners as a post-conflict context, with many actors finding this problematisation too convenient to be challenged. Thus, 'in 2001–2002, there was a kind of euphoria in the country that NGOs could go out working under the banner ... of the liberated Afghanistan' (interview, 14 June 2010). Therefore, an uncoordinated flood of new and inexperienced NGOs into 'post-conflict' Afghanistan was not surprising (e.g. Marsden, 2009). In addition, the perceived end of the conflict influenced the conduct of military operations and the rules regarded as applicable. For example, a belief that International Humanitarian Law (IHL), including the rules concerning the neutrality of medical facilities, did not apply, was widespread.

The UN played an important role first in legitimising the intervention and then in the implementation of the Bonn Agreement, which called for, *inter alia*, a UN mandated international military force. The International Security Assistance Force (ISAF) was established on the basis of the UNSC Resolution 1386 of 20 December 2001 'to assist the Afghan Interim Authority in the maintenance of security in Kabul and its surrounding areas' (para. 1). While signalling a further alignment of the UN with the interveners, the ISAF's model as a force with a 'light footprint', confined to a specific area, proved counterproductive in terms of fulfilling its overall mandate (Rubin and Hamidzada, 2007; Goodhand and Sedra, 2009). These limitations were the important reasons for the establishment of Provincial Reconstruction Teams (PRTs), civil-military hybrids, which, in addition to the original mandate of security provision, engaged in assistance provision. In 2003, the ISAF mandate was extended beyond Kabul (UNSC Resolution 1510 of 13 October 2003) as NATO assumed overall command, using PRTs as 'the template for expansion' (Rubin and Hamidzada, 2007: 12). In 2011, 48 countries were contributing over 132,000 troops (90,000 were provided by the USA) to the ISAF, and the ISAF was operating in 28 PRTs (ISAF, 2011a). The responsibility for security was to be transferred to the Afghan National Security Forces by the end of 2014 (UNSC, 2011a).

The United Nations Assistance Mission in Afghanistan (UNAMA) further cemented the lead role that the UN was to take in supporting the 'post-conflict' transition (Marsden, 2009). UNAMA was established by the UNSC Resolution No. 1401 of 28 March 2002,[1] with its mandate outlined in the Secretary General's (SG) Report of 18 March 2002, which recommended that '[t]he next step, to ensure that all United Nations efforts are harnessed to fully support the implementation of the Bonn Agreement, would be to integrate all the existing United Nations elements in Afghanistan into a single mission' (UNSC, 2002a: 15). The Mission was to be 'a unified, integrated structure under the authority and leadership of the Special Representative for Afghanistan', and was to have a political affairs pillar and a humanitarian and development pillar (UNSC, 2002a: 16). The Head of the second pillar was given the responsibility for 'the direction and oversight of United Nations relief, recovery and reconstruction activities in Afghanistan, ... and of the offices, agencies, funds and programmes undertaking those activities' (UNSC, 2002a: 17).

UNAMA was the first UN mission influenced by the wars on terrorism and the first fully integrated one[2] (Johnson and Leslie, 2004; Donini, 2006). More importantly, UNAMA replaced UN OCHA, which had worked in Afghanistan since 1988 (Donini, 2009); within the UNAMA, the political wing was prioritised to the detriment of humanitarian issues. As some critics argued, the mandate of the Mission was to be 'aid-induced pacification' (Costy, 2004: 146). Being 'a child of the UN Security Council' (Donini, 2010: 9), UNAMA was supposed to act in coordination with both the ISAF and the OEF forces, which led to fundamental tensions, aptly summarised in a question, 'How can you do humanitarian work in the same organisation ... that does logistics for air strikes?'[3] (interview, 10 August 2010).

As a result of the folding of UN OCHA into UNAMA, oversight, coordination and a bigger picture of the humanitarian situation were lost (Marsden, 2009), as was the humanitarian information-gathering and analysis capacity (Donini, 2010). Crucially, the closure of the independent UN OCHA was simultaneously an outcome of the discourse about a post-conflict environment with no humanitarian crisis, and a powerful factor that made widespread suffering invisible through the continued denial of urgent humanitarian needs. Thus, in 2002, according to UNAMA, in the absence of a humanitarian crisis, there was even no need for a Consolidated Appeal Process for Afghanistan (Donini, 2006: 32). Overall, '[w]ithdrawing [OCHA] at a time when it was most crucial to have a coordinated humanitarian approach was ... really destructive for the humanitarian voice in Afghanistan' (interview, 7 June 2010). As a former high-level UN official elaborated, 'if OCHA capacity had been maintained, maybe ... the aid community would have woken up a bit earlier ... than 2009[4] [and realised] that there was, indeed, a humanitarian crisis in the country, and we were not collectively equipped to address it' (interview, 18 May 2010). The reluctance of the UN and donors to recognise large-scale humanitarian needs in Afghanistan was evident up until 2009–2010, as demonstrated by the difficulties associated with the re-opening of the UN OCHA: 'surprisingly enough we had a large fight trying to get UN OCHA to re-open its office in Afghanistan, and that [was] ... a very clear example of the denial of [the] humanitarian crisis' (interview, 10 August 2010).

As for the wider aid community, while many organisations were arguably forced to change their programming and become multi-mandated, given the lack of humanitarian funding and availability of other types of funding, they also played an important role in supporting and sustaining dominant problematisations. Thus, according to a representative of a major donor organisation, at the time many NGOs were not sending experienced humanitarian staff to Afghanistan, which made it very difficult for donors to find the right partners (interview, 6 June 2010). As a result, 'by the end of 2002 the majority of assistance agencies working in the country were in fact no longer engaging in humanitarian operation strictly defined, despite the use of bureaucratically defined 'humanitarian' funding instruments by donors' (Costy, 2004: 160).

At first, this may seem surprising, given the humanitarian rhetoric surrounding the OEF. As Ayub and Kouvo noted, '[d]espite the fact that the US-led war in Afghanistan was explicitly *not* a humanitarian intervention, American policymakers [came] to embrace the language and rhetoric of a humanitarian cause' (Ayub and Kouvo, 2008: 647; original emphasis; also Johnson and Leslie, 2004). Moreover, from the very start of the campaign, it was made clear that the military and the humanitarian missions were part of the same whole. If, however, we were to take into account the counter-terrorist priorities discussed above, there would be little surprise in the initial de-prioritisation of humanitarian needs. Even in 2009 there were very few 'purely humanitarian', Dunantist-type agencies, in Afghanistan, as the majority of actors were multi-mandated (Donini, 2009).

Overall, in the first few years after Bonn, international engagement in Afghanistan was characterised 'by competing and largely incompatible agendas, with major actors remaining involved for reasons other than humanitarian ideals and state-building' (Ayub and Kouvo, 2008: 647). However, it was the subsequent re-definition of the situation in Afghanistan, and, consequently, of the purpose of international engagement, that had the most significant impact on the assistance effort in Afghanistan.

COIN and its overall implications for the assistance effort

As the security situation in Afghanistan deteriorated, especially after 2006, it became obvious that the conflict was not over. This belated recognition resulted in the situation being re-defined as an insurgency, and COIN[5] became the focus of the international engagement in Afghanistan. As a population-centric doctrine, COIN is about weakening the support for the insurgency by winning the hearts and minds (WHAM) of the population, and is based on military engagement in assistance provision, along with integrating military and civilian activities (e.g. 2006 *FM 3–24*). In practice, this meant that COIN strategies not just encouraged, but were also reliant on, the use of assistance, paving the way for aid militarisation and securitisation. Thus, the UNSC Resolution No. 1746 of 23 March 2007[6] stressed 'the synergies in the objectives of UNAMA and ... ISAF', along with 'the need for continued cooperation and coordination' (UNSC, 2007a).

In the case of ISAF, PRTs served as one of the main vehicles for implementing the COIN strategy. Although established to focus on security provision as enabling/facilitating the assistance effort, PRTs were extensively engaged in direct assistance provision, often through the so-called QIPs[7] (Quick Impact Projects) (e.g. Braem, 2008; Waldman, 2009). This involvement, along with the attempts to use all humanitarian and development activities to achieve overall security objectives, had a number of important implications, and attracted a number of criticisms, both practical (e.g. high cost, poor quality and unsustainable nature of the projects) and principled (e.g. military objectives vs the humanitarian imperative; creation of 'perverse incentives' by targeting the least stable areas; blurring the differences between the military and humanitarian actors).

Another, more recent, but related, doctrine that informed international engagement in Afghanistan was that of stabilisation. Gordon (2009:116) defined stabilisation as 'the military pursuit of "soft security" instruments sufficient to transform its tactical successes in the battlefield into more sustainable forms of stability ... and a conflict management/containment strategy drawn from the "new humanitarianism"'. According to a representative of a major donor organisation, this meant that assistance provision 'ha[d] to be tied to counter-insurgency and stabilisation' (interview, 6 June 2010).

Arguably, the most important general implication of both COIN and stabilisation strategies for the assistance effort is the danger of sacrificing the humanitarian imperative in favour of military objectives. After all, as suggested by

Egnell (2010: 289), '[a]lthough improvements in terms of humanitarian and development situations are important, they are not the main concerns of hearts and minds activities'. Indeed, these activities are often carried out for purposes other than those of addressing urgent needs or providing sustainable development (Bricknell, 2009). For instance, according to an influential report published by the Development Initiatives (2010: 99), the US DoD aid expenditure was 'primarily guided by military doctrine and tactical advantage rather than by poverty reduction or humanitarian goals'. According to some humanitarian actors, this leads to weaponisation of aid, whereby '[a]ssistance ... becomes just another weapon at the service of the military, which can condition, deny or reward relief to those who fall in or out of line with its larger security agenda' (MSF, 2010: 4; interview, 21 June 2010).

The widespread practices of geographic targeting of assistance in Afghanistan were a telling example of the above, with humanitarian and reconstruction interventions concentrated in those areas where COIN operations were taking place, rather than in more stable locations, which were more likely to benefit from external aid, thus creating widely noted 'perverse incentives' (Barakat *et al.*, 2008, in Barakat *et al.*, 2010: 312; Wilder, 2009; Thompson, 2010). Indeed, the stabilisation agenda created a massive redirection of development resources. As a representative of a major donor organisation explained with respect to the situation in 2010:

> It [was] very clear that ... a large portion of what was considered development money ... [was] very specifically being targeted towards what [was] called 'stabilisation activities', and [those activities]... [were] not about development.... The purpose of the money [was] to win the war, whatever that mean[t]. And winning the war ... [was] not going to be done only through military force ... the entire development enterprise ... [was] being turned to a completely different agenda ... called stabilisation.
>
> (interview, 6 June 2010)

The 2003 UN OCHA *Guidelines on the Use of Military and Civil Defence Assets to Support United Nations Humanitarian Activities in Complex Emergencies* (revised in 2006) could have served as a basis for challenging the negative impact of COIN and stabilisation strategies on the assistance effort. The *Guidelines* reiterated the importance of the humanitarian imperative and humanitarian principles and emphasised the need to maintain 'a clear distinction between the role and function of humanitarian actors from that of the military', as it 'is the determining factor in creating an operating environment in which humanitarian organisations can discharge their responsibilities both effectively and safely' (UN OCHA, 2003: para. 3). The document expressed a serious concern with possible motivations for military engagement in assistance provision and their implications:

> Many international military forces provide assistance to the civilian population.... While motivation for this can be.... Humanitarian, ... assistance can

also be motivated by a desire to legitimize missions, gain intelligence, and/ or enhance protection of forces, [which] can be inappropriate, lack longevity, and can disrupt assistance.

(UN OCHA, 2003: para. 35)

Consequently, the *Guidelines* limited the use of military assets to situations 'where there is no comparable civilian alternative and only the use of military assets can meet a critical humanitarian need' (UN OCHA, 2003: para. 7). Ultimately, the document stated that 'the use of military and civil defence resources should under no circumstances undermine the perceived neutrality or impartiality of the humanitarian actors, nor jeopardize current or future access to affected populations' (UN OCHA, 2003: para. 28).

In 2008, specific *Guidelines for the Interaction and Coordination of Humanitarian Actors and Military Actors in Afghanistan* were signed by UNAMA and UN agencies, the Agency Coordinating Body for Afghan Relief (ACBAR), ISAF, OEF forces and Afghan National Security Forces to 'support the development of a relationship between military and humanitarian actors in which differences are recognized and respected' (UNAMA *et al.*, 2008: 3). However, despite a lot of effort that went into adopting the *Guidelines*, they were rarely adhered to, which could be partly attributed to the power imbalance between the military and the humanitarian community, with the latter lacking in numbers, organisation and resources (e.g. Donini, 2010).

In 2010–2011, following the US 'surge' of 2009, which saw the deployment of tens of thousands of additional US troops and civilians, the security situation in the country was again deteriorating, as the attacks by armed opposition groups continued to rise (ANSO, 2011a; also UNSC, 2011a; UN OCHA, 2011), as did the numbers of civilian casualties. Thus, in 2010 attacks by armed opposition groups were 69 per cent higher than in 2009, which represented the highest growth rate recorded by the Afghanistan NGO Safety Office (ANSO) (ANSO, 2011a). In the first quarter of 2011, the attacks grew by 51 per cent on 2010 (ANSO, 2011b). The increased insecurity took its toll in civilian casualties. According to UNAMA, in 2010, 2,412 civilians became casualties of the conflict, which represented a 14 per cent increase on the previous year (UN OCHA, 2011).

Violent attacks affected not just civilians, but also the aid community. Thus, in 2010 'NGOs were involved in 126 incidents', which resulted in 28 fatalities and additional 33 people being injured (ANSO, 2011a: 1). Despite the overall fall in the number of incidents compared to 2009, they were becoming deadlier, with 'an alarming 42 per cent increase in fatalities' (ANSO, 2011a: 1). As violent attacks against civilians and humanitarians spread to traditionally calm areas (UN OCHA, 2011), only four provinces in Afghanistan were considered to be of low insecurity (ANSO, 2011a). The implications of the increasing insecurity were twofold, as it increased humanitarian need, while limiting the access for humanitarian organisations (UN OCHA, 2011). For instance, according to the UN OCHA (2011: 7), 'operations ... such as *Operation Moshtarak* in February

2010 or *Operation Hamkari* in August 2010 led to significant population displacements and civilian casualties in the south with little humanitarian opportunity to respond due to insecurity'.

The increased insecurity was one of the reasons humanitarian agencies were forced to retreat, resulting in what Duffield termed a 'bunkering' of the aid industry (Duffield, 2010a, 2010b; also Donini, 2010a). As the conflict was becoming more complex, even humanitarian agencies with a long history of presence on the ground '[did] not have a concrete, comprehensive picture on the different groups operating in some areas' (interview, 14 June 2010), let alone a comprehensive picture of the humanitarian caseload (interview, 15 May 2010). The inability to build such a picture was also due to the previously discussed loss of the humanitarian information-gathering and analysis capacity, along with the ability to negotiate with all parties to the conflict, due to the UN alignment with one side of the conflict and the closure of the independent UN OCHA in 2002 (Donini, 2010). Although the UN OCHA was re-opened in 2009, it lacked authority, capabilities and support from the UN OCHA Headquarters to co-ordinate the assistance effort effectively.

At the same time, the affected populations considered the provision of humanitarian assistance as essential, and often suggested that its provision meant 'the difference between life and death' (ICRC/IPSOS, 2009: 9). Important considerations for Afghan beneficiaries included the perceived impartiality of assistance and the long-term commitment (ICRC/IPSOS, 2009: 9). In terms of priorities, 63 per cent mentioned food as the most urgent need, 'followed by protection/ security (53 per cent) and medical treatment/care (48 per cent)' (ICRC/IPSOS, 2009: 28). While improved physical security was definitely regarded a priority by the population, the deteriorated security situation would suggest that this need had not been given a priority by those responsible for its provision. This could be considered surprising, given that the international military presence was arguably there 'to provide security for the population' (Stirrup, in Meikle *et al.*, 2010; ISAF, 2011b), and given the amount of resources that came with it. As one of my interviewees commented, the main reason aid was coming into Afghanistan was because of the military involvement, and if there had been no military involvement, aid would have been a small fraction of what it was (interview, 14 March 2010). In fact, in 2010 all major donors in Afghanistan were also belligerents[8] (Donini, 2010a), and the US DoD managed multiple funds 'significantly higher than both official humanitarian and development aid' (Development Initiatives, 2010: 9). Thus, the 2010 budget of the Commander's Emergency Response Program (CERP) alone exceeded both the 2010 Afghanistan and Iraq CAPs (Consolidated Appeals) combined (Development Initiatives, 2010). As a high-level UN official pointed out, in 2010 '[i]n Afghanistan, the military [had] about 1.4–1.8 billion US$ to spend.... They [did] not need the humanitarian community' (interview, 21 March 2010).

Policies and practices of the securitisation and militarisation of aid in Afghanistan post-2001

Many developments and practices, along with the dominant problematisations of the situation in Afghanistan post-2001, can be said to have established the conditions of possibility for the securitisation and militarisation of aid. Thus, as has been previously discussed, new agendas for humanitarians had emerged out of a number of post-Cold War developments in the 1990s (e.g. coherence agenda, comprehensive approaches and integrated missions), which implied that humanitarian action would assume new roles, such as conflict resolution or peace-building. In addition, with the new interventionism of the 1990s, humanitarianism had been also used as a justification for wars, and had become military humanitarianism. Such justifications also characterised the military campaign in Afghanistan. Indeed, 'military humanitarianism ... was catapulted onto the international scene most forcefully in Kosovo in 1999 and in Afghanistan, since 2001' (Ankersen, 2008: 2).

However, there is more to military humanitarianism than just the use of humanitarian rhetoric, as it also implies engagement of the military forces in assistance provision and closer civil–military cooperation (as in an integrated mission, e.g. UNAMA) in pursuit of a comprehensive approach. Indeed, according to Ankersen (2008: 1), '[c]ivil-military cooperation [CIMIC] [was] on the rise, and ha[d] been since the 1990s and the conception of modern "peace support operations"'. Parallel developments had also been taking place in donor countries themselves, where attempts had been made to bring together 'armed forces, diplomacy and national relief agencies' (e.g. the UK 'whole of the government' or Canadian '3D' – diplomacy, defence, development – approaches) (Braem, 2008: 41). Gordon (2009) also acknowledged the importance of integrated or comprehensive approaches for making possible both the establishment of particular structures, such as the Stabilisation Unit in the UK, and for the emergence of strategies like stabilisation. According to Howell and Lind (2009: 92–93), 'development of new cross-departmental institutions ... point[ed] to the increasing securitisation of aid policy and practice'. Furthermore, some suggested that direct provision of assistance by some armed forces, or their engagement in the assistance efforts of others, had become their 'mainstream, non-combat function' (Rana, 2008: 226), whereby humanitarian aid had been used as a WHAM tool (Kett and van Tulleken, 2009).

As has been previously stressed, post-2001 COIN and stabilisation strategies in Afghanistan were reliant on the use of humanitarian, reconstruction and development assistance in order to win over populations. However, according to Barakat *et al.* (2010: 297), those strategies were not entirely new, and 'civilian and military actors ha[d] collaborated both to bring an end to small- and large-scale conflicts and to promote durable dispensations in their aftermath', although this 'collaboration' might not have always been called COIN or stabilisation. Historical examples included the Philippines (1898–1902) and Vietnam (1967–1975). Even some of the structures were not new, with PRTs in Afghanistan being based on Provincial

Advisory Teams in Vietnam and QIPs first used in the Philippines (Barakat, Deely and Zyck, 2010). More specifically, as Bricknell (2009: 49) pointed out, '[m]ilitary medical services ha[d] a long history of being involved in providing humanitarian medical assistance to local civilian populations'. For the UK, examples included Jordan in 1970, East Nepal in 1988, Iraq in 1991 and 2003, Rwanda in 1994, and Kosovo in 1999. The USA ran a variety of programmes during the Vietnam War (Bricknell, 2009).

In addition, in the case of Afghanistan, aid had been used as an instrument of foreign policy in the country well before 2001 (Atmar and Goodhand, 2002; Johnson and Leslie, 2004; Marsden, 2009; Howell and Lind, 2009). This was very much the case during the Cold War,[9] when 'refugee and cross border programmes were seen by many as the non-lethal component of aid to the Afghan resistance' (Atmar and Goodhand, 2002: 23). As Baitenmann's (1990: 63) research demonstrated, '[a]part from Pakistan, two major official players who carried out the relief effort and influenced the work of NGOs [were] the UNHCR and the USA (the largest donor government)'. However, the scale of the relief effort meant that many more actors were involved, including NGOs. At the same time as they were providing life-saving assistance, there was also no denying that NGOs actively supported an armed resistance (Baitenmann, 1990; also Marsden, 2009). Importantly, the relationship between the US government and some NGOs was very close, and extended beyond funding, as NGOs were expected to assist in bringing down the Soviet-backed Afghan regime. It was this objective that arguably resulted in the assistance effort being focused on refugees in Pakistan rather than civilians in the government-controlled areas in Afghanistan, who were also in urgent need of aid (Baitenmann, 1990). Although European NGOs were receiving funding independent from the USA, the whole assistance effort became associated with the US government and its foreign policy objectives in Afghanistan (Marsden, 2009). Interestingly, that assistance effort was also one of the pre-1990 examples of aid privatisation, with the UNHCR contracting NGOs for projects, and USAID using contractors (Baitenmann, 1990).

The consequent evolution of the assistance effort in Afghanistan saw it shifting from Cold War alliances to a more coordinated, system-wide response, whereby the assistance community would 'speak with one voice' (Johnson and Leslie, 2004: 95). However, after 1993, when Afghanistan was no longer a strategic priority for the US foreign policy, continued support was not required, despite the fact that the country was severely damaged (Marsden, 2009). This situation changed again in 2001, and dramatically so. Crucially then, given the above discussion, were the policies and practices of securitisation and militarisation of assistance in Afghanistan post-2001 anything new and, if so, how are we to understand them?

The scale of securitisation and militarisation of the post-2001 assistance effort in Afghanistan needs to be understood in terms of the amount of resources, nature and variety of policies and practices and the range of actors involved. Some indication of the resources available to military actors for various forms of assistance has already been provided, and, according to the Development Initiatives (2010: 98), the volume of resources was so significant that 'it warrant[ed] a separate study'. In addition, what distinguished the post-2001 assistance effort in Afghanistan from previous examples of aid securitisation and militarisation was the explicit treatment of aid as a weapons system (Wilder, 2009; Barakat *et al.*, 2010), the systematic nature of the military involvement in assistance provision and a concerted effort to promote civilian-military cooperation and coordination (Howell and Lind, 2009).

Interpretations of the general logic behind military engagement in assistance provision usually focus on political and operational reasons, with the latter including force protection, force 'happiness' and possible contribution to information operations (Ankersen, 2008). Political reasons, in turn, have to do with the need to win hearts and minds of the international media and international and domestic publics (Neuhaus, 2008). Egnell (2010: 284) suggests that with the 'new' COIN, WHAM (and, consequently, assistance provision) becomes a necessity due to limited manpower and the inability to use highly coercive methods. While counter-terrorism is often characterised by 'the adoption of increasingly illiberal measures to achieve a ... liberal peace' (Goodhand and Sedra, 2007: 53), I suggest that COIN and stabilisation as population-centric doctrines are characterised by their reliance on assistance provision. Indeed, military engagement in assistance provision is required by biopolitical justifications of care and protection offered to the 'assisted' populations. However, in this way, biopolitical concerns also justify sovereign violence, and the resultant combination of sovereignty and biopolitics can be said to represent a clear example of what Foucault termed a 'demonic project'. In this particular project in Afghanistan, direct provision of assistance and co-optation of humanitarian agencies allowed the military a different kind of access to the body of the Afghan population as a collective body containing threats, both to other societies and to itself. The use of biopolitical concerns of care and protection facilitated the transcendence of sovereign borders and the double legitimisation of pacification and containment, whereby the threats emanating from underdeveloped societies were addressed in the hope of achieving transformation, or betterment, of these societies, something I come back to later. As for the threatening elements, they were made subject to disciplining and, if proven resistant to it, to selective, but necessary, killing (Dillon, 2008; Anderson, 2011; Kienscherf, 2011). This discussion can help us understand why, while the military in Afghanistan were engaging in the assistance provision, which was believed to create stability, they were not focusing on security provision as much as would have been expected if they had taken protection of Afghan civilians seriously. For instance, it was argued that 'the local population, as well as NGOs and aid agencies, found it difficult to understand why the military was focusing on building schools when security was degrading' (Parker, former development adviser to the commander of ISAF, in Egnell, 2010: 296).

As for the specific policies and practices of aid securitisation and militarisation, they were diverse, with one of them being direct engagement of military forces in provision of medical care. Arguably, medical care is one of the most controversial areas of military engagement in the provision of humanitarian assistance, as the purpose of such engagement can be 'to achieve support for political and military objectives rather than solely saving lives and alleviating suffering of a crisis-affected population' (Bricknell, 2009: 51–52). The impossibility of impartiality and neutrality, including the impossibility of following the humanitarian imperative (e.g. because supporting the deployed force is the priority (Neuhaus, 2008)), is one of the most important principled objections to such practices.[10] Thus, the ICRC's concern relates to the fact that 'responding to the needs of part of the population comes to be seen as a component of a broader strategy designed to defeat an opponent or enemy' (Krähenbühl, 2004: 512). One of the starkest examples of this in Afghanistan came in 2004, when the Coalition forces used leaflets threatening a withdrawal of assistance 'unless the population provided information on al-Qaeda and Taliban leaders' (MSF, 2010: 4). Further issues involved: PRTs providing assistance in NGO-led hospitals,[11] without informing the NGOs (Braem, 2008); Afghan and NATO forces raiding a clinic in 2009; and US forces raiding a hospital (MSF, 2010). Not only did such actions violate IHL, but they also reinforced the link between health services and the COIN agenda, and made the former another dimension of the latter (Gordon, 2010). As MSF (2010: 4) argued, with 'a competition for the support of a population, the provision (or denial) of health services [became] a key asset for all belligerents. This ... led warring parties in Afghanistan to see healthcare workers and facilities a part of the battlefield'.

This had important implications in terms of endangering both healthcare staff and beneficiaries. In the case of healthcare staff, such blurring of the lines could be seen as an instance of a bigger trend when securitisation of assistance eroded their consent-based, carefully negotiated access and acceptance by the communities they served (Cornish, 2007; Bricknell, 2009; Waldman, 2009) and could result in increased attacks by insurgents[12] (Donini, 2009; also Cornish, 2007; Howell and Lind, 2009). As for beneficiaries, they could be affected in a number of ways, as, medical facilities where they received assistance came under attack, often because they were constructed/refurbished/used by PRTs or military forces, but also because of being persecuted by insurgents for having used the services provided by military forces or by organisations 'associated' with them or with the Afghan government. As one of my interviewees explained in detail:

> patients [were] scared to go to those clinics ... for two reasons: ... either the clinic [would] be targeted while they [were] actually physically in it, but, perhaps, even more significantly, they [were] scared of what [would] happen when they [went] back to the home villages ... the very fact that they ha[d] sought out health care in what [was] seen as a politicised facility then open[ed] them up for retribution.... What kind of choice [was] that for people? As a result, they tend[ed] to seek health care very late, because they [were] very scared of the consequences.

> (interview, 21 June 2010)

Such endangerment of beneficiaries can also be seen as a clear example of bio-political abandonment, as lives of beneficiaries did not matter, and they could be left to die or left to be killed by anti-government forces, and all in the name of their security and well-being. Furthermore, the possible endangerment of beneficiaries was not limited to medical services, and similar concerns were expressed about the National Solidarity Programme, widely perceived as successful: 'NSP [was] being co-opted for stabilisation.... It [became] a victim of its own success.... NSP [was] seen as an instrument of weakening the Taliban, [which would] make it a target for insurgents' (interview, 31 July 2010).

Military medical aid programmes were one of the main ways in which the UK military engaged in assistance provision in Helmand; they also ran medical outreach clinics, but those were discontinued in an attempt to preserve humanitarian space (Gordon, 2010). Importantly, by 2010, the ICRC and MSF were running medical programmes in Helmand, which suggested that eventually there was some space for assistance provision based on humanitarian principles (Gordon, 2010).

Another practice of aid securitisation that threatened these principles in post-2001 Afghanistan was the so-called 'post-battlefield clean-up', whereby humanitarian agencies were expected to follow military forces and selectively provide assistance in the aftermath of major military offensives. Several of my interviewees admitted that they were under pressure to work in the conflict-affected areas (interviews, 14 March 2010 and 7 June 2010). Refugees International (2009) also drew attention to a significant (five-year, US$150 million) 2008 USAID project, applications for which were required to show the ability to implement 'post-battlefield clean-up', including operating alongside PRTs and delivering a specific US government-endorsed message to affected communities. The danger of such practices was that they neither followed the humanitarian imperative, nor respected humanitarian principles of independence, neutrality and impartiality. It can be argued that it was down to humanitarian actors to resist such practices and the co-optation involved, for instance, by refusing the funding provided by PRTs. Indeed, some humanitarian actors, including the ICRC and MSF, as well as several multi-mandated organisations, did so:

> Why would we bid for funding that they [PRTs] [were] providing?... They [were] a belligerent, we [could not] take funding from them, so, of course, we [were] not going to bid for that money.... We [did not] actually agree on the prioritisation process in terms of the projects that they [were] doing.... We want[ed] money through the development departments... We [were there] for a long-term, [they were] not.
>
> (interview, 7 June 2010)

However, invariably in Afghanistan all assistance providers, from the UN family organisations to multi-mandated INGOs and NGOs, found themselves working alongside military forces. As mentioned previously, the 2008 *Guidelines* had been adopted in order to avoid blurring the lines between military and humanitarian actors. However, the document did not stop some military actors[13] from engaging in assistance provision, further eroding the distinction between military forces and other assistance providers, which had serious implications in terms of humanitarian access and community acceptance. Erosion of access and acceptance, in turn, further contributed to the so-called bunkering of aid (Duffield, 2010a, 2010b; also Donini, 2010a). For Donini (2009), the life inside the fortified compound[14] represented 'the virtual Afghanistan'. As one of my interviews explained:

> people [were] hiding behind tall walls [with] barbed wire, and a lot of the international aid community ... never [met] Afghans beside their own drivers, and ... you [could] definitely see that you [were] working in a pretty extreme situation, but it also mean[t] that you [did not] get a full picture of what [was] happening ... in the rest of the country.
>
> (interview, 10 August 2010)

For Duffield (2010b: 467), fortified aid compounds mark the point where 'the international space of aid flows physically confronts underdevelopment as dangerous'. This very architectural form is emblematic of occupation and pacification, and, as such, does little to overcome the divide between development (the inside) and underdevelopment (the outside); instead, it reproduces it, while signalling its further institutionalisation. If we follow Kelly (2010: 6), compounds are better understood as outposts of the biopolitical border, which divides populations rather than states and ensures advantage to the inside.

At the same time, traditional COIN doctrine recommends to military forces that '[p]resence should be established by living in close proximity to the populations' (Kilcullen, in Egnell, 2010: 291). In Afghanistan, this was a source of concern, with civilians 'killed and injured as a result of their proximity to military bases, homes and property ... damaged or destroyed' (UNAMA, 2010: 3). Such positioning of military bases also violated IHL, as 'military bases should be placed outside residential and commercial areas in order to minimize the effects of the conflict on civilians' (UNAMA, 2010: 3). What happened in Afghanistan was a kind of reversal, whereby military forces were venturing out, as it was necessary for achieving COIN objectives, while humanitarians were withdrawing into the fortified compounds due to increased insecurity. As Thompson (2010: 19) noted, 'through the COIN strategy, the military [was] becoming more 'civilianised' at the same time that the aid agencies [were] becoming more risk averse, and disconnected from the populations concerned'. In this respect Bell (2011) argues that what is commonly termed militarisation of development and humanitarianism should instead be understood as civilianisation of warfare. I would argue that COIN doctrine and the way it was practiced in the-post 2001 Afghanistan brought the humanitarian and development enterprise and the military intervention incredibly close together, with transformative effects for both, which meant that aid securitisation and militarisation was simultaneously a condition of possibility for, and an outcome of, civilianisation of warfare.

In turn, the disconnect between aid providers and beneficiaries was reflected in organisations switching to remote programming/monitoring, whereby they worked through local 'implementing partners' and had much less contact with their beneficiaries (e.g. Montgomery, 2009, in Duffield, 2010b: 470; interview, 10 August 2010). To access insecure areas, many agencies had to resort to using military forces or security contractors for protection, although not all organisations were prepared to do so. This dynamic created a vicious cycle: less contact with beneficiaries had a negative impact on trust and acceptance and led to a further erosion of access and further distancing. This was an instance of biopolitical violence, which, unlike sovereign violence, did not have to involve killing, but rather resulted in increased vulnerability. Indeed, many argued that the assumptions informing the use of aid as an important stabilisation tool had been untested, unsupported and/or flawed (Wilder, 2009; Goodhand and Sedra, 2009; Waldman, 2009; Thompson, 2010). This concern was also shared by one of my interviewees:

> our government, and that include[d] the military and … the civilian side of the government, [had] made a huge assumption that you [could] use development money and development tools in order to win a war and create a stable [environment] … I think [the development department] ha[d] been hijacked … for a completely different purpose that it was never designed to do. So, how [could] it possibly succeed?
>
> (interview, 6 June 2010)

Furthermore, according to Rietjens (2008: 97), assistance provision by ISAF did not even contribute in any significant way to force protection, let alone produce any genuine development, which, one may argue, it was not designed to achieve. Indeed, in trying to win the hearts and minds of the population, the military engaged in quick impact programming, which proved to be both ineffective and unsustainable for a number of reasons. First, as a military actor, PRTs were not well-positioned for conducting development activities; second, they were not able to achieve the necessary level of local engagement and ownership given the overall mistrust of the population; third, they diverted funds away from civilian development institutions; fourth, they were unable to create a nation-wide consistent development framework, which resulted in geographical disparities; and, finally, the tensions between the WHAM and COIN approaches and the principles of sustainable development meant that even intended security objectives were unlikely to be achieved (Waldman, 2009). In addition, as QIPs were often of poor quality (Rietjens, 2008; Jackson, 2010), they contributed to the overall disillusionment of local populations.

Another reason for disillusionment came from the major differences in the amount of resources provided to different regions and in the speed of their allocation. Too much money provided too quickly to insecure regions of the country could not be absorbed, and had delegitimising and destabilising effects by fuelling corruption[15] and creating perverse incentives to either maintain the levels of insecurity or destabilise relatively stable areas (Thompson, 2010), based on the conclusion that violence was necessary to receive assistance (Barakat, 2008: 54). In addition, when large funds have to be spent quickly, the effectiveness of their development impacts is not a priority (Thompson, 2010). As one of my interviewees remarked with respect to the post-2006 situation:

> Military success [was] the key priority for all international actors who are engaged militarily in Afghanistan. They [could] 'blah-blah' about development, and rights, and people of Afghanistan as much as they want[ed], but they want[ed] success ... because they seem[ed] to have failed ... in the War on Terror.... So, they need[ed] military success, and they believe[d] [that], in order to get that military success, [they] need[ed] to throw a lot of money around those communities where [they were] trying to win, and that's what they [had] done.
>
> (interview, 7 June 2010)

This statement captured well the rationale for the adoption of WHAM policies (the inability to succeed in other ways) and the assumptions on which it was based (i.e. that people's loyalties could be bought, also implying a particular type of subjectivity, that of a rational and calculating subject), as well as pointing to some of the consequences of such policies (i.e. the geographical targeting of aid and aid instrumentalisation in general). As for the specific examples of the consequences, according to Save the Children (2010: 3), in 2010 '[i]n per capita terms, Helmand [was] among the most heavily aided places, ... while other provinces with comparably poor indicators for child survival, education and nutrition [were] largely bypassed by ... donors'. For Wilder (2009), such geographical targeting of aid was one of the starkest pieces of evidence of the securitisation of aid in Afghanistan, along with the channelling of resources through military forces or PRTs. Arguably geographical targeting of aid in the post-2001 Afghanistan can be best understood as a biopolitical triage and abandonment. In this triage, the decisions were dictated not by positive biopolitical criteria (the humanitarian imperative), but by the securitised criteria that prioritised other populations and their security over the assisted ones, because the latter represented a threat to the former. As a result, many communities in need were abandoned, but such abandonment was an outcome of both the global biopolitical triage (as discussed by Duffield, 2007 onwards; Dillon and Reid, 2009; Bell and Evans, 2010) and the one taking place within the targeted population itself (Anderson, 2011; Kienscherf, 2011).

The level of involvement of humanitarian agencies in the COIN campaign was another distinguishing feature, according to Slim (2004). He is also one of a number of scholars who rightly pointed out that this involvement was not all down to co-optation, and it was agencies themselves who often made it possible. For Braem (2008: 45), the arrival of NGOs en masse into the post-Taliban Afghanistan 'soon after military deployments and bombing campaigns, show[ed] on what side of the conflict' they were, i.e. that 'they were participating in the

US led occupation and reconstruction of the territory, even if they claimed the contrary'. Marsden (2009: 218) also blamed humanitarian actors for failing 'to dissociate themselves from the international military presence'. Some (e.g. Slim, 2004; Cornish, 2007; Donini, 2009; MSF, 2010) see multi-mandated agencies as an important cause of the problem, as they are more vulnerable to co-optation, given their focus on state-building and development, which also made abiding by humanitarian principles of independence, impartiality and neutrality very difficult, if not impossible. The key issue here seems to be the tension between alleviating suffering and transforming societies. Duffield (2001) commented on this shift from deontological to consequentialist thinking, associated with the rise of 'new' humanitarianism, in *Global Governance and the New Wars*. According to MSF (2010: 6), '[w]hile both relief and development may be well-intentioned and are not necessarily opposed to one another, there is a major operational incompatibility between the two in war'. Consequently, if humanitarian space is to be preserved, all organisations operating in a conflict zone should make a choice between relief and development, a 'choice between saving lives today or saving societies tomorrow' (MSF, 2010: 6). For some, in the post-2001 Afghanistan this choice was clear. As a former high-level UN official argued, 'there [was] no dilemma, ... if your priority lie[d] with the people who [were] most at risk, then ... you ha[d] to be principled, ... you ha[d] to abide by ... humanitarian principles' (interview, 15 May 2010).

However, while criticising NGOs operating in Afghanistan for 'wanting it both ways' in that, although uncomfortable with being associated with the government's projects, they still accepted the funding, Johnson and Leslie (2004) acknowledged that many NGOs did not have much choice, as funding was not readily available for those who choose to remain independent. Furthermore, some organisations choose to coordinate with other actors, including the international military forces, 'mainly to prevent duplication of humanitarian effort and to avoid *doing harm* to the local population' (Rietjens, 2008: 86; original emphasis). Also, as has been mentioned, while some humanitarian actors might have been complicit in creating the conditions for aid securitisation and militarisation, the dominant problematisations of the situation in Afghanistan, and the general direction of the assistance effort, were indeed challenged. Unfortunately, the space for alternative problematisations and for challenging securitisation and militarisation of assistance had been circumscribed, and the ability of humanitarian actors to contest these practices had been largely eroded (e.g. Johnson and Leslie, 2004; Rana, 2008).

At the same time, Slim (2004: 2) drew attention to stark similarities between NGO policy documents and COIN manuals, and suggested that 'there [was] a considerable overlap of moral "ends" between the Coalition, humanitarian, human rights and development agencies in Iraq and Afghanistan', one that 'UN agencies, NGOs and other humanitarian commentators' did no fully acknowledge (Slim, 2004: 2–3). Bringing the argument to bear on the COIN campaign in Afghanistan, Slim (2004: 8) contended that humanitarians also represented one of the groups 'who compete[d] for access, acceptance and the support of the people', and they sometimes used the same public goods to achieve the above objectives, as did insurgents and international military forces. However, he did recognise the important differences in terms of the means used. I suggest that differences were also in the ends, and such differences were informed by the consideration that humanitarian agencies had for the assisted population, their main concern; they treated the population as an end in itself, not as a means of securing another population. Therefore, even if they could be said to be complicit in maintaining the gap between the developed and underdeveloped populations (Duffield, 2008), as the biopolitical care they provided was limited and inferior to that available to the developed populations (Kelly, 2010), their efforts were largely based on the urgency and severity of the need, and they opposed the use of assistance as a reward for compliance, or its withdrawal as a punishment.

The heavy presence of private military/security contractors (PMCs) in Afghanistan further complicated the operational environment, and had implications for humanitarian access, and for the assistance effort overall, signalling its further privatisation, informed by a neoliberal logic. The amount of resources channelled through PMCs was significant. Thus, in 2010, British private security companies in Afghanistan received contracts worth a record £29 million, which suggested an increased reliance on private companies in conducting the military operation in Afghanistan (Townsend, 2011). PMCs represented 'a very complicated area: they had more money than NGOs, their work [was] uncontrolled in many ways, [which was] quite challenging, ... as they engage[d] in very similar activities [to those of NGOs], while their accountability [was] next to none' (interview, 14 March 2010).

Understandably, 'the nature of a private contractor [was] that [it was a] for-profit company', and, for private contractors, 'humanitarian principles [were] not part of the equation' (interview, 6 June 2010). But more importantly, the use of PMCs was believed to increase insecurity both for NGOs and the communities they serve, as '[t]hey pay[ed] for access ... they [bought] their way; ... the more private contractors you use, the more you fuel the conflict economy' (interview, 21 March 2010). Barakat, Deely and Zyck (2010: 313) argue that private companies involved in stabilisation activities were set to benefit from the continuation of violence. For Slim (2004: 10), 'the massive presence of commercial corporations and private military companies' was something that, along with the scale of military involvement and funds available, distinguished the COIN campaigns in Iraq and Afghanistan from previous ones. Privatisation and commercialisation had important implications for the assistance effort, both in terms of availability of the resources due to the increased competition and high transaction costs of assistance, and in terms of its quality. Thus, the resources were often being given to contractors who spent a substantial proportion of them on establishing their presence in Afghanistan, while their services were often of poor quality (Rubin and Hamidzada, 2007). As Tondini (2010: 88) argued, 'the transaction costs of international assistance' in Afghanistan were very high, compared to other countries, and '[t]he cost of mentors, advisors, consultants and trainers ... absorb[ed] about 25 per cent of all aid'.

Overall, policies and practices of securitisation and militarisation of the assistance effort in Afghanistan were diverse and widespread, and they had a transformative impact on the assistance effort. They also constructed the people to be 'assisted' in a number of ways, which, in turn, informed the assistance they received.

Population as a battleground: biopolitical triage and its implications

COIN and the population as information

The population-centric nature of COIN was reflected in the *ISAF Commander's Counterinsurgency Guidance*, which stated that '[t]he will of the people is the Objective. An effective "offensive" operation in counter-insurgency, therefore, is one that takes from the insurgent what he cannot afford to lose – control of the population' (ISAF, 2009: 3). Similarly, UK MOD *Joint Doctrine Publication (JDP) 3–40 Security and Stabilisation: the Military Contribution* considered the population as 'the focus' (para. 249: 2–24). It all suggests that COIN signals a restrategising of power to the level of society (Bell, 2009). For Anderson (2011), COIN doctrine sees the population as a source of insurgency in two ways: first, as a collective of potential enemies or potential friends; and, second, as a resource provider. This understanding of the population has important implications, as, given that everybody has a potential to become an enemy or a friend, intervention needs to become anticipatory – it needs to address not just the existing insurgency, but also the conditions of insurgency formation (Anderson, 2011). Doing so involves securing popular support for COIN, which, in turn, is reliant on knowing the population. With COIN, the population is perceived as a complex set of factors, including basic needs, essential services and the way of life, and, by acting upon them, popular support can be achieved (Anderson, 2011). This also implies that, in addition to, and in the process of implementing the global biopolitical triage, COIN needs to constantly triage the targeted population (Kienscherf, 2011) with a view to pre-empting, identifying, transforming or eliminating threats.

The need to gain information about the population encourages approaches like Human Terrain Mapping[16] (Bell, 2009; Anderson, 2011; Kienscherf, 2011; Zehfuss, 2012). Indeed, information gathering about the population became a 'big thing' in Afghanistan, as the military were trying to build a picture of the human terrain (the so-called 'White Cell') by establishing not just what the enemy was doing, but also what the population was doing and why. In the UK, *JDP-3–40* population was considered as 'a rich source of intelligence'. In Afghanistan, all international military forces (both the OEF and ISAF through PRTs) were actively seeking intelligence in return for assistance provision. Indeed, assistance provision was regarded as an important way of securing information essential for achieving COIN objectives. As it was explained with respect to rubble-clearing projects run by PRTs:

we [were] not too fussed about clearing that rubble; but, by clearing the rubble, the people [were not] fighting, or they [were] sharing some information about an area, or telling us where this IED [improvised explosive device] ha[d] been filled, ... kind of intelligence, ... and we buil[t] trust and relationships, and [it was] more about that than clearing the rubble.

(interview, 17 May 2010)

Such actions amounted to a rather specific biopolitical triage, different to that based on the humanitarian imperative; a triage that divided the population into deserving and undeserving victims depending on their cooperation, and prioritised certain types of knowledge production over others (that required for COIN, as opposed to humanitarian needs assessments), thereby contributing to the invisibility of suffering that remained unaddressed. As a high-level UN official emphasised, '[t]he nature of the information we need[ed] [was] different' (interview, 21 March 2010). In addition to people's needs being abused to gain intelligence, using them in such a way also put them and assistance providers at risk, given that armed opposition groups punished those they suspected of supplying intelligence (Azarbaijani-Moghaddam *et al.*, 2008).

A further development in this area was based on the idea that although it was local men who were ordinarily used for intelligence purposes, women could also be a rich source of intelligence; furthermore, given their unique role in raising children, they could be worked with so that they would influence their children's decisions in not joining the fighting. Such initiatives can be seen as an example of securitised biopolitical governing aimed at transforming the society from within by colonising and instrumentalising some of the most intimate relationships. The importance of instrumentalising relations also informed *JDP-3–40* emphasis on establishing intelligence networks, which suggested using NGOs for that purpose in addition to the population by persuading them to engage for their own protection. This risked using humanitarian information as intelligence for reasons different to those of alleviating suffering based on the humanitarian imperative. Furthermore, this complicated the information gathering activities of humanitarian NGOs (Azarbaijani-Moghaddam *et al.*, 2008).

As one of the interviewees admitted, in Afghanistan NGOs were supposed to report to donors, but they had no control over how that information was used (which, arguably, was more of a problem where donor countries were also belligerents). While some military forces exerted pressure on NGOs to share information, a high-level UN official insisted:

we [would] not share information with the military that [would] lead to a political or military advantage, and we [would] not share the information with the opposition groups [for the same reasons]. We [would] not share the information with the donors, if that information [was] going to find its way to the military, because we want[ed] to save communities' lives ... we want[ed] to safeguard communities at risk.

(interview, 21 March 2010)

Biopolitical triage in action: necessary killing, violent transformation and inevitable abandonment

Although the description of COIN in the *US Army Field Manual 3–24* suggests a therapeutic nature and reliance on an emergency triage not unlike the one performed by humanitarian actors (Gregory, 2008), this biopolitical triage is not informed by the humanitarian imperative and involves necessary killing. While the killing is mostly reserved for threatening elements incapable of being transformed, its effects cannot be contained. Thus, commenting on the killing of 12 Afghan civilians by NATO rockets in February 2010, the then Air Chief-Marshal Sir Jock Stirrup was reported as saying that 'the incident had damaged efforts to win the support of local communities', but 'that accidents were inevitable during conflict' (in Meikle *et al.*, 2010). The reason that the incident was considered a setback in the war effort was because, in Chief-Marshal's words, they were 'there to provide security for the population'. The Operation, he told the *BBC Today*, was 'not about battling the Taliban, it [was] about protecting the local population, and you don't protect them when you kill them' (in Meikle *et al.*, 2010). I suggest that, in light of the biopolitical nature of COIN, the statement 'you don't protect them when you kill them' can be reversed to read 'to protect them you have to kill some of them', which, by now, should not appear paradoxical. Although that particular loss of life could have well been accidental, written off as collateral damage, it can be suggested that, in a bigger scheme of things, the killing that was taking place in Afghanistan was not accidental – it was a calculated necessity. While some see the assassination ('kill or capture') of insurgents as a sign of COIN disintegration, a move away from protecting the population (Wimpelmann, 2013), such practices form an integral part of COIN.

However, given the positive biopolitical justifications of care and protection, killing, and the use of violence in general, need to be carefully calculated in COIN interventions, to avoid exposing the tension inherent in the sovereignty/biopolitics nexus to both the Western and local audiences. The risk of adverse consequences of the use of violence in terms of contributing to insurgency formation can be reduced should killing remain invisible. This can be achieved in a variety of ways, one of which is preventing its possible targets from being visible. Thus, Afghanistan was turned into a 'de-corporealised space', where people were made invisible, with the invisibility of casualties achieved through aerial strikes and suppression and control of images (Gregory, 2004).

In addition, further blurring of the lines between civilians and legitimate targets (and not just due to the nature of insurgency warfare) contributes to creating the conditions under which civilian casualties can be justified and accepted. According to Mansour (2009), new security discourses compromised the protection civilians previously enjoyed by either considering them as collateral damage or even human shields, or by taking the 'total enemy' view, which turns them into legitimate targets. Normalisation of civilian deaths as collateral damage or accidents also plays an important role in removing responsibility for deaths, as, should a civilian death occur, it will result just in a monetary compensation

(Owens, 2003). This was something that prompted the following comment: '[y]ou can't get past an air strike with a hundred civilian casualties and make a statement ... "we are sorry," ... but we still think it was proportionate according to IHL' (interview, 10 August 2010).

The view that civilians can be legitimate targets comes centre-stage with COIN, which potentially makes the whole population a target and fuels insurgency. As one interviewee put it with respect to the situation in Afghanistan, '[b]y making the shift [from the counter-terrorism to the COIN] ... whole areas [were made into] targets' (interview, 14 June 2010). Furthermore, as already discussed, essential facilities also became part of the battlefield: '[b]uilding schools in highly insecure areas often turn[ed] them into targets for the insurgency; healthcare clinics [were] bombed, mined and occupied by all sides' (Jackson, 2010: 6).

In 2009–2010, the number of civilian deaths in Afghanistan was rising. In 2009, UNAMA recorded 2,412 civilian deaths, an increase of 14 per cent on the previous year (UNAMA, 2010). In 2010, 2,777 civilian deaths were recorded, a 15 per cent increase on 2009 (UNAMA, 2011). Although the number of deaths attributed to pro-government forces was declining (by 26 per cent in 2010 compared to 2009), it remained significant, with the largest percent of deaths caused by aerial attacks (UNAMA, 2011). A 2009 tactical directive restricting the use of airstrikes was the main measure undertaken by the international militaries to reduce civilian casualties (Jackson, 2010). However, the motivations behind the decision to reduce civilian casualties were believed to be more pragmatic than humanitarian, and more to do with force protection (Dilanian, 2010). Interestingly, insurgents mirrored these policies, as 'an updated Taliban code of conduct[17] urge[d] fighters to avoid killing civilians, ... a directive aimed at winning hearts and minds of Afghans' (Achakzail, 3 August 2010). As an NGO representative remarked in this respect: 'it [was] uncanny how they [directives regarding civilian casualties] resemble[d] each other' (interview, 10 August 2010).

Apart from airstrikes, clearance operations were also responsible for the overall increase in civilian casualties in the provinces where they were conducted (e.g. Marja and Nad Ali in Helmand in 2010) (UNAMA, 2011). Clearance operations are one of the starkest manifestations of the COIN logic as biopolitical, with the whole population as a target, in need of protection from itself, which requires a constant process of dividing into groups, and the necessary killing of threatening elements, along with inevitable civilian casualties. In Afghanistan, in addition to casualties such operations resulted in wide-spread damage, such as 'large scale destruction of homes, crops, and irrigation systems', along with displacement (UNAMA, 2011: vi). The aftermath of such operations was a clear case of biopolitical abandonment ('letting die'), where the population was left in a precarious situation with humanitarian access difficult or impossible due to insecurity.

While COIN and stabilisation were based on the assumption that assistance was capable of securing the population's support both towards the external involvement and their own authorities (Barakat *et al.*, 2010), what was often being ignored was that '[a]id ... tends to be unacceptable when it is accompanied by force, brutality or by behaviour which is disrespectful' (Marsden, 2009: 131). With COIN and stabilisation, certain assumptions were made not just about the role that the assistance could play, but also about its recipients. Thus, according to Marsden (2009: 131), '[t]he assumption ... that the desire for material benefit [would] prevail over all other considerations, [was] ... deeply flawed'. The reliance on assistance in COIN meant that it was used as a negative biopolitical tool, involved in a different kind of triage of who lived and who was left to die. As has been demonstrated, in that triage the decisions about what and where got funded and who got assistance and who did not were not dictated by positive biopolitical criteria (the humanitarian imperative). For instance, in Afghanistan food did get funded, because, as one of the donors put it crudely to one of my interviewees, 'people who [were] not hungry [were] less likely to go over to the other side' (interview, 28 February 2010). Furthermore, with the geographical targeting of aid, considered in the previous section, communities in need were subject to biopolitical abandonment. This complicated the dilemmas humanitarian agencies faced on a daily basis, as reflected in the rhetorical question posed by one interviewee: 'what about the most vulnerable places, or the most [remote] tribes, or the people who'd never been a part of the insurgency in their life, but ... had the worst mortality figures in the region?' (interview, 7 June 2010). In fact, in the post-2001 Afghanistan one did not have to venture far to find examples of biopolitical abandonment, as the implications of COIN and stabilisation-driven assistance gravitating towards the areas where the conflict was at its height was evident in Kabul. Thus, according to another interviewee, Kabul had

> been seriously underfunded, despite the fact that ... the international community [was] resident in Kabul and [would] barely leave the place. The needs of [some] hidden part of the Kabul population [returnees and IDPs] ha[d] not been addressed at all.
>
> (interview, 21 June 2010)

In Afghanistan, as in other similar contexts, neoliberal governmentality also laid the foundations for future biopolitical abandonment on a larger scale by creating conditions for the centrality of the market in the absence of a viable state. Johnson and Leslie (2004) drew attention to the evidence of how privatisation of essential services was occurring without much debate and opportunity for Afghans to have their say regarding the future of these services, and of how resources were being absorbed by new layers of management and international consultants, which provided an indication of the type of state being created in Afghanistan. According to Howell and Lind (2009), a close examination of documents such as the *National Development Framework* of 2002, *Securing Afghanistan Future* of 2004 or the *Afghanistan National Development Strategy* of 2008, revealed a profoundly neoliberal vision. With a limited role in delivering social welfare, the state was 'to manage at arm's length an array of sub-contracted private and non-profit agencies' (Howell and Lind, 2009: 109). Privatisation and commercialisation of the assistance effort, demonstrated by NGO proliferation and use of private contractors, was also evident in Afghanistan and was a clear reflection of the effects of neoliberal governing, taking place through an assemblage of a variety of actors. According to Johnson and Leslie (2004: 101), '[w]hat [was] notable in Afghanistan [was] how far both the multilateral agencies, and even many of the supposedly independent NGOs, ha[d] been pulled into the free market project'.

Neoliberal governing as biopolitical abandonment was also evident in the promotion of community defence initiatives, which were supposed to replace the need for external security provision with increased resilience, but, in practice, represented an instance of neoliberal responsibilisation (i.e. transfer of responsibility without creating necessary conditions for fulfilling this responsibility). Such initiatives proved to be at best ineffective, and at worst endangering the communities. Thus, according to Jackson (2010: 14, 15), community defence initiatives in Afghanistan 'ha[d] all too often failed to improve security', and 'often result[ed] in abuses against civilians'. Often such initiatives were scaled up without trial and lacked accountability mechanisms (Jackson, 2010; also Waldman, 2009). Other concerns included lack of training of such forces, risk of infiltration[18] and reversing gains produced by the disarmament and demobilisation, along with damaging efforts to establish adequate state security forces (Waldman, 2009). The attempts to foster self-protection culminated with the Afghan Local Police Programme (ALP), which, according to Hakimi (2013: 389), was a case of what Duffield (2005) termed 'getting savages to fight barbarians', i.e. a mobilisation of local 'savages' (Afghan villagers) to protect not just themselves, but the civilised world as a whole, against 'barbarians' (insurgents). In practice, this meant that 'Afghan villagers were used as cheap and dispensable auxiliaries to fight America's war' (Hakimi, 2013: 392). Like its predecessors, not only did the ALP programme, which lasted until 2012–2013, fail to improve security, but it lso contributed to the increased insecurity and endangerment that characterise the 'violently transformed landscape peppered with local militias' which the US forces are leaving behind (Hakimi, 2013: 400).

Conclusion

This chapter has analysed the post-2001 assistance effort in Afghanistan, with a specific focus on the policies and practices of securitisation and militarisation of assistance. It has shown that the way in which the post-2001 situation in Afghanistan was problematised, first as terrorism, requiring a counter-terrorist operation in a post-conflict context, then as an insurgency, requiring COIN and stabilisation, had a significant impact on the assistance effort in creating conditions for its securitisation and militarisation. While many policies and practices of securitisation and militarisation were not new, their diversity and the range of actors involved suggested an unprecedented instrumentalisation of aid. I have suggested that the policies and practices of aid securitisation and militarisation in the post-2001 Afghanistan can be seen as an example of biopolitics where assistance provision was not informed by the humanitarian imperative, but by security objectives that prioritised the populations of the intervening countries. While positive biopolitical concerns (to protect and assist Afghans) were invoked, they were used to justify sovereign violence against the population that was accompanied by biopolitical violence (endangerment and abandonment). The pressures for transformation and betterment of the population for its own good pursued the same goal, i.e. for this 'underdeveloped' population ceasing to represent a threat to developed populations of the intervening countries.

In some ways, Afghanistan '[stood] out as a defining moment ... in the evolution of the theory and practice of global ordering' (Donini, Niland and Wermester, 2004: 2). While the COIN model applied in Afghanistan may have been a 'temporary and partial experiment' (Wimpelmann, 2013: 418), its elements were replicated in stabilisation efforts elsewhere, in places like Haiti, the Democratic Republic of Congo, Kenya (Collinson *et al.*, 2010) and Somalia (Menkhaus, 2010), with serious consequences for the humanitarian enterprise. Therefore, Afghanistan was arguably an extreme example of the recent aid instrumentalisation, but it was not the only one. As a former high-level UN official argued,

> Iraq, Sudan, Somalia [indicated] similar trends.... There [was] a bigger trend at work ... that ma[de] it more difficult to uphold humanitarian principles, particularly in crises that ha[d] high visibility or high stakes for the West.
>
> (interview, 18 May 2010)

For him, the reason why what happened in the post-2001 Afghanistan was very important for the future of humanitarian action was that unless something was done urgently to consolidate and protect the independent humanitarian voice, humanitarians would be increasingly seen by the people they were trying to help as useless, and by the military and donors as an obstacle, which could be replaced by a different form of relief, more efficient and easier to control (interview, 18 May 2010).

In addition, it was pointed out that both individual organisations and the humanitarian enterprise overall was and would be judged by their actions in Afghanistan. Thus, according to one interviewee,

> we feel that what we do and say in those contexts particularly feeds in and shapes the global perception of who we are and what we do. The impacts of that instrumentalisation of assistance in Afghanistan [went] way beyond our ability to work in that context.
>
> (interview, 21 June 2010)

Overall, the legacy of the post-2001 international intervention in Afghanistan, like that of its predecessors, will continue to inform the processes of statebuilding in Afghanistan and the region as a whole, along with debates on exogenous statebuilding (Goodhand and Sedra, 2013: 239). As for the future of the assistance effort in Afghanistan, it does not seem likely that it will ever be possible to achieve something that a high-level UN official believed was absolutely essential for the future, namely 'to convince the donor community that the humanitarian situation in Afghanistan requires a more creative, unorthodox approach' (interview, 21 March 2010).

Some humanitarians hoped that when the international military forces were gone, some issues would go away with them (interview, 28 February 2010). However, in 2011 UN OCHA expressed concerns that the withdrawal of the international militaries could both disrupt local economies and have a negative impact on humanitarian and development action (UN OCHA, 2011). As the humanitarian situation continues to worsen (UN OCHA, 2013), the availability of resources to meet the growing humanitarian needs will be absolutely crucial, but whether they will be forthcoming remains to be seen, despite the promises laid down in the 2012 *USA–Afghanistan Strategic Partnership Agreement*. Overall, Afghanistan is much more likely to remain a post-interventionary society in Duffield's terms, where 'pacifying low-intensity insurgency is a long-term policing problem for the international community' (Duffield, 2008: 159). Indeed, if we follow Duffield's thinking closely, then even when the majority of the international militaries are gone,[19] humanitarians will still remain implicated in the processes of pacification and containment, as they will be relied upon to provide 'an international insurance of last resort' and to improve the ability of the underdeveloped life 'to survive *in situ*' (Duffield, 2008: 151, 153). This suggests that the communities in need of assistance are likely to be abandoned to face a deteriorating security situation and unmet needs.

Notes

1 The UNAMA's mandate was extended by a series of subsequent UNSC resolutions, with the latest of 17 March 2014 extending it until 2015 (UNSC, 2014).
2 UNAMA was not, however, the very first attempt at integration in Afghanistan, as the Strategic Framework (SF) for Afghanistan of 1997 was designed to bridge the gap between humanitarian and political responses (Atmar and Goodhand, 2002: 28). It was at the same time an outcome and a reflection of coherence agendas of previous years. For a detailed analysis of the SF see Duffield (2007) and Donini (2003). Importantly, Johnson and Leslie (2004) also argued that, by linking humanitarian and political agendas, in the way that the SF did, the UN created conditions under which the humanitarian community was perceived as being partial even before the start of the Afghanistan campaign.
3 The same fundamental tension characterises military involvement in assistance provision, and is considered in more detail in the next section.
4 In 2009, UN OCHA was reopened in Afghanistan, following the campaign of the humanitarian community. In January 2009, the first CAP since 2002 was issued (Donini, 2009).
5 In 2006, the *U.S. Army and Marine Corps Counterinsurgency Field Manual* (3–24) was published. The UK COIN doctrine was laid out in the UK Joint Doctrine Publication 3–40 *Security and Stabilisation: the Military Contribution* of 2009. The ISAF Commander's COIN Guidance was of the same year.

6 Subsequent UNSC resolutions, such as No. 1776 of 19 September 2007, No. 1806 of 20 March 2008, No. 1833 of 22 September 2008, No. 1868 of 23 March 2009, No. 1890 of 8 October 2009, etc., reiterated these points.

7 In fact, QIPs were introduced in Afghanistan as early on as 2002 (Oliker *et al.*, 2004).

8 Donini's point is that many donors were also involved in the international military effort in Afghanistan (e.g. USA, UK). There were, however, donors that were not part of the military effort, e.g. Russia and India, who contributed around US$10m each in 2009 (Development Initiatives, 2010).

9 For a detailed analysis see Donini (2003).

10 A more pragmatic objection relates to the fact that military health services often have facilities different from those required (Neuhaus, 2008).

11 On such occasions, a hospital in the battlefield presented itself as an intense biopolitical space *par excellence*, where the positive biopolitical criterion (severity and urgency of need) was replaced with a securitised one (security of the populations of intervening states and of the armed forces).

12 The existence of such a link is, however, a matter of some debate, and further research is required to provide more evidence, not so much of its existence, but rather of the relative contribution of aid securitisation, in a variety of forms, to the increased attacks on aid workers in conflict environments.

13 Examples included US Special Forces and some ISAF contingents. It should be noted, however, that not all militaries contingents had the same position or engaged in similar practices. Thus, the UK doctrinal publication *Sharing the Space: a Guide to Constructive Engagement with Non-governmental Organisations and the Aid Community* (UK MOD, 2009b) reflected a considerable progress in recognising the important differences between the military and humanitarian actors.

14 Fortified aid compounds were not limited to Afghanistan, as Duffield's (2010b) research with respect to Sudan has shown.

15 Indeed, important consequences of massive resource flows into the post-2001 Afghanistan in general included creation of the *rentier* state and widespread corruption (e.g. Suhrke, 2013; Maley, 2013; also the 2012 and 2013 Asia Foundation Afghanistan Surveys).

16 The Human Terrain System (HTS) was a programme of the US military that relied on social sciences experts to provide the military with a more nuanced understanding of the local population. The Programme was opposed, in particular, by the *American Anthropological Association* (www.aaanet.org/pdf/EB_Resolution_110807.pdf).

17 The Code of Conduct was *The Islamic Emirate of Afghanistan Rules for Mujahideen*, issued by Mullah Omar to limit 'the use of suicide attacks to important targets' and set 'guidelines for abductions' (UNAMA, 2010:2).

18 Even Afghan security forces turned against NATO troops on a number of occasions (Rodrigues, 2011), one incident taking place in April 2011, when an Afghan pilot shot eight NATO troops and a civilian contractor in Kabul (Boone, 2011).

19 At the end of September 2014, the Bilateral Security Agreement (BSA) between the USA and Afghanistan was signed, securing US and NATO military presence until at least 2024, with the counterterrorism operations set to continue.

References

Achakzail, M. (*Associated Press*). 3 August 2010. *Taliban code of conduct seeks to win hearts, minds* [online]. [Accessed 11 January 2011]. www.newsday.com/news/world/taliban-code-of-conduct-seeks-to-win-hearts-minds-1.2169078.

American Anthropological Association. 2007. *American Anthropological Association's Executive Board Statement on the Human Terrain System Project* [online]. [Accessed 2 June 2014]. www.aaanet.org/pdf/EB_Resolution_110807.pdf.

Anderson, B. 2011. Population and the affective perception: biopolitics and anticipatory action in US counterinsurgency doctrine. *Antipode*, **43**(2): 205–236.
Ankersen, C. 2008. Introduction: interrogating civil-military co-operation. *In*: C. Ankersen (ed.). *Civil-military cooperation in post-conflict operations: emerging theory and practice*. London: Routledge, pp. 1–11.
ANSO (the Afghanistan NGO Safety Office). 2011a. *ANSO quarterly data report. Q4 2010 (1 January–31 December 2010)* [online]. [Accessed 11 May 2011]. www.afgnso.org/2010Q/ANSO%20Quarterly%20Data%20Report%20(Q4%202010).pdf.
ANSO (the Afghanistan NGO Safety Office). 2011b. *ANSO quarterly data report. Q1 2011 (1 January–31 March 2011)* [online]. [Accessed 11 May 2011]. www.afgnso.org/2011/ANSO%20Q1%202011.pdf.
Atmar, H. and J. Goodhand. 2002. *Aid, conflict and peacebuilding in Afghanistan: what lessons can be learned?* London: International Alert.
Ayub, F. and S. Kouvo. 2008. Righting the course? Humanitarian intervention, the war on terror and the future of Afghanistan. *International Affairs*, **84**(4): 641–657.
Azarbaijani-Moghaddam, S. *et al.* (for ENNA and BAAG). 2008. *Afghan hearts, Afghan minds: exploring Afghan perceptions of civil-military relations* [online]. [Accessed 16 March 2011]. www.baag.org.uk/publications/category/reports.
Baitenmann, H. 1990. NGOs and the Afghan war: the politicisation of humanitarian aid. *Third World Quarterly*, **12**(1): 62–85.
Barakat, S. 2008. *Synthesis Report. Understanding Afghanistan: the Consolidated Findings of a Research Project Commissioned by Her Majesty's Government* [online]. [Accessed 21 March 2011]. www.york.ac.uk/politics/centres/prdu/publications/.
Barakat, S. *et al.* 2008. *A Strategic Conflict Assessment of Afghanistan* [Accessed 21 March 2011]. www.york.ac.uk/politics/centres/prdu/publications/.
Barakat, S., S. Deely and S.A. Zyck. 2010. 'A tradition of forgetting: stabilisation and humanitarian action in historical perspective. *Disasters*, **34**(S3): 297–319.
Bell, C. 2009. *War by other means: the problem of the population and the civilianisation of coalition intervention. Working Paper 02–09 Department of Politics University of Bristol* [online]. [Accessed 11 May 2011]. www.bristol.ac.uk/spais/research/working-papers/wpspaisfiles/bell0209.pdf.
Bell, C. 2011. Civilianising warfare: ways of war and peace in modern counterinsurgency. *Journal of International Relations and Development*, **14**: 309–332.
Bell, C. and B. Evans. 2010. Terrorism to insurgency: mapping the post-intervention security terrain. *Journal of Intervention and Statebuilding*, **4**(4): 371–390.
Boone, J. (*Guardian*). 27 April 2011. *Afghan pilot shoots dead eight NATO troops* [online]. [Accessed 11 May 2011]. www.guardian.co.uk/world/2011/apr/27/nato-soldiers-shootout-afghan-officer.
Braem, Y. 2008. Managing territories with rival brothers: the geopolitical stakes of military-humanitarian relations. *In*: C. Ankersen (ed.). *Civil-military cooperation in post-conflict operations: emerging theory and practice*. London: Routledge, pp. 31–51.
Bricknell, M.C.M. 2009. Military medical assistance to civilian health sectors. *In*: A.P.C.C. Hopperus Buma *et al.* (eds). *Conflict and catastrophe medicine: a practical guide*. London: Springer, pp. 49–60.
Collinson, S., S. Elhawary and R. Muggah. 2010. States of fragility: stabilisation and its implications for humanitarian action. *Disasters*, **34**(S3): 275–296.
Cornish, S. 2007. No room for humanitarianism in 3D polices; have forcible humanitarian interventions and integrated approaches lost their way? *Journal of Military and Strategic Studies*, **10**(1): 1–48.

Costy, A. 2004. The dilemma of humanitarianism in the post-Taliban transition. *In*: A. Donini, N. Niland and K. Wermester (eds). *Nation-building unravelled? Aid, peace and justice in Afghanistan*. Bloomfield, CT: Kumarian, pp. 143–165.

Development Initiatives. 2010. *Global Humanitarian Assistance Report 2010* [online]. [Accessed 10 May 2011]. www.globalhumanitarianassistance.org/reports.

Dilanian, K. (*Los Angeles Times*). 2 August 2010. *Study: Military efforts to prevent Afghan civilian casualties help U.S. troops too* [online]. [Accessed 11 January 2011]. http://articles.latimes.com/2010/aug/02/world/la-fg-afghan-civilians-20100803.

Dillon, M. 2008. Security, race and war. *In*: M. Dillon and A.W. Neal (eds). *Foucault on politics, security and war*. Basingstoke: Palgrave Macmillan, pp. 166–196.

Dillon, M. and J. Reid. 2009. *The liberal way of war: killing to make life live*. Abingdon: Routledge.

Donini, A. 2003. *Learning the lessons? A retrospective analysis of humanitarian principles and practice in Afghanistan* [online]. [Accessed 10 April 2011]. www.relief web.int.

Donini, A. 2006. *Humanitarian agenda 2015: Afghanistan country study* [online]. [Accessed 11 March 2011]. https://wikis.uit.tufts.edu/confluence/display/FIC/Human-itarian+Agenda+2015+-+Afghanistan+Country+Study.

Donini, A. 2009. *NGOs and Humanitarian Reform: Mapping Study, Afghanistan Report* [online]. [Accessed 4 April 2011]. www.actionaid.org/docs/mapping%20study.pdf.

Donini, A. 2010. *Afghanistan: Humanitarianism unravelled?* [online]. [Accessed 22 March 2011]. https://wikis.uit.tufts.edu/confluence/pages/viewpage.action?pageId=36675386.

Donini, A., N. Niland and K. Wermester. 2004. Introduction. *In*: A. Donini, N. Niland and K. Wermester (eds). *Nation-building unravelled? Aid, peace and justice in Afghanistan*. Bloomfield, CT: Kumarian, pp. 1–8.

Duffield, M. 2001. *Global governance and the new wars: the merging of development and security*. London: Zed Books.

Duffield, M. 2005. Getting savages to fight barbarians: development, security and the colonial present. *Conflict, Security and Development*, 5(2): 141–160.

Duffield, M. 2007. *Development, security and the unending war: governing the world of peoples*. Cambridge: Polity Press.

Duffield, M. 2008. Global civil war: the non-insured, international containment and post-interventionary society. *Journal of Refugee Studies*, 21(2): 145–165.

Duffield, M. 2010a. The liberal way of development and the development-security impasse: exploring the global life-chance divide. *Security Dialogue*, 41(1): 53–76.

Duffield, M. 2010b. Risk management and the fortified aid compound: everyday life in post-interventionary society. *Journal of Intervention and Statebuilding*, 4(4): 453–474.

Egnell, R. 2010. Winning 'hearts and minds'? A critical analysis of counter-insurgency operations in Afghanistan. *Civil Wars*, 12(3): 282–303.

Goodhand, J. and M. Sedra. 2007. Bribes or bargains? Peace conditionalities and 'post-conflict' reconstruction in Afghanistan. *International Peacekeeping*, 14(1): 41–61.

Goodhand, J. and M. Sedra. 2009. Who owns the peace? Aid, reconstruction, and peace-building in Afghanistan. *Disasters*, 34: 78–102.

Goodhand, J. and M. Sedra. 2013. Rethinking liberal peacebuilding, statebuilding and transition in Afghanistan: an introduction. *Central Asian Survey*, 32(3): 239–254.

Gordon, S. 2009. Civil society, the 'new humanitarianism', and the stabilization debate: judging the impact of the Afghan war. *In*: J. Howell and J. Lind (eds). *Civil society under strain: counter-terrorism policy, civil society and aid post-2001*. Bloomfield, CT: Kumarian, pp. 109–126.

Gordon, S. 2010. The United Kingdom's stabilisation model and Afghanistan: the impact on humanitarian actors. *Disasters*, **34**(S3): 368–387.

Greentree, T.R. 2013. A war examined: Afghanistan. *Parameters*, **43**(3): 87–98.

Gregory, D. 2004. *The colonial present: Afghanistan, Palestine, Iraq*. Oxford: Blackwell.

Gregory, D. 2008. The biopolitics of Baghdad: counterinsurgency and the counter-city [online]. [Accessed 11 May 2011]. http://web.mac.com/derekgregory/iWeb/Site/The%20biopolitics%20of%20Baghdad.html

Hakimi, A.A. 2013. Getting savages to fight barbarians: counterinsurgency and the remaking of Afghanistan. *Central Asian Survey*, **32**(3): 388–405.

Howell, J. and J. Lind. 2009. *Counter-terrorism, aid and civil society*. Basingstoke: Palgrave Macmillan.

ICRC/IPSOS (*International Committee of the Red Cross/IPSOS*). 2009. *Afghanistan: Opinion survey and in-depth research* [online]. [Accessed 15 March 2011]. www.icrc.org/eng/assets/files/other/our-world-views-from-afghanistan-i-icrc.pdf.

Interview with a British military representative, 17 May 2010.

Interview with a British NGO policy officer, 7 June 2010.

Interview with a deputy head of INGO, with extensive experience of direct involvement in the assistance effort in Afghanistan, 14 June 2010.

Interview with a former high-level UN official, with extensive experience of coordinating the assistance effort in Afghanistan, 18 May 2010.

Interview with a former high-level UN official, with extensive experience of working in Afghanistan, 15 May 2010.

Interview with a former UN officer, a head of an NGO, with extensive experience of direct involvement in the assistance effort in Afghanistan, 31 July 2010.

Interview with a high-level UN official, directly involved in the coordination of the assistance effort in Afghanistan (at the time of the interview), 21 March 2010.

Interview with an INGO officer, with an extensive experience of direct involvement in assistance provision in Afghanistan, 14 March 2010.

Interview with an INGO senior policy officer, with extensive knowledge of and involvement in the assistance effort in Afghanistan, 21 June 2010.

Interview with a policy officer, representative of a consortium of INGOs working in Afghanistan, 28 February 2010.

Interview with a representative of a major donor organisation, 6 June 2010.

Interview with a representative of an NGO, with a long history of working in Afghanistan, 10 August 2010.

ISAF (International Security Assistance Force). 2009. *ISAF Commander's counterinsurgency guidance* [online]. [Accessed 10 May 2011]. www.nato.int/isaf/docu/official_texts/counterinsurgency_guidance.pdf.

ISAF. 2011a. *About ISAF: Troops numbers and contributions* [online]. [Accessed 10 May 2011]. www.isaf.nato.int/troop-numbers-and-contributions/index.php.

ISAF. 2011b. *About ISAF: Mission* [online]. [Accessed 10 May 2011]. www.isaf.nato.int/mission.html.

Jackson, A. 2010. *Nowhere to turn: the failure to protect civilians in Afghanistan. A Joint Briefing Paper by 29 aid organizations working in Afghanistan for the NATO Heads of Government Summit, Lisbon, November 19–20, 2010* [online]. [Accessed 11 January 2011]. www.oxfam.org.uk/resources/policy/conflict_disasters/nowhere-to-turn-afghanistan.html.

Johnson C. and J. Leslie. 2004. *Afghanistan: the mirage of peace*. London: Zed Books.

Kelly, M.G.E. 2010. International biopolitics: Foucault, globalisation and imperialism. *Theoria*, **57**(123): 1–26.

Kett, M. and A. van Tulleken, A. 2009. Humanitarian organizations and their coordination in humanitarian assistance. *In*: A.P.C.C. Hopperus Buma *et al.* (eds) *Conflict and Catastrophe Medicine: a Practical Guide*. London: Springer-Verlag, pp. 31–48.

Kienscherf, M. 2011. A programme of global pacification: US counterinsurgency doctrine and the biopolitics of human (in)security. *Security Dialogue*, **42**(6): 517–535.

Krähenbühl, P. 2004. The ICRC's approach to contemporary security challenges: a future for independent and neutral humanitarian action. *International Review of the Red Cross*, **86**(855): 505–514.

Leader, N. and H. Atmar. 2004. Political projects: reform, aid, and the state in Afghanistan. *In*: A. Donini, N. Niland and K. Wermester (eds). *Nation-building unravelled? Aid, peace and justice in Afghanistan*. Bloomfield, CT: Kumarian pp. 166–186.

Maley, W. (2013) Statebuilding in Afghanistan: challenges and pathologies. *Central Asian Survey*, **32**(3): 255–270.

Mansour, N. 2009. Only 'civilians' count: the influence of GWOT discourses on governments' humanitarian responses to 'terror'-related conflicts. *In*: J. Howell and J. Lind (eds). *Civil society under strain: counter-terrorism policy, civil society and aid post-2001*. Bloomfield, CT: Kumarian, pp. 191–207.

Marsden, P. 2009. *Afghanistan; aid, armies and empires*. London: Tauris.

Meikle, J., D. Walsh and S. Bates (*Guardian*). 2010. *Five civilians killed in NATO rocket attack in Afghanistan* [online]. [Accessed 15 February 2010]. www.guardian.co.uk/world/2010/feb/15/afghanistan-civilian-deaths-nato-taliban.

Menkhaus, K. 2010. Stabilisation and humanitarian access in a collapsed state: the Somali case. *Disasters*, **34**(S3): 320–341.

MSF (*Médecins Sans Frontières*). 2010. *Focus on Afghanistan* [online]. [Accessed 10 May 2011]. www.msf.org.uk/afghanistan.focus.

Neuhaus, S.J. 2008. Medical aspects of civil-military operations: the challenges of military health support to civilian populations on operations. *In*: C. Ankersen (ed.). *Civil-military cooperation in post-conflict operations: emerging theory and practice*. London: Routledge, pp. 201–224.

Oliker, O. *et al.* 2004. *Aid during conflict: interaction between military and civilian assistance providers in Afghanistan, September 2001–June 2002*. Santa Monica, CA: Rand.

Paris, R. 2013. Afghanistan: what went wrong? *Perspectives on Politics*, **11**(2): 538–548.

Poole, L. (Development Initiatives). 2011. *Afghanistan: Tracking Major Resource Flows 2002–2010* [online]. [Accessed 18 June 2012]. www.globalhumanitarianassistance.org/wpcontent/uploads/2011/02/gha-Afghanistan-2011-major-resource-flows.pdf.

Rana, R. 2008. At a crossroads or a dead-end? Considering the civil-military relationship in times of armed conflict. *In*: C. Ankersen (ed.). *Civil-military cooperation in post-conflict operations: emerging theory and practice*. London: Routledge, pp. 225–239.

Rietjens, S.J.H. 2008. *In*: C. Ankersen (ed.). *Civil-military cooperation in post-conflict operations: emerging theory and practice*. London: Routledge, pp. 75–99.

Rodrigues, J. (*Guardian*). 27 April 2011. *NATO troops record 20 incidents where Afghan security forces have 'turned'* [online]. [Accessed 11 May 2011]. www.guardian.co.uk/world/2011/apr/27/nato-troops-afghan-forces-incidents.

Rubin, B.R. and H. Hamidzada. 2007. From Bonn to London: governance challenge and the future of statebuilding in Afghanistan. *International Peacekeeping*, **14**(1): 8–25.

Save the Children. 2010. *A child survival emergency – refocusing Britain's objectives in Afghanistan: general election briefing* [online]. [Accessed 22 March 2011]. www.savethechildren.org.uk/en/docs/Afg_election_briefing_FE_edit_GG.pdf.

116   *'Caring' for the population of Afghanistan*

Sedra, M. 2013. The hollowing-out of the liberal peace project in Afghanistan: the case of security sector reform. *Central Asian Survey*, **32**(33): 371–387.

Slim, H. 2004. *With or against? Humanitarian agencies and Coalition counter-insurgency* [online]. Centre for Humanitarian Dialogue. [Accessed 10 January 2011]. www.hdcentre.org.

Suhrke, A. 2013. Statebuilding in Afghanistan: a contradictory engagement. *Central Asian Survey*, **32**(3): 271–286.

The Asia Foundation. 2012. *Afghanistan in 2012: A survey of the Afghan people* [online]. [Accessed 2 June 2014]. http://asiafoundation.org/country/afghanistan/2012-poll.php.

The Asia Foundation. 2013. *Afghanistan in 2013: A survey of the Afghan people* [online]. [Accessed 2 June 2014]. http://asiafoundation.org/country/afghanistan/2013-poll.php.

The Refugees International. 2009. *Afghanistan: open eyes to humanitarian needs* [online]. [Accessed 11 May 2011]. www.refugeesinternational.org/policy/field-report/afghanistan-open-eyes-humanitarian-needs.

Thompson, E. 2010. *Winning 'hearts and minds in Afghanistan: assessing the effectiveness of development aid in COIN operations. Report on Wilton Park Conference 1022, 11–14 March 2010* [online]. [Accessed 15 March 2011]. http://kingsofwar.org.uk/wp-content/uploads/2010/04/WP1022-Final-Report.pdf.

Tondini, M. 2010. *Statebuilding and justice reform: post-conflict reconstruction in Afghanistan*. London: Routledge.

Townsend, M. (Guardian). 2011. *Afghan private security bill soars*. 6 March 2011.

UK MOD (Ministry of Defence). 2009a. *Joint Doctrine Publication 3–40 (JDP 3–40). Security and stabilisation: the military contribution*. Swindon: MOD.

UK MOD. 2009b. *Sharing the space: a guide to constructive engagement with non-governmental organisations and the aid community* [online]. [Accessed 11 May 2011]. www.mod.uk/DefenceInternet/MicroSite/DCDC/OurPublications/Concepts/SharingTheSpaceAGuideToConstructiveEngagementWithNongovernmentalOrganisationsAndTheAidCommunity.htm.

UNAMA (United Nations Assistance Mission in Afghanistan) *et al.* 2008. *Guidelines for the Interaction and Coordination of Humanitarian Actors and Military Actors in Afghanistan* [online]. [Accessed 10 May 2011]. www.afgana.org/showart.php?id=323&rubrica=223.

UNAMA. 2010. *Afghanistan: Annual Report 2009 on Protection of Civilians in Armed Conflict* [online]. [Accessed 10 May 2011]. http://unama.unmissions.org/Portals/UNAMA/human%20rights/Protection%20of%20Civilian%202009%20report%20English.pdf.

UNAMA. 2011. *Afghanistan: Annual Report 2010 on Protection of civilians in armed conflict* [online]. [Accessed 11 May 2011]. http://unama.unmissions.org/Portals/UNAMA/human%20rights/March%20PoC%20Annual%20Report%20Final.pdf.

UNDP (United Nations Development Programme). 2011. *Human Development Report* [online]. [Accessed 11 June 2014]. www.undp.org/content/undp/en/home/librarypage/hdr/human_developmentreport2011.html.

UN OCHA (United Nations Office for the Coordination of Humanitarian Affairs). 2003. *Guidelines on the use of military and civil defence assets to support United Nations humanitarian activities in complex emergencies* [online]. [Accessed 10 May 2011]. www.ochaonline.un.org/OchaLinkClick.aspx?link=ocha&docId=1112407.

UN OCHA. 2011. *Afghanistan Consolidated Appeal* [online]. [Accessed 10 January 2011]. http://ochaonline.un.org/.

UN OCHA. 2013. *Common Humanitarian Action Plan for Afghanistan 2013* [online]. [Accessed 2 June 2014]. www.unocha.org/cap/common-humanitarian-action-plan-afghanistan-2013.

UNSC (United Nations Security Council). 2003. *Resolution of 13 October 2003 No 1510* (S/RES/1510 (2003)) [online]. [Accessed 10 May 2011]. http://unama.unmissions.org/Portals/UNAMA/Security%20Council%20Resolutions/13%20October%202003.pdf.

UNSC. 2001. *Resolution of 20 December 2001 No 1386* (S/RES/1386 (2001)) [online]. [Accessed 10 May 2011]. http://unama.unmissions.org/Portals/UNAMA/Security%20Council%20Resolutions/20%20December%202001.pdf.

UNSC. 2002a. *The situation in Afghanistan and its implications for international peace and security: Report of the Secretary General, 18 March 2002* (A/56/875–S/2002/278) [online]. [Accessed 10 May 2011]. http://unama.unmissions.org/Portals/UNAMA/SG%20Reports/18%20March%202002.pdf.

UNSC. 2002b. *Resolution of 28 March 2002 No 1401* (S/RES/1401 (2002)) [online]. [Accessed 10 May 2011]. http://unama.unmissions.org/Portals/UNAMA/Security%20Council%20Resolutions/SC1401.pdf.

UNSC. 2007a. *Resolution No 1746 of 23 March 2007* (S/RES/1746 (2007)) [online]. [Accessed 10 May 2011]. http://unama.unmissions.org/Portals/UNAMA/Security%20Council%20Resolutions/sc1746.pdf.

UNSC. 2007b. *Resolution No 1776 of 19 September 2007* (S/RES/1776 (2007)) [online]. [Accessed 10 May 2011]. http://unama.unmissions.org/Portals/UNAMA/Security%20Council%20Resolutions/07sep19-1776.pdf.

UNSC. 2008a. *Resolution No 1806 of 20 March 2008* (S/RES/1806 (2008)) [online]. [Accessed 10 May 2011]. http://unama.unmissions.org/Portals/UNAMA/Security%20Council%20Resolutions/sc-1806-20-march-english.pdf.

UNSC. 2008b. *Resolution No 1833 of 22 September 2008* (S/RES/1833 (2008)) [online]. [Accessed 10 May 2011]. http://unama.unmissions.org/Portals/UNAMA/08sep22-no-1833.pdf.

UNSC. 2009a. *Resolution No 1868 of 23 March 2009* (S/RES/1868 (2009)) [online]. [Accessed 10 May 2011]. http://unama.unmissions.org/Portals/UNAMA/Security%20Council%20Resolutions/sc-1868-23march-2009.pdf.

UNSC. 2009b. *Resolution No 1890 of 8 October 2009* (S/RES/1890 (2009)) [online]. [Accessed 10 May 2011]. http://unama.unmissions.org/Portals/UNAMA/Security%20Council%20Resolutions/oct2009_UNSC_ISAF_RES1890.pdf.

UNSC. 2011a. *The situation in Afghanistan and its implications for international peace and security: Report of the Secretary General, 9 March 2011* (S/2011/120) [online]. [Accessed 10 May 2011]. http://unama.unmissions.org/Portals/UNAMA/SG%20Reports/SG_Report_to_Security_Council_March_2011.pdf.

UNSC. 2014. *Resolution No 2145 of 17 March 2014* (S/RES/2145 (2014)) [online]. [Accessed 2 June 2014]. www.un.org/en/ga/search/view_doc.asp?symbol=S/RES/2145(2014).

Waldman, M. 2009. *Caught in the conflict: civilians and the international security strategy in Afghanistan. A briefing paper by ten NGOs operating in Afghanistan for the NATO Heads of States and Government Summit, 3–4 April 2009* [online]. [Accessed 20 May 2014]. www.rescue.org/sites/default/files/migrated/resources/2009/caught-in-the-conflict-afghanistan-report-april-2009-pdf.pdf.

Wilder, A. 2009. Money can't buy America love. *Foreign Policy* [online]. [Accessed 10 January 2011]. www.foreignpolicy.com/articles/2009/12/01/money_cant_buy_america_love.

Wimpelmann, T. 2013. Nexuses of knowledge and power in Afghanistan: the rise and fall of the informal justice assemblage. *Central Asian Survey*, **32**(3): 406–422.

Zehfuss, M. 2012. Culturally sensitive war? The Human Terrain System and the seduction of ethics. *Security Dialogue*, **43**(2): 175–190.

4 'Caring' for the population of Belarus

Problematisations that matter and Chernobyl's 'ghosts'

> the experts found that fear of radiation, rather than radiation itself, continues to poison the lives of many Chernobyl survivors.
>
> (UNDP, 2009)

> Potential health effects resulting from exposure(s) to low doses of ionizing radiation have been, and continue to be the focus of scientific research, intense debate and significant controversy.
>
> (Morgan and Blair, 2013: 502)

Introduction

On 26 April 1986, during a test of the cooling system, one of the reactors at the Chernobyl Nuclear Power Plant (NPP) in Ukraine became out of control, which led to an explosion and fire that destroyed the reactor building and released large amounts of radioactive material into the atmosphere. The Chernobyl accident is still regarded as the worst nuclear power plant disaster in history. The explosion and subsequent fire released 400 times more radioactive material than in Hiroshima (IAEA, 1997: 8); the material included more than forty different radionuclides, with iodine-131 (I-131), caesium-137 (Cs-137) and strontium-90 (Sr-90) among the most serious in terms of the radiation exposure of the population (IAEA, 1997; UNSCEAR, 2000). Given its geographical proximity to the Chernobyl NPP and the prevailing winds, Belarus was severely affected, with 70 per cent of the total radioactive fallout that left 23 per cent of its territory contaminated (IAEA, 1997; UN OCHA, 2000). I-131 affected the whole territory of Belarus and, although short-lived (its half-life is just eight days), it was responsible for the sharp rise in thyroid cancer (e.g. IAEA, 1997).

Following the accident, around 25,000 people from over 100 villages in Belarus were evacuated from what became the exclusion zone, where 70 villages were buried, and a further 110,000 people were resettled, making the total displaced around 135,000 (Belarus Chernobyl Committee, 2001). Approximately 1.3 million, including 500,000 children, still live in areas affected by the accident (Belarus MFA, 2009). These are large numbers, especially given that the population of Belarus is just over nine million people. In addition, some 110,000 people from Belarus took part in mitigating the consequences of the accident as emergency clean-up workers, or, as they are more commonly known, 'liquidators' (Belarus Chernobyl Committee, 2006).

In 2000, the UN repeated its call for the accident not to be forgotten. However, since then, a number of high-level international reports have suggested that the consequences of the accident were not as serious as had been previously feared (e.g. UNSCEAR, 2000; the Chernobyl Forum 2003–2005), and, in 2007, the UN declared that 'a return to normal life is a realistic prospect for most people living in Chernobyl-affected regions' (UN, 2007: 8, 16).

With a view to revealing the conditions of possibility for the 'forgetting' of the Chernobyl accident, this chapter critically analyses the dominant, post-2000, problematisations of the accident and its health consequences and their implications for the affected people and for the international assistance effort during the 2000–2011 decade. In so doing, it deploys the tools of the analytics of government to examine: conflicting ways in which the Chernobyl accident and its consequences were problematised and systems of knowledge underpinning such problematisations (e.g. statistics, radiation protection, epidemiology); the strategies and technologies of governing used during assistance interventions (e.g. neoliberal responsibilisation, psychologisation and mentality change, etc.) and the role of the actors carrying out these interventions; and, finally, the ways in which people in need of assistance were constructed (dependent, passive and irresponsible victims, as opposed to self-reliant, active and entrepreneurial individuals and resilient self-sufficient communities).

The central argument advanced here is that the dominant problematisations of the accident and its consequences, sustained, in particular, by such influential UN-family organisations as the International Atomic Energy Agency (IAEA), the United Nations Scientific Committee on the Effects of Atomic Radiation (UNSCEAR) and the United Nations Development Programme (UNDP), were crucial for making the accident and its victims 'disappear' from the radar of the international assistance community, and that the related assistance effort was profoundly informed by a biopolitics of invisibility and abandonment.

In the spirit of a Foucauldian critique, I do not aim to substitute one 'truth' about Chernobyl with another (or, indeed, reveal the ultimate 'truth' or to prescribe the ways in which affected individuals or communities should be helped); rather, I seek to demonstrate that the ways in which the accident and its consequences were problematised did matter. Not only do the dominant problematisations inform the assistance offered or withdrawn, but also the disruption of prevalent problematisations makes other possibilities visible and opens up a space for alternative problematisations and, consequently, alternative actions.

The Chernobyl accident and health consequences in Belarus: dominant problematisations

As has been previously discussed, Foucault's concept of problematisation both establishes and activates a power/knowledge nexus, where the two 'directly imply one another' (Foucault, 1977: 27), and identifying dominant problematisations represents an important step for any analytics of government (Foucault, 1987: 223–224; Dean, 1999; Miller and Rose, 2008). This section offers a critical account of the ways in which the accident and its health consequences in Belarus were problematised in the international expert discourse. This account is organised chronologically, to enable us to identify some important shifts and conflicts in the dominant discourse, but it is by no means exhaustive, as it covers on the most significant reports produced by the UN-family organisations, with a special focus on the 2000–2011 decade.

In 2000, the UNSCEAR issued its major report on the Chernobyl accident, *Exposures and Effects of the Chernobyl Accident*, which was its first evaluation of its consequences since 1988. The importance of the 2000 UNSCEAR findings should not be underestimated, as they served to shape the dominant problematisations of the accident and its consequences for years to come. While recognising that the overall impact of the accident as 'both serious and enormous' (453), in terms of the health consequences due to the radiation exposures the Report only confirmed the link between radiation and thyroid cancer. The Report's message was an optimistic one. While referring to the limited nature of the existing knowledge of the late effects of protracted exposures to ionising radiation, it nevertheless stated that 'the vast majority of the population need not live in fear of serious health consequences from the Chernobyl accident', and, although '[l]ives have been disrupted by the Chernobyl accident, ... from the radiological point of view ... generally positive prospects for the future health of most individuals should prevail' (UNSCEAR, 2000: 517).

The 2000 UNSCEAR Report was not well-received in the affected countries, as local scientists disagreed with the UN-affiliated scientists about the consequences of Chernobyl (for more details see Petryna, 2002). Thus, one of the official Belarusian responses to the Report expressed in the 2001 *National Report 15 Years after [the] Chernobyl Catastrophe: Consequences in the Republic of Belarus and Their Overcoming* stated that the 2000 UNSCEAR Report was '[a] vivid example of a prejudiced attitude to the consequences of the Chernobyl catastrophe', as '[b]ased on arbitrary selection of data, on individual publications, which included practically no works [*sic*] of Belarusian scientists, [it] treats incompletely and pretentiously the post-Chernobyl situation in the three affected countries' (Belarus Chernobyl Committee, 2001: 107).

The year 2000 also saw the publication of the UN Office for Coordination of Humanitarian Affairs (UN OCHA) Report *Chernobyl: a Continuing Catastrophe,* which had the aim of drawing the attention of the international community to the on-going plight of the people of the three most affected countries: Belarus, Ukraine and Russia. The Report argued that while, in terms of the health effects, the worst was still to come, the Chernobyl accident had been forgotten, and only a fraction of the required external resources had been mobilised (1). Importantly, it emphasised uncertainties surrounding the long-term effects of radiation (6) and the need for continuing medical research (8). However, while calling for a wider appreciation of the scale and complexities of the accident's consequences, the Report still presented them rather narrowly and unproblematically, without recognising that many numbers were contingent on the prevailing interpretations of the consequences.

The 2002 Report *The Human Consequences of the Chernobyl Nuclear Accident: a Strategy for Recovery* was jointly prepared by the UNDP, United Nations Children's Fund (UNICEF), UN OCHA and World Health Organisation (WHO). Its findings with respect to the health effects differ significantly from many subsequent reports. For instance, the Report warned that the doses received by some high risk groups of people, as well as their numbers, could actually be increasing, despite the decrease in radioactive contamination, as poverty was forcing people to switch to locally-grown produce, to abandon remediation measures and to rely more on forest products (41). This observation is in stark contrast with the subsequent 2003–2005 Chernobyl Forum Report that claimed that the majority of the doses had already been received and further exposure was negligible (13). The Report was also one of a few to recognise that thyroid cancer, although normally not fatal, still posed a problem in terms of resources (49). However, it failed to consider the complex effects that having thyroid cancer and/or one's thyroid removed partially or completely had on its sufferer.

Importantly, the Report argued that the absence of statistical evidence with respect to the increase in specific health effects should not be 'a reason to dismiss such claims' (49), thereby leaving the door open to future findings to the contrary. It also acknowledged the differences between the effects of high and low doses of radiation, with the latter being less well known, as well as the lack of consensus on the health effects of the accident, some of which might only become apparent in the future (52). Addressing the psychological effects of the accident (59–60), the Report did not claim that such effects resulted from unjustified fears, as subsequent reports would, but, instead, provided an analysis of the distress experienced by resettlers.

In contrast, the central message of the 2003–2005 Chernobyl Forum Report *Chernobyl's Legacy* was that for the majority of the affected populations the radiation dose was low (it did not consider that many remained exposed). While health effects were interpreted carefully overall, 'there is no *clearly* demonstrated increase in the incidence of solid cancers or leukaemia due to radiation on the *most* affected populations' (7; emphasis added), the main argument remained that there was no evidence of serious effects. While the Report did not deny the possibility of some people developing solid cancers or leukaemia, it also indicated that such effects were unlikely ever to be rendered visible and recognised as caused by radiation. The likelihood of such recognition with respect to the health effects of an individual was lower still, as their visibility and recognition reside at the level of the population.

The Report largely supported the previous findings of the UNSCEAR, and was criticised by some national scientists, independent experts, environmental and relief organisations, who claimed that it had disregarded data that opposed its overall position and had downplayed the consequences of the accident (e.g. Fairlie and Sumner, 2006). Some also pointed out that the Report was produced under IAEA coordination and reflected its interests. Thus a senior INGO official with a long history of involvement in the assistance effort said:

> the UN ... too quickly made statements that underplayed the negative effects of Chernobyl. In my opinion, the UN assessment and report lacked sensitivity, to say the least. The fact remains that thyroid cancers were on the increase, ... and yet, the big report ... seemed to have been done mainly for the benefit of [the] IAEA. That is certainly my perception.
>
> (interview, 27 April 2010)

Alternative interpretations were offered in response to the Report, but they never had the same amount of exposure as the Report, produced by the most authoritative international expert bodies. In this way, the Report can be seen as 'the reassertion of scientific control over an apparent chaos of reported health and environmental consequences of the Chernobyl accident' (Stephens, 2002: 108). The Q&A section of the UNDP webpage on Chernobyl[1] demonstrates this, especially by dismissing other interpretations as unscientific. It begins by stressing that the Chernobyl Forum was 'to conduct a rigorous review of all available scientific evidence to arrive at 'authoritative consensual statements' on the impact of the accident'. It then points out that '[t]he scientific effort that has gone into Chernobyl Forum is unrivalled in both its breadth and depth, and in the renown of the experts involved', while alternative claims 'are not supported by reputable scientific evidence'. These discursive framings are responsible for marginalising and excluding other types of knowledges, produced by national and international scientists and scholars, local medical doctors, government officials and humanitarian agencies, knowledges that challenged the dominant problematisations and the 'speaking with one voice' stance of the Chernobyl Forum. In Foucault's terms, such knowledges can be seen as subjugated. Foucault (1980) distinguished between two types of subjugated knowledges: those that have fallen victim to various processes of systematisation; and those that have been deemed insufficiently scientific. These, therefore, are subjugated knowledges of the first category.

While stressing the lack of information regarding the doses received by liquidators and the general public, the Chernobyl Forum Report nevertheless concluded that they 'received relatively low whole-body radiation doses, comparable to background radiation levels accumulated ... since the accident' (11). In addressing the health effects, the Report argued that the evidence presented in studies suggesting a radiation-induced increase in general population mortality and in emergency and recovery workers, was not 'clear and convincing' or was in need of future confirmation from 'better designed studies' (16). Such an interpretation contrasted with the way in which the numbers of the acute radiation syndrome (ARS) deaths were presented, numbers that migrated, unchallenged, from initial Soviet reports. At the same time, the Report showed some appreciation of the fact that all the health effects might not yet be known, and that an absence of solid evidence did not mean that there was no increase in some conditions, such as cancer.

Given that certain health effects in the affected populations were not recognised as caused by radiation, the Report interpreted them as psychological, arguing that 'the mental health impact of Chernobyl is the largest public health problem unleashed by the accident to date' (36). This argument was in line with the 2000 UNSCEAR findings,[2] and was replicated and reinforced in the UNDP official discourse. Thus, the previously mentioned Q&A section of the UNDP webpage informs the reader that the Chernobyl Forum found 'an alarming increase in mental health problems in the affected communities .... including symptoms of stress, depression, anxiety, and psychosomatic disorders [that are] are typical among populations that have fallen victims to disasters';[3] therefore, not only did these problems have nothing to do with radiation, but neither were they *sui generis*.

As Kuchinskaya (2007: 88) argued in this respect, statements by international experts 'suggest[ed] that estimating 'psychological pressure' requires no proof ... the authority of nuclear experts is presumed sufficient for diagnosing populations with anxiety and radiophobia'. This also points to depoliticising effects of expertise, making the power/knowledge nexus especially visible, with laypeople's ideas and perceptions deligitimised and marginalised. Kuchinskaya (2007: 89) further argued that:

> The references locating the problem 'in the head' are never adequately substantiated ... the causes of poor health no longer have to be or can be investigated in the world external to the affected populations and are now fully contained within the individuals themselves.

The Report was also instrumental in shifting the blame onto the residents, which can be seen as an instance of neoliberal responsibilisation, i.e. transfer of responsibility without creating opportunities for its meaningful fulfilment. In particular, the residents were accused of 'neglect[ing] the role of personal behaviour in maintaining health', which was evident in continued foraging and 'misuse of alcohol and tobacco' (37). The Report demonstrated a significant lack of understanding of the local context, when it suggested that the main reason people continue foraging was because they were fatalistic (41) (i.e. not because they had been doing so for generations or because if they did not, they would find it impossible to provide for their families).

Another important message of the Chernobyl Forum Report was that of normalisation: 'the majority of the "contaminated" territories are now safe for resettlement and economic activity' (8; the positioning of the parentheses is significant, as it implicitly challenges the designation of the territories as contaminated). This message had very significant implications, and was reinforced in the UNDP official discourse and in the 2008 *UN Action Plan on Chernobyl to 2016*. The Plan served to express 'the common vision and shared principles' for the UN Chernobyl-related assistance effort (UN, 2008: 1). It was based on the assumption that 'the vast majority of people living in "contaminated" areas are in fact highly unlikely to experience negative health effects from radiation exposure and can safely raise families where they are today' (UN, 2008: 2). At the same time, the Plan stressed that these people suffered from the Chernobyl victim's syndrome, which it described as a condition characterised by passivity and helplessness, brought about by the dependency syndrome combined with 'widespread (and often unfounded) fears about the health impact of radiation' (UN, 2008: 2). So, they needed to hear 'the message of reassurance' of the Chernobyl Forum, and the leading UN agencies were tasked with disseminating it (UN, 2008). Overall, the return to normality is expected by 2016.

The implications of strategies of responsibilisation and normalisation for the affected people and the assistance effort are further discussed in the sections that follow. What needs to be emphasised here is the role of these strategies in producing another category of subjugated knowledges, knowledges of 'ordinary' people, who, despite having an understanding of their circumstances and an ability to express themselves, are prohibited from doing so (Smart, 1985: 67). For Foucault (1980: 85), subjugation of such knowledges raises important questions:

> What types of knowledge do you want to disqualify in the very instant of your demand: 'Is it a science?' Which speaking, discoursing subjects – which subjects of experience and knowledge – do you want to 'diminish' when you say: 'I who conduct this discourse am conducting a scientific discourse, and I am a scientist'?

While one of the main examples elaborated in Foucault's work is the disqualified knowledge of psychiatric patients, in this case we have an example of disqualification and marginalisation of perspectives and voices of the people affected by the Chernobyl accident concerning its impact on their health and their lives in general.

In 2006, WHO issued the Report of the Chernobyl Forum Expert Group 'Health', *Health Effects of the Chernobyl Accident and Special Care Programmes*. The Report was important as it updated the 2000 UNSCEAR Report using more recent information (iii), and as the WHO, unlike the IAEA, does not have the promotion of peaceful uses of nuclear energy as one of its objectives. However, the overall message of the Report was not dissimilar to that of the 2000 UNSCEAR and the 2003–2005 Chernobyl Forum reports with respect to the number of deaths attributed to the accident and with respect to its health effects, largely limited to thyroid cancer. The Report did not find any increased risk of leukaemia linked to radiation in either children, clean-up workers or the general population (3).

However, on a number of occasions, the Report took a somewhat different approach to evaluating health risks from that of the main Chernobyl Forum Report. It emphasised that, at the time, absence of evidence did not constitute evidence of absence, and that, for instance, 'presently, it is not possible to exclude an excess risk of thyroid cancer in persons exposed to Chernobyl accident as adults' (38). In this respect, the position expressed in the Report has more affinity with the 2002 Report than with either UNSCEAR reports or that of the Chernobyl Forum. In this case, the impossibility of proving the negative, i.e. the absence of any health effects, is compounded by uncertainties about the health risks of low doses of radiation, as well as economic and political implications of carrying out further research, which means that a decision must be made as to when the search for evidence should stop. However, such a decision is both scientific and ethico-political, and has wide-ranging implications; suggesting otherwise, as was the case in the main Chernobyl Forum Report, results in depoliticisation and obscuring of the fact that such a decision is never solely based on assessing the accuracy of, and confidence in, the existing scientific findings. This is an important point, as abandonment of research programmes, in the absence of a commitment to regular re-evaluations of the situation in line with development of scientific knowledge on effects of low doses, forecloses any possibility of fully appreciating the health effects of the accident. Finally, claims about the absence of health effects based on the existing absence of evidence shift the burden of proof to those arguing that such effects are real, while their ability to substantiate their arguments is often already impaired due the marginalisation of their knowledges and ways of their production.

The 2006 WHO Report also drew attention to the inherent unsuitability of some types of studies for detecting small increases in uncommon health conditions, such as childhood leukaemia (58). Addressing solid cancers, it pointed out that although most scientists would agree that there had been an increase in risk for radiosensitive cancers, it 'has not manifested itself in the various epidemiological studies due to their lack of statistical power' (67). Another important conclusion was that, first, given the latency period, solid cancers would only begin to appear around 2006, and, second, there were studies providing evidence of 'a significant increase in the incidence of pre-menopausal breast cancer among women exposed before the age of 45 in the most contaminated districts' (64).

Another conclusion regarding solid cancers, which acknowledged the existing gaps in knowledge, is very important:

> The current knowledge concerning the effects of radiation on such cancers is based largely on acute external exposures to relatively high doses. Such exposures are quite different from those caused by Chernobyl, and consequently the extent to which risk estimates derived from them can be applied to the Chernobyl experience is unknown. This is particularly true for the populations that have lived in contaminated regions, which have accumulated radiation doses from both internal and external exposure at low dose rates over prolonged periods. However it is also true for liquidation workers. Even though many liquidation workers received higher doses than the general populations of contaminated regions, and at higher dose rates, their exposures were generally much less acute and more likely to include internal exposure than those of the Japanese atomic-bomb survivors or medically irradiated cohorts. Moreover, many liquidation workers have also lived in contaminated regions and consequently accumulated additional radiation doses (65).

This position echoed that expressed in the 2002 Report, and was also used by many critics who challenged the appropriateness of applying projections based on exposures of A-bomb survivors to Chernobyl-related exposures, due to important differences between them (65). Furthermore, some scientists challenged the linear, no-threshold, dose-response model currently in use with respect to stochastic radiation health effects,[4] by arguing that protracted exposure to low doses of radiation might be more harmful (e.g. Nussbaum, 1998; Burlakova and Nazarov, 2006). The 2006 WHO Report briefly referred to this as 'a matter of some dispute' (62). For Proctor (1995: 153), however, this is not just a minor technical issue, but the most hard-fought cancer war. He argues that the significance of the issue of thresholds and shapes of the dose-response curve lies in the policy implications, as, for instance, given that in most cases exposures cannot be reduced to zero, the assumption that most cancers are caused by low-level exposures can have very serious implications for public health, environment and economy (Proctor, 1995). Nussbaum further points out that '[e]xpert positions on health effects of ionizing radiation have for a long time been influenced by powerful, mutually conflicting interests', with the interest of protecting the public health on the one hand, and the interest of the industry, regulatory authorities and scientific advisory bodies on the other (Nussbaum, 1998: 291; see also Morgan and Bair, 2013).

The accepted linear, no-threshold model is based on the assumption that even very low doses may produce health effects proportionate to the dose, reflects the current scientific consensus and can be said to embrace the precautionary principle. Indeed, this model is less permissible than the threshold model (low doses are not hazardous) and even less so than the hormesis thesis (low doses may be beneficial), but it is also more restrictive than the supralinear model where low-level doses are believed to be disproportionally damaging. These models inform different ways in which the risk-based biopolitics can be operationalised in this area, showing that a risk-based biopolitics relies on a multiplicity of competing approaches to protecting collective life. Importantly, given that most Chernobyl-related exposures are protracted low-dose ones, the application of different dose-response models (i.e. linear no-threshold, threshold or supralinear) would result in diverging risk estimates and, consequently, different overall assessments of the health impact of the accident. As the above discussion makes clear, the choice of a model is as much a political issue as it is a scientific one; however, with the emphasis on experts 'speaking with one voice', it is unlikely to be further discussed with respect to Chernobyl-related exposures and their effects. The existence of different dose-response models also suggests that in the area of radiation protection in general, and in the Chernobyl case in particular, the precautionary principle itself can have different interpretations, some of which would arguably better reflect the interests of those affected by the accident. If we further compare the ways in which this principle is interpreted in radiation protection and in the domain of security, for instance, as reflected in the so-called 'one per cent doctrine' attributed to Dick Cheney and used to justify the Bush Administration counter-terrorist policies and practices (Suskind, 2007), we will be able to appreciate not just the contextual specificity of the risk-based governing, but also the sustained prioritisation of risks to the state sovereignty, however low their probability.

The 2006 WHO Report also considered the evidence regarding non-cancer and non-thyroid health effects, and concluded, that, while the 2000 UNSCEAR Report only mentioned cataracts, scarring and ulceration as occurring in acute radiation sickness survivors, the available evidence suggested that cataracts in children and liquidators were also 'associated with exposure to radiation from the Chernobyl accident' (72). It also concluded that, based on the available evidence, '[l]iquidators who recovered from the acute radiation syndrome and received high doses are likely to be at increased risk for cardiovascular disease' (76). These findings are important, as the system of radiation protection currently privileges cancer risks over noncancerous effects while, according to recent studies, the latter effects at low doses may also be important, with the threshold for these effects being lower than previously suggested (Morgan and Bair, 2013: 507).

The 2008 reassessment of the Chernobyl health effects by the UNSCEAR endorsed the previous findings of its 2000 Report. While recognising 'indications of an increase in incidence of leukaemia and of cataracts among those [recovery workers] who received higher doses' and that they, along with persons exposed as children to radioiodine, 'are at increased risk of radiation-induced effects', it maintained that most people 'were exposed to low-level radiation' and, therefore, 'need not live in fear of serious health consequences' (UNSCEAR, 2008: 26–28).

Overall, the official problematisations of the Chernobyl accident in the last decade for the most part suggested that it did not produce serious radiation-induced health consequences, apart from the thyroid cancer in children, and that the biggest impact was on the mental health of the affected populations. The following sections will explore the implications of these problematisations for the affected people and for the nature of the assistance interventions.

The biopolitics of invisibility: tracking Chernobyl's 'ghosts'

For biopolitics, the reliance on the sciences of the aggregate, such as demography and epidemiology, is crucial. I would suggest that, to an extent, biopolitics erases the individual body in the process of creating a collective body, that of the population. This has important implications, because, as Casper and Moore (2009: 18) argue, '[d]ue to the predominance of science of the aggregate … individual stories and bodies are often lost'. Indeed, for biopolitics, individual suffering does not exist and does not matter. This appreciation could shed some light on the seemingly paradoxical situation, invoked in a conversation I had with a French expert directly involved in the assistance effort in Belarus. He reported that when they visited the affected settlements everybody knew somebody who had cancer or who had died before their time following the accident, but that this had virtually no impact on the Chernobyl-related morbidity and mortality rates, being statistically insignificant or not being unambiguously linked to radiation.

Furthermore, as Foucault contended, with biopolitics while life is supported, death is hidden (e.g. Foucault, 2003). While they remain alive, people's suffering is obscured. In its ability to reveal the limits of biopolitical care, death is an important way of rendering the suffering visible, at least to some extent, but to achieve this kind of visibility statistically significant numbers are required. Letting people survive obscures not only the suffering itself, but also the conditions that make continued suffering possible. To illustrate the way in which the Chernobyl-related suffering is obscured because it does not normally result in death, we can consider the case of thyroid cancer survivors.

Thyroid cancer remains one of a very few conditions with respect to which the causal link with radiation was established, although the process of recognising such a link was not straightforward.[5] However, the fact that those affected 'only' had thyroid cancer, which is rarely fatal and generally curable (in about 95 per cent of cases), renders their suffering invisible. As Bertell (2006: 245) points out, 'this tragedy is not dealt with in ... death estimates'. That these people had their thyroid glands partially or completely removed, that they need to be constantly taking medications, that they will bear scars, referred to as the 'Belarusian necklace', that so many of them are children, is somehow not as important. 'My driver,[6] for instance, he died – thyroid cancer; I myself only have half of my thyroid, and new nodules have recently been discovered, but I won't be going through another operation ... I will just live with it', said Vladimir, a clean-up worker I interviewed (28 May 2009). At the same time, a 2005 UNDP press-release on the finding of the Chernobyl Forum boldly states:

> the five million residents living in Chernobyl-affected areas received low doses of radiation.... This level of exposure *resulted in no observable radiation-induced health effects, aside from a rise in the incidence of thyroid cancer (successfully treated [in] virtually all cases)*.
>
> (UNDP, 2005; emphasis added)

So, what is addressed here is the level of mortality in a population and not individual deaths or the suffering of the survivors. Similarly, according to the 2008 UNSCEAR Report, '[a]lthough thyroid cancer incidence continues to increase ... up to 2005 *only 15 cases had proved fatal*' (UNSCEAR, 2008: 27; emphasis added). One of the few instances of recognition of the problems of thyroid cancer survivors measured them in economic terms, as a problem of resources (UNDP *et al.*, 2002: 49). In addition, WHO, while considering clinical aspects of thyroid disease, drew attention to difficulties of treatment in terms of side- and after-effects (WHO, 2006).

Furthermore, the almost exclusive focus on children prevents the suffering of the adult thyroid cancer survivors from being acknowledged[7] (e.g. Pflugbeil, 2006: 307; interviews, 28 May 2009), and international recognition of thyroid cancer as caused by radiation has not been followed by recognition of the same origin of other health conditions; instead, as Kuchinskaya (2007:63) observed, '"thyroid" [became] a common reference for Chernobyl problems, to the exclusion of anything else'.

As Casper and Moore (2009: 180) argue:

> visibility and invisibility are stratified in manifold ways. Bodies – seen and hidden, lost and found, alive and dead, actual and virtual – bear the marks of power and the many local and global processes through which it produces subjects.

Importantly, visibility and invisibility are also mutually constituted, with 'invisibility … folded into the condition of visibility from the beginning'; '[t]here is no visibility that is not also invisible, no visibility that is not in some way always spectral' (Lippit on Derrida, 2008: 244). An exploration of the fields of visibility and invisibility with respect to the Chernobyl health effects allows us to track Chernobyl's 'ghosts' and to reveal the conditions of their 'disappearance'. They are ghosts as they are not in full view, but they have left traces that concern us, that cannot be ignored, and therefore they act as a spectre in the Derridian sense: both visible and invisible. They are 'a trace that marks the present with its absence in advance', but also 'a someone who watches or concerns me without any possible reciprocity' (Derrida, 2002, in Lippit, 2008: 242). As far as the state is concerned, they are the 'unmissed missing' in Edkins' (2011) terms. Chernobyl 'ghosts' include those who are physically absent (in a particular location or have died); those whose health effects are not officially linked to the accident; those whose health effects are linked to the accident, but their numbers are statistically insignificant; and/or those who may be accounted for statistically, but visible only as numbers, as an aggregate phenomenon.

Possibly nowhere else is the presence of the first category of Chernobyl's ghosts so strongly felt as in the resettled villages of the exclusion zone. In Belarus, the exclusion zone is currently occupied by the Polessky State Radiological and Ecological Reserve (the Reserve). The territory of the Reserve consists of parts of the three administrative districts of the Gomel region of Belarus: Narovlya, Bragin and Khoiniki. The overall territory is $2,162 \, km^2$; there used to be 92 settlements with over 20,000 people there prior to the accident. It comprises the so-called 10 and 3 km zones. The exclusion zone contains around 30 per cent of all caesium (Cs-137) in Belarus, over 70 per cent of strontium (Sr-90) and around 90 per cent of transuranic elements (official website of the Reserve).

The testimonies of the liquidators, who were in the exclusion zone at different times in 1986, the year of the accident, are most appropriate here. This is just a short fragment of what they had to say about their experiences:

> people were given three hours to leave their village. They took their cows to the collective farm, but the cows broke through the farm gates and each of them was running home howling. People could not take anything with them, neither dogs nor cows, and animals could feel that, and it was scary.
>
> (Aliaksandr V., 26 May 2009)

we saw those resettled villages, empty houses with gardens full with apples that were falling and rotting; it created an awful impression as if everything had died out, had died.

(Aliaksandr P., 18 May 2009)

It was depressing: abandoned dogs and cats; allotments not tended to; everything overgrown. One could not even pass through for the branches of cherry, pear and plum trees: everything had gone wild; ... that's how it was like there.

(Anatoliy G., 28 May 2009)

So, what happened to the people who used to live in the exclusion zone? In the first few months after the accident, in Belarus around 25,000 people were evacuated from what became the exclusion zone, and a further 110,000 were later resettled (Belarus Chernobyl Committee, 2001). Overall, the response of the authorities was characterised by damaging secrecy, unjustified delays[8] (e.g. Medvedev, 1990; Yaroshinskaya, 1994; Marples, 1996) and other actions or inactions best understood as biopolitical abandonment. Thus, belated evacuations were hastily conducted and poorly organised: due to the lack of information (e.g. Marples, 1996), the overall unpreparedness of the authorities to deal with the consequences of a significant accident at a nuclear facility (interview, 28 May 2009; Abalkina and Panchenko, 2005); and general challenges that any mass-scale evacuation would present. Often, evacuations were taking place in stages, with people brought from the 10 to the 30 km zone first, before they would be taken elsewhere. Many of them were hoping that the evacuation would be temporary and that they would come back, and to see them realise that they would not be able to return was heart-breaking (interview, 19 January 2010).

Further resettlements were incomplete, mainly due to the lack of available housing. In addition, a number of residents, mostly elderly people, either refused to leave or later returned to their old houses without permission (Marples, 1996). In parallel to the organised evacuations, there was a mass exodus of people from the affected areas to the capital, Minsk, where resettlers, or 'Chernobylites', as they were, and sometimes still are, called, were made much less welcome. Apart from the tensions between new and old residents in places of resettlement, people suffered from the trauma of relocation, the loss of livelihoods, combined with inability to find employment, which could not be redressed by the free housing and compensations provided by the government. However, once they had been relocated, they officially ceased to be a problem (Marples, 1996).

Radiation is an invisible killer, and so are its effects at lower doses, especially at an early stage, but it is not this that plays the major role in creating most of Chernobyl's ghosts. These are people whose health effects are not officially linked to the accident or, if linked, their numbers are statistically insignificant. Thus, Chernobyl liquidators were mostly men, aged 25–45 at the time (IAEA, 2005), both military and civilian, who were used for clean-up operations following the accident. They performed various tasks, from decontamination to medical

care, often with no adequate information about the risks and no special protection (e.g. interviews, 18, 26 and 28 May 2009). As a result, they received doses
of radiation that are difficult to determine with certainty, with many records lost
or accidently or deliberately distorted (SDC, 2006). It has been estimated that
less than 10 per cent of them 'had reliable estimates of their doses' (Pitkevitch *et
al.*, 1995, 1996, in Cardis *et al.*, 2003: 2).

As of 2001, there were around 110,000 registered liquidators in Belarus, of
which about 12,000 were registered as having a disability (Belarus Chernobyl
Committee, 2001). Despite the fact that they represented one of the most seriously affected categories, and despite their deteriorating health and dwindling
numbers, they were often overlooked because of the assumption that their deaths
and their health problems were not caused by the accident, that they were receiving social benefits from the state, and were, therefore, taken care of. The absence
of reliable dose estimates for the majority of liquidators had important implications for establishing the link between radiation exposure and their health conditions, but it was not the only reason why such a link was not established, as it
was often denied in the absence of evidence to the contrary. The 2003–2005
Chernobyl Forum Report went even further by suggesting that 'most recovery
workers ... received relatively low whole-body radiation doses, comparable to
background radiation levels accumulated ... since the accident' (11). The 2000
UNSCEAR Report found no increased risk in liquidators of either leukaemia or
solid tumours related to radiation, while the 2006 WHO Report acknowledged
that cataracts in liquidators could be 'associated with exposure to radiation from
the Chernobyl accident' (72), and that, based on the available evidence, '[l]iqui-
dators who recovered from the acute radiation syndrome and received high doses
are likely to be at increased risk for cardiovascular disease' (76). The IAEA
(2005) maintains that 'cancer and death rate studies that have been conducted
among samples of the recorded liquidators have shown no direct correlation
between radiation exposure at Chernobyl and increased cancer or death rates',
and describes their health problems as psychological or related to post-traumatic
stress disorder.

According to national reports, liquidators suffered from all types of cancer
more often than the control group (e.g. Belarus Chernobyl Committee, 2001).
However, such recognition only made them partially visible as health statistics,
and, in addition, each of them had to go through numerous checks and committees for the link between cancer and exposure to be officially established. Such
processes are processes of objectification, of 'the production of people as nothing
but objects of administration' (Edkins, 2011: 7), processes on which biopolitical
governing is reliant.

Tellingly, the Head of the Epidemiological Laboratory of the Republican Scientific Centre of Radiation Medicine and Human Ecology (Belarus) several
years ago announced that the list of the health conditions used in the process of
granting Chernobyl-related disability status would be reduced to a minimum
(*BelaPAN News Agency*, 18 April 2008). The decision was justified, he said, as
the link between radiation and cancer had not been proven statistically, and

many health conditions caused by radiation had the same clinical symptoms as those unrelated to it.

Liquidators were mentioned in the 2003–2005 Chernobyl Forum Report, albeit combined with the denial of the radiation origin of their health conditions. The Report used the category of 'exposed' and identified three groups of people as belonging to this category (11): emergency and recovery operation workers who worked at the Chernobyl NPP and in the exclusion zone after the accident; inhabitants evacuated from contaminated areas; and inhabitants of contaminated areas who were not evacuated from those areas. Given that virtually the whole population was exposed to some extent – for example, through consumption of contaminated produce – it would possibly be more appropriate to call the above categories the most exposed. In any case, this categorisation rendered invisible many instances of exposure, sufficient to have potentially produced serious health effects, such as thyroid cancer in children residing outside the areas officially recognised as contaminated. This latter issue is important for another reason. The categorisation was based on the territorial principle, with the presence in a particular area linked to a particular status. However, the Chernobyl contamination was non-uniform, while the establishment and subsequent changes in the status of territories are always political, and often have little connection with doses received by the population (Marples, 1996; Kuchinskaya, 2007). Finally, as the areas officially considered contaminated shrink, partly for economic reasons, partly in response to the criticisms voiced in the international reports discussed in the previous section,[9] so do the numbers of people considered exposed.

In addition to categorisations, we should also be aware of such strategies[10] considered, in particular, by Kuchinskaya (2007), as the dissolution of the consequences of the accident into individual health problems of unspecified origin, or locating the problem in the people's head (as with 'radiophobia'). The latter strategy, as previously mentioned, was often accompanied by blaming the victim (for unhealthy lifestyles, or risky behaviour, such as consumption of contaminated foodstuffs). Finally, the strategy of normalisation was also very prominent; by using this strategy various actors attempted to, and cooperated in, governing through the seemingly depoliticised norm of radiation protection and in normalising the effects of the accident by reinterpreting, and redefining, what is considered normal and safe (see Marples, 1996; Kuchinskaya, 2007, for examples).

From fatalistic victims to entrepreneurial individuals and resilient communities: strategies and technologies of neoliberal governing

Importantly, the consistent 'erasure' of radiation effects was crucial for making the Chernobyl accident and its victims 'disappear' from the radar of the international assistance community. As Kuchinskaya (2007: 94) argued:

> the results of ... international studies [on Chernobyl-related health effects] affected humanitarian assistance for which the Belarusian government was

appealing. In turn, the lack of international recognition and assistance affected the politics of the Belarusian government, including the official reframing of Chernobyl as a socio-economic problem.

This shift in framing the problem further decreased the visibility of Chernobyl's consequences (Kuchinskaya, 2007). The first major international report to reframe Chernobyl as a socio-economic problem was the previously mentioned 2002 Report. It marked a paradigmatic development in the international Chernobyl-related assistance effort by announcing the change of strategy from emergency assistance to sustainable development and by emphasising 'a return to normality' (4).

The strategy outlined in the Report was supposed to promote 'long-term recovery through ... new partnerships and a new generation of initiatives designed to assist the individuals and the communities concerned to take their future in their own hands' (3). While this sounded like empowerment, such pronouncements, made in the knowledge that the opportunities for the people to influence their lives were extremely limited, should rather be interpreted as a negative responsibilisation, i.e. a transfer of responsibility without creating necessary conditions to make its acquisition meaningful. Thus, one of my interviewees, an INGO official, expressed some reservations about this solution to Chernobyl-related problems:

> development should most definitely be the way forward.... I would be somewhat pessimistic about such an ambitious plan [the 2008 UN Action Plan] for such a short period of time though, especially bearing in mind the donor disinterest. Also, how is the progress being measured? Have the decision-makers consulted with the population about what they think about the plan? Who is funding the development? Is there international commitment towards it?... So, it is hard to see the region being transformed back to normal just like that.
>
> (interview, 27 April 2010)

The introduction of the new approach in the Report was based on the understanding that radioactive contamination would remain for the years to come, informing the need for humanitarian assistance; however, the Report made it clear that the assistance could not be open-ended (16), although even a World Bank Report (2002: 25) recognised that 'Belarus has carried the burden of Chernobyl expenditures, while international assistance has played a relatively minor role'. A comparison of the official requests for assistance and the funds pledged demonstrates the unwillingness of the international community to provide assistance in the first decade after the accident. For instance, in 1991, at the UN Chernobyl Pledging Conference in New York, out of over US$646m requested by the three most affected Soviet Republics, only US$670,000 was collected (with the then Czechoslovakia making a contribution of US$500,000); in 1998, again, less than 2 per cent of the requested amount was pledged at the 2nd International

Pledging Meeting in Geneva (Belarus Chernobyl Committee, 2001: 87). Importantly, the first of the Conferences took place after the release of the 1991 International Chernobyl Project Report, which did not find evidence of radiation-induced health effects. In addition, Chernobyl has always been associated with Ukraine in the first place,[11] and, in Belarus, with Gomel, even though other regions were also contaminated. These perceptions had a profound impact on aid flows, as more aid was given to Ukraine and, in Belarus, to Gomel region.

Having taken a relatively balanced approach with respect to the health effects of the accident, the 2002 Report nevertheless called on the respective governments to reform the existing health care provision with a view to not prolonging the so-called dependency culture (8). It also engaged in a critique, informed by a cost-benefit approach, of the measures undertaken to mitigate the consequences of the accident, by stating that 'countries ... became locked into a disruptive and an expensive programme of resettlement and compensation without adequate examination of the costs and benefits involved' (33). Criticising the mass screening policies (57), the Report ignored the positive effect of saving lives, as well as reassuring people and making them feel that they had not been abandoned (e.g. International Federation of the Red Cross and Red Crescent Societies (IFRC), 2006). Overall, this can be seen as an example of a conflict between the two different systems of biopolitical governing, informed and driven by different rationalities, i.e. a Soviet project of social welfare, with its management of the collective life in all spheres through total planning and its focus (even if oftentimes more declaratory than real) on universal and equitable access to public goods and support systems, and neoliberalism, with its critique of inefficiencies associated with 'governing too much' and its reliance on market mechanisms and individual entrepreneurship as way of establishing, in Collier's (2011) words, 'a novel pattern of correlation between choice mechanisms and social welfare'.

The 2003–2005 Chernobyl Forum Report also clearly espoused the neoliberal stance in its critique of the measures undertaken by the affected countries, which, it suggested, had 'undermined the capacity of the individuals and communities concerned to tackle their own economic and social problems' (37). It called on to the respective governments to scale down medical and social benefit programmes and to reduce the areas excluded from the economic use. The latter was to be achieved not through decontamination, but through a change in the legal status of the territories, as the existing 'delimitations [were] far more restrictive than demonstrated radiation levels [could] justify' (54). A related recommendation was that 'large-scale monitoring of foodstuffs, whole-body counting of individuals, and provision of dosimeters [were] no longer necessary' (49). The 2008 *UN Action Plan on Chernobyl* also criticised the national efforts as excessive and creating a dependency syndrome; what was required instead was 'a restored sense of community self-reliance' (UN, 2008: 2). Such criticisms were made even more explicit in the 2013 UNDP's 'knowledge product' *Recovery from Chernobyl and other Nuclear Emergencies: Experiences and Lessons Learnt*, which provided an overview of the agency's involvement in recovery efforts following nuclear emergencies.

Being an essential element of the psychologisation of the consequences of the accident, the Chernobyl victim, or Chernobyl dependency syndrome, received a lot of attention in the international discourse. While it is easy to blame people for becoming dependent, doing so ignores the complex effects of the accident, along with the authoritarian past and current policies and practices of normalisation. As an officer from a UN-family organisation pointed out (interview, 1 April 2008), the affected regions in Belarus had been largely reliant on agriculture and the accident took their livelihoods away. In addition, in some places problems were compounded by the migration of young people away from the affected areas and a serious lack of qualified specialists due to a considerable brain-drain. A senior INGO officer, who visited the affected regions, commented: 'these are not exactly the most motivating environments to be part of! So, if there is passivity, I think it's understandable' (interview, 27 April 2010).

However, as the problem was located in people's mentality and attitudes, it was concluded that something was wrong with them and had to be rectified through what Pupavac termed 'therapeutic governing', associated with the demise of genuine development and used 'to foster personalities able to cope with risk and insecurity' (Pupavac, 2005: 162). Thus, to combat the Chernobyl victim syndrome, interventions were supposed to transform passive, dependent and fatalistic people into active and entrepreneurial individuals and resilient and self-reliant communities. As stated by the World Bank (2002: IV; emphasis added):

> [p]rograms should shift from those that create a victim and dependency mentality to those that support opportunity, promote local initiatives, involve the people and *spur their confidence in shaping their destiny*.

The orientation of such therapeutic interventions towards the future[12] with a focus on 'transformation' and 'moving on' can be seen as an attempt to erase accident-related memories, 'a refusal of memory' (Edkins, 2011). Such interventions rely on linear temporality that stands in contrast to what Edkins (2003) aptly termed 'trauma time' – a time which is non-homogenous and non-linear and which allows for a different kind of response, '*encircling* of the trauma, a refusal to forget the lessons, an insistence on acknowledgement that, however impossible to understand, what happened happened' (Edkins, 2011: 4; original emphasis). For Edkins (forthcoming), it is this temporality that is capable of disrupting the dominant linear narrative and opening up space for questioning and challenging the forms of power that produce it. However, the Chernobyl-related assistance effort did not display much appreciation of the trauma time and its radical potential.

One of the first major programmes to embrace a 'transformative' approach was the CORE (Cooperation for Rehabilitation) Programme, hailed as a new generation programme in international Chernobyl co-operation (Tsalko *et al.*, 2005: 5; author's translation from Russian). It was argued that none of the previous efforts had involved active participation of the affected population in rehabilitation and improvement of their living conditions, and this had resulted in the dependency syndrome (Trafimchik *et al.*, 2009: 3; author's translation from Russian). The Programme was expected to lift the affected population from the position of victim and put them into the position of a partner (interview, 27 May 2009). In practice, 'working with the people' often implied governing them, through responsibilisation and often through their children and those community members more capable of self-governing.

According to the 2003 CORE *Declaration of Principles*, the objective was 'to improve the living conditions of the inhabitants of selected districts by reaching out to people themselves, *helping them to contribute to formulating specific individual and common project proposals*' (2; emphasis added). Thus, in order to receive anything, people had to learn how to formulate projects, which reflected the unequal distribution of power between the donors and the recipients, as well as illustrating a growing reliance on project management in the humanitarian and development sector. The very fact that people learned how to formulate projects was considered to be an important achievement of the CORE programme (interview, 27 May 2009).

The projects of the CORE Programme were to focus on such priority area as: 'Health care and surveillance', 'Economic and social development in the rural contaminated areas', 'Culture and education' and 'Radiological quality'. The rationale for health care as a priority was that people in the contaminated areas were worried about their health and the health of their children, while health statistics demonstrated low birth rates, decreases in longevity and increases in morbidity levels (Tsalko *et al.*, 2005: 13; author's translation from Russian). At the same time, it was argued that it was wrong to perceive health as a medical problem, and people had to look after themselves (Tsalko *et al.*, 2005: 13; author's translation from Russian). This was in line with the *National Strategy of Sustainable Social-Economic Development to 2020*, which declared it to be a strategic goal 'to create a state mechanism of support for the healthy lifestyle, to develop high demand for personal health and create conditions for its satisfaction' and which was supposed to contribute to the 'development of *personal responsibility for one's own health protection* and that of others' (in Tsalko *et al.*, 2005: 13; emphasis added; author's translation from Russian). This is a clear example of the previously mentioned responsibilisation strategy. While justifiable under different circumstances, the application of such principles to people living in the contaminated areas raises additional ethical concerns. An attempt to consider radiation as another factor among numerous life-style *choices*, something that, by definition, people are responsible for (and can be blamed for) is problematic: while they did not choose to live with high levels of radiation, people were expected to avoid receiving high doses, and, should they fail to do so, it was their problem and their responsibility. This was reinforced by the suggestion that people fell ill not because they lived in the contaminated areas, but because they smoked, drank and led otherwise unhealthy lifestyles (e.g. UNSCEAR, 2008; UN, 2008).

When considering examples of projects, strategies such as responsibilisation and mentality change become even more apparent. Virtually all CORE projects examined had an element of 'mentality change' and were aimed at creating new neoliberal subjects, active, full of initiative and hope, enterprising, self-sufficient, assuming responsibility for themselves, capable of managing their own risks, resilient, etc. According to the 2006 *CORE Annual review*, participants in the projects in the priority area of health care and surveillance got truly 'transformed', as they 'develop[ed] a more proactive life stance, show[ed] greater willingness to follow radiation safety measures and to contribute to improving the living environment in their communities' (5). This alleged mentality change did not translate into project sustainability however, which demonstrates the inherent failings of the project of manufacturing new neoliberal subjects, especially when attempted in the absence of a strong commitment to support genuine development.

Tellingly, the next stage in the international Chernobyl assistance effort was informed by the same approach, as evident in the *UNDP Belarus Area Based Development of Programme (2008–2010)*. The Programme outline stressed that, so far, no attention had been paid to 'stimulating active life position and personal responsibility for their own future' among people affected by the Chernobyl accident, as 'many still perceive themselves as helpless, weak people, lacking the ability to influence their own future' (UNDP, 2008: 4, 36; author's translation from Russian). The project activities were focused on information and training provision, with most of the budget of just over €1.5 million allocated to various meetings, consultations, expert evaluations and monitoring. The previously mentioned 2013 UNDP evaluation document further emphasised the role of information dissemination in 'improve[ing] population's mentality' and 'help[ing] people to re-energize, re-direct their lives' (3).

The psychological turn in the evaluation of Chernobyl health effects had far reaching implications, and even a mass screening programme, one of the longest running and most inclusive and non-discriminatory of all humanitarian programmes, the *Chernobyl Humanitarian Assistance and Rehabilitation Programme (CHARP) of the IFRC and the Red Cross Societies of Belarus, Ukraine and Russia*, was marked by psychologisation. The psychosocial support as an element of the CHARP represented an example of therapeutic governing aimed at normalising conditions that would not otherwise be perceived as normal. It was informed by the assumption that exposure to radiation and associated consequences were not so much a real problem, but rather a problem of perception. It also suggested that people living in the affected territories, who were concerned about their living conditions, suffered from mental health problems, and, therefore, needed help to understand that there was nothing to be afraid of. Thus, the rationale behind the psychological support was presented as addressing 'increased levels of depression, anxiety and *medically unexplained physical symptoms* ... [in] Chernobyl-exposed populations' (IFRC, *CHARP Fact Sheet*: 2; emphasis added). The psychosocial support for the population affected by the Chernobyl disaster was 'to diminish stress in the population by delivering accurate information about the long-term health effects of the accident' (IFRC, *CHARP Plan 2009–2010*: 6).

The idea that information provision can be the solution of all the Chernobyl-related problems also informed the International Chernobyl Research and Information Network (ICRIN). The concept of ICRIN was developed by the *Swiss Agency for Development and Cooperation* (SDC) and endorsed in 2003 by the *UN Inter-Agency Task Force on Chernobyl* (Kuchinskaya, 2007: 110). The first stage of the ICRIN was completed in 2004–2005, with the establishment of the National Committees in the three most affected countries (UNDP, 2006). The ICRIN 'was planned as a structured network of scientists that would identify the gaps in Chernobyl-related research, provide recommendations for future studies, and assist in the information provision efforts' (UNDP, 2006: 4). However, following the release of the *2003–2005 Chernobyl Forum Report*, the ICRIN was modified, with the focus on information dissemination, as opposed to new research (UNDP, 2006: 4). It was to 'address the lack of accurate, accessible information on how to live, work and have family in Chernobyl-affected territories' (www.chernobyl.info) by distributing information to the public in a way that '*encourage[d] a change in behaviour and helps to overcome fatalistic attitudes*', as its end goal was

> to tackle the *'Chernobyl victim syndrome'*, uncertainties and fatalism about health as well as *deep-seated misconceptions* that exist in the minds of people living on Chernobyl-affected territories with regard to the dangers to their livelihoods as result of the accident.
>
> (www.chernobyl.info; emphasis added)

However, according to *An Information Needs Assessment of the Chernobyl-affected Population of the Republic of Belarus*, conducted by the UNDP in cooperation with the Belarus Chernobyl Committee, UN OCHA and SDC, respondents did not suggest that the lack of information was something that worried them, unlike health concerns (74.2 per cent of all respondents), low living standards (50.5 per cent) or radioactive contamination (21.8 per cent) (UNDP, 2004: 26). When asked what could improve their living conditions, respondents did not mention information provision either, suggesting instead such measures as health care improvement (68.4 per cent), area decontamination (20.8 per cent), job creation (18.4 per cent) and new research (13.5 per cent) (UNDP, 2004: 28).

It should be mentioned that the earlier stages of the ICRIN development produced a platform in the form of the 'www.chernobyl.info' website, which covered information coming from a variety of sources, including independent ones. The website used to be maintained by the SDC Office, but, following the Office's closure in 2010, the UNDP became responsible for it. Predictably, a more recent stage of the ICRIN Project included provision of '[i]nformation on healthy lifestyles ... through locally-based information and education initiatives' and '[c]ommunity-driven "safer-living" initiatives' (UNDP, 2006: 6–7). These were to be achieved with the support of a US$2.5 million programme, launched in 2009[13] to meet the priority information needs of affected communities through the introduction of a sustainable response mechanism that link the information needs ... with corresponding *internationally-recognized, objective scientific knowledge, adapted to be understandable to information consumers.*

(www.chernobyl.info; emphasis added)

This focus on the vaguely defined information needs of 'information consumers' instead of the declared needs of individuals and communities signals a further objectification of the suffering (defined narrowly as a lack of objective scientific knowledge) and a further distancing from those affected in an attempt to govern them through information. Unsurprisingly, however, the efforts of the implementing agencies 'in produc[ing] numerous information materials for a variety of local stakeholders', all checked to ensure that they were 'factually accurate, up to date, consistent and convincing', were duly noted in the 2013 Report of the UN Secretary General *Optimizing the international effort to study, mitigate and minimize the consequences of the Chernobyl disaster* (UN, 2013: 5).

Conclusion

This chapter has established a recent (2000–2010) genealogy of the response to the Chernobyl accident in in Belarus with the focus on the health effects of the accident and relevant assistance projects. In particular, the tools of the analytics of government have been deployed to critically examine the dominant problematisations of the accident and its consequences and their implications for those affected and for the assistance effort. I have shown that the consistent 'erasure' of radiation effects undertaken in a number of reports by relevant international expert bodies and in the official discourse of influential organisations of the UN family, was crucial in making the accident and its victims 'disappear' from the radar of the international humanitarian assistance community. Interpreting the 'disappearance' of Chernobyl and its consequences through the analytical lenses offered by the theorising on biopolitics and governmentality has proved to be helpful in making visible Chernobyl's 'ghosts' and the conditions of their 'disappearance', along with the deliberate strategies and technologies aimed at radically transforming individuals and communities living with the aftermath of the accident from dependent, passive and irresponsible victims to self-reliant, active and entrepreneurial survivors.

As the chapter has demonstrated, there are not many reasons to be optimistic about the future of the individuals and communities affected by the accident. When asked what can be done so that the accident and those affected by are not completely forgotten, a senior INGO officer said:

I think very little. Commitment is just not there. Everyone is like – well, tough ... it happened so long ago. We moved on ... poor people of Chernobyl ... etc. More advocacy is needed, but the question is to whom? Governments are not interested really. Pro-nuclear energy lobbyists are very strong and there is a very considerable economic factor in all this. Chernobyl is sort of a nuisance if you like.... It's fading away in people's memories.

(interview, 27 April 2010)

This prospect, along with the 2011 nuclear accident at Fukushima Daiichi NPP in Japan, make it even more important that the Chernobyl accident and its consequences are not treated as closed matters, and reminding us of the enormity and complexity of its impact is one of the few ways of 'being accountable to those people affected' (Petryna, 2011: 30).

Notes

1 http://europeandcis.undp.org.
2 Interpretations of the Chernobyl health effects as predominantly psychological go back to the official Soviet reports and first international assessments, such as that of the 1989 WHO team or the 1991 *International Chernobyl Project Report* by the International Advisory Committee set up under the auspices of the IAEA. Importantly, much more data on the health consequences were available to the UNSCEAR in 2000 and to the Chernobyl Forum.
3 Perhaps unsurprisingly a 'mental health crisis' has also been declared among Fukushima residents affected by the 2011 accident at Fukushima Daiichi NPP (McCurry, 2013).
4 Radiation health effects are divided into deterministic and stochastic. Deterministic effects are effects of cell death, and, for them to occur, 'the radiation dose must be large enough to kill a sufficient number of cells' (Lindell, 1996: 159). For such effects, 'there is a dose threshold below which the harm cannot arise and the risk is zero' (Lindell, 1996: 159), while the dose-effect relationship is linear, as the severity of the effect depends on the dose (Gofman, 1981, in Petryna, 2002: 10). For stochastic effects, such as solid cancers, leukaemia or hereditary effects, 'the dose-response relation is assumed to show no threshold', and the dose-response effects 'can only be established on probabilistic grounds' (Lindell, 1996: 159). Furthermore, 'health effects depend on sex, age at exposure, time since exposure and organ in question', and other factors, such as 'diet, lifestyle, genetic and epigenetic factors will all influence the consequences of radiation exposure' (Morgan and Bair, 2013: 504, 505).
5 This also appears to be the case with the situation in Japan post-Fukushima, where newly detected cases of thyroid cancer are not attributed to the radiation released during the 2011 accident at Fukushima Daiichi NPP (e.g. McCurry, 2013).
6 He is referring not to a personal driver, but a person with whom he worked in the exclusion zone.
7 Not the people who were exposed as children or adolescences and who are adults now, but those exposed as adults, for instance, liquidators.
8 For example, according to a recent large-scale study of the thyroid doses received by those exposed as children, out of the entire cohort of 11,732, only 803, or 7 per cent, 'reported intake of stable iodine shortly after the accident ... when blockade of radioactive iodine uptake was the most effective to prevent thyroid exposure' (Drozdovitch *et al.*, 2013: 606–607).
9 For instance, the 2003–2005 Chernobyl Forum Report recommended that the governments of the three most affected countries 'should urgently revisit the classification of Chernobyl-affected zones, as current legislation is too restrictive, given the low radiation levels that now prevail in most territories' (50).

10 In fact, some of these strategies are not new. However, in the Chernobyl case, the systems of knowledge that underpin such strategies, the ways in which they are deployed and their implications, are rather unique.
11 The tendency towards so-called 'Ukranisation' of the Chernobyl assistance was perceived in Belarus as worrying and unfair. At the same time, the interests of donors were focused on the Chernobyl NPP, which was considered a threat to the whole Europe. With the closure of the NPP, the interest of the international community in Chernobyl-related issues has further diminished (World Bank, 2002: 20).
12 Even the 'return to normal', declared both possible and desirable in the reports produced by the international expert bodies, with its implied reference to the past, in fact presupposes a 'return' to a 'new', and therefore, future, normality.
13 Currently, the website contains very little information, most of which is focused on Ukraine.

References

Abalkina I.L. and S.V. Panchenko. 2005. *Chernobyl radiation in questions and answers* (in Russian). Moscow: Komtekhprint.

BelaPAN (Belarusian Information Company). 18 April 2008. *The link between disability and consequences of the Chernobyl accident will be reconsidered* [online in Russian]. [Accessed 16 August 2010]. http://news.tut.by/107382.html.

Belarus Chernobyl Committee (Committee on the Problems of the Consequences of the Catastrophe at the Chernobyl NPP). 2001. *15 Years after Chernobyl Disaster: Consequences in the Republic of Belarus and Their Overcoming [sic]. National Report.* Shevchouk, V.E. and V.L. Gourachevskiy (eds). Minsk: Belarus Chernobyl Committee.

Belarus Chernobyl Committee (Committee on the Problems of the Consequences of the Catastrophe at the Chernobyl NPP). 2006. *20 Years after Chernobyl Disaster: Consequences in the Republic of Belarus and Their Overcoming [sic]. National Report.* Shevchouk, V.E. and V.L. Gourachevskiy (eds). Minsk: Belarus Chernobyl Committee.

Belarus MFA (Ministry of Foreign Affairs). 2009. *Chernobyl Disaster: Why Are the Consequences Still Observed? and Why Is the International Assistance Still Critical?* [online]. [Accessed 1 May 2009]. www.un.int/belarus/chernobyl.htm.

Bertell, R. 2006. The death toll of the Chernobyl accident. *In*: C.C. Busby and A.V. Yablokov (eds). 2006. *Chernobyl: 20 years on. Health effects of the Chernobyl accident. Documents of the ECRP 2006 No 1.* Aberystwyth: Green Audit Press on behalf of the European Committee on Radiation Risk, pp. 245–248.

Burlakova, E.B. and A.G. Nazarov. 2006. Is it safe to live in territories contaminated with radioactivity? Consequences of the Chernobyl accident 20 years later. *In*: C.C. Busby and A.V. Yablokov (eds). *Chernobyl: 20 years on. Health effects of the Chernobyl accident. Documents of the ECRP 2006 No. 1.* Aberystwyth: Green Audit Press on behalf of the European Committee on Radiation Risk, pp. 49–60.

Burlakova, E.B. and V.I. Naidich (eds). 2006. *20 years after the Chernobyl accident: past, present and future.* New York: Nova Science Publishers.

Busby, C.C. and A.V. Yablokov (eds). 2006. *Chernobyl: 20 years on. Health effects of the Chernobyl accident. Documents of the ECRP 2006 No. 1.* Aberystwyth: Green Audit Press on behalf of the European Committee on Radiation Risk.

Cardis, *et al.* 2003. *Reconstruction of Doses for Chernobyl Liquidators. Final Performance Report of 20 March 2003.* Unit of Radiation and Cancer, International Agency for

Research on Cancer, Lyon, France [online]. [Accessed 17 August 2010]. www.cdc. gov/niosh/oerp/pdfs/FinalPerformanceReport.pdf.

Casper, M.J. and L.J. Moore. 2009. *Missing bodies: the politics of visibility*. London: New York University Press.

Collier, S.J. 2011. *Post-Soviet social: neoliberalism, social modernity, biopolitics.* Oxford: Princeton University Press.

CORE. 2003. *Declaration of Principles on (sic) the CORE Programme 'Cooperation for Rehabilitation of Living Conditions in Chernobyl Affected Areas in Belarus'*. Minsk: UNDP *et al.*

CORE. 2006. *2005 CORE Annual Review*. Minsk: UNDP *et al.*

Dean, M. 1999. *Governmentality: power and rule in modern society*. London: SAGE.

Drozdovitch, V. *et al.* 2013. Thyroid dose estimates for a cohort of Belarusian children exposed to radiation from the Chernobyl accident. *Radiation Research*, **179**(5): 597–609.

Edkins, J. 2003. *Trauma and the memory of politics*. Cambridge: Cambridge University Press.

Edkins, J. 2011. *Missing: persons and politics*. London: Cornell University Press.

Edkins, J. (forthcoming). Reflections on memory and the future: time and trauma in Chris Marker's *La Jetée. Memory Studies.*

Fairlie, I. and D. Sumner. 2006. *TORCH: the Other Report on Chernobyl: an Independent Scientific Evaluation of Health and Environmental Effects 20 Years after the Nuclear Disaster Providing Critical Analysis of a Recent Report by the International Atomic Energy Agency (IAEA) and the World Health Organisation (WHO)* [online]. [Accessed 10 May 2009]. www.chernobylreport.org/torch.pdf.

Foucault, M. 1997. Discipline and punish: the birth of the prison. London: Allen Lane.

Foucault, M. 1980. Two lectures. Lecture one: 7 January 1976. *In*: C. Gordon (ed.). *Power/knowledge: selected interviews and other writings 1972–1977. Michel Foucault.* Harvester Press Limited, pp. 78–92.

Foucault, M. 1987. Nietzsche, genealogy, history. *In*: M. T. Gibbons (ed.). *Interpreting politics*. Oxford: Basil Blackwell, pp. 221–240.

Foucault, M. 2003. *Society must be defended: Lectures at the Collège de France, 1975–76.* London: Penguin.

IAC (International Advisory Committee). 1991. *The International Chernobyl Project. Assessment of Radiological Consequences and Evaluation of Protective Measures. Summary Brochure*. Vienna: IAEA.

IAEA (International Atomic Energy Agency). 1997. *Ten Years after Chernobyl: What Do We Really Know? Based on the Proceedings of the IAEA/WHO/EC International Conference, Vienna, April 1996*. Vienna: IAEA.

IAEA. 2005. *Chernobyl's 700,000 'liquidators' struggle with psychological and social consequences* [online]. [Accessed 16 August 2010]. www.iaea.org/NewsCenter/Features/Chernobyl-15/liquidators.shtml.

IFRC (International Federation of Red Cross and Red Crescent Societies). *Chernobyl Humanitarian Assistance and Rehabilitation Programme (CHARP): fact sheet* [online]. [Accessed 17 August 2010]. www.ifrc.org/Docs/pubs/health/charp-fact-sheet-0406.pdf.

IFRC. 2006. *CHARP focus: 15 years of the Chernobyl Humanitarian Assistance and Rehabilitation Programme. 20 years after the Chernobyl disaster*. Geneva: IFRC.

IFRC. Plan 2009–2010. *Chernobyl Humanitarian Assistance and Rehabilitation Programme (CHARP).*

Interview with Aliaksandr P., a clean-up worker (liquidator), 18 May 2009.

Interview with Aliaksandr V., a clean-up worker (liquidator), 26 May 2009.

Interview with Anatoliy G., a clean-up worker (liquidator), Head of the USSR Civil Defence Headquarters in 1988, 28 May 2009.

Interview with a donor organisation officer, 18 May 2009.

Interview with a former CORE Programme Coordinator, 27 May 2009.

Interview with a former head of a local council, 19 January 2010.

Interview with a Polessky State Radiological and Ecological Reserve officer, 12 January 2010.

Interview with a senior INGO official with prior experience of direct involvement in the assistance effort, 27 April 2010.

Interview with a UN family organisation (UNDP) officer, 1 April 2008.

Interview with Vladimir F., a clean-up worker (liquidator), 28 May 2009.

Kuchinskaya, O. 2007. *'We will die and become science': the production of invisibility and public knowledge about Chernobyl radiation effects in Belarus*. PhD Thesis. The University of California, San Diego.

Lindell, B. 1996. The risk philosophy of radiation protection. *Radiation Protection Dosimetry*, **68**(3/4): 157–163.

Lippit, A.M. 2008. Reflections on spectral life. *Discourse*, **30**(1&2): 242–254.

Marples, D.A. 1996. *Belarus: from Soviet rule to nuclear catastrophe*. Basingstoke: Macmillan.

McCurry, J. 2013. Fukushima residents still struggling 2 years after disaster. *The Lancet*, **381**(9869): 791–792 [online]. [Accessed 10 June 2013]. www.thelancet.com/journals/lancet/article/PIIS0140-6736(13)60611-X/fulltext.

Medvedev, Z.A. 1990. *The legacy of Chernobyl*. Oxford: Basil Blackwell.

Miller, P. and N. Rose. 2008. *Governing the present: administering economic, social and personal life*. Cambridge: Polity Press.

Morgan, W.F. and W.J. Bair. 2013. Issues in low dose radiation biology: the controversy continues. A Perspective. *Radiation Research*, **179**(5): 501–510.

Nussbaum, R. 1998. The linear no-threshold dose-response relation: is it relevant to radiation protection regulation? *Medical Physics*, **25**(3): 291–299.

Petryna, A. 2002. *Life exposed: biological citizens after Chernobyl*. Princeton: Princeton University Press.

Petryna, A. 2011. Chernobyl's survivors: paralyzed by fatalism or overlooked by science? *Bulletin of Atomic Scientists*, **67**(2): 30–37.

Pflugbeil, S. 2006. Chernobyl – looking back to look forwards: the September 2005 IAEA Conference. *Medicine, Conflict and Survival*, **22**(4): 299–309.

Proctor, R.N. 1995. *Cancer wars: how politics shapes what we know and don't know about cancer*. New York: BasicBooks.

Pupavac, V. 2005. Human security and the rise of global therapeutic governance. *Conflict, Security & Development*, **5**(2): 161–181.

SDC (Swiss Agency for Development and Cooperation). 2006. *55 questions and answers to the Chernobyl disaster*. Bern: SDC.

SDC (no date). *ICRIN goals and tasks* [online]. [Accessed 17 August 2010]. www.chernobyl.info/index.php?userhash=713409&navID=342&lID=2.

Smart, B. 1985. *Michel Foucault*. London: Routledge.

Stephens, S. 2002. Bounding uncertainty: the post-Chernobyl culture of radiation protection experts. *In*: S.M. Hoffman and A. Oliver-Smith (eds). *Catastrophe & culture: the anthropology of disaster*. Oxford: James Currey, pp. 91–112.

Suskind, R. 2007. *The one percent doctrine: deep inside America's pursuit of its enemies since 9/11*. New York: Simon & Schuster.

The Chernobyl Forum. 2003–2005. *Chernobyl's Legacy: Health, Environmental and Socio-economic Impacts and Recommendations to the Governments of Belarus, the Russian Federation and Ukraine.* Vienna: IAEA.

Trafimchik, Z.I., *et al.* 2009. *On the outcomes of the CORE Programme, specifics of the CORE approach and its development in the Republic of Belarus: analytical summary* (in Russian). Minsk.

Tsalko, V.G., *et al.* 2005. *2004 CORE Programme annual review: strategy, initiatives, partnership (in Russian).* Minsk: Unipack.

UN. 2007. *Optimizing the International Effort to Study, Mitigate and Minimize the Consequences of the Chernobyl Disaster. Report of the Secretary General. A/62/467* [online]. [Accessed 1 March 2009]. http://chernobyl.undp.org/english/sg_reports.html.

UN. 2008. *UN Action Plan on Chernobyl to 2016* [online]. [Accessed 16 August 2010]. http://chernobyl.undp.org/english/docs/action_plan_final_nov08.pdf.

UN. 2013. *Optimizing the international effort to study, mitigate and minimize the consequences of the Chernobyl disaster: Report of the Secretary-General (A/68/498)* [online]. [Accessed 7 June 2014]. http://chernobyl.undp.org/english/docs/a_68_498_e. pdf.

UNDP (United Nations Development Programme). 2004. *Report. An Information Needs Assessment of the Chernobyl-Affected Population in the Republic of Belarus.* Minsk: Unipack.

UNDP. 2005. *Chernobyl Forum opening statement by Kalman Mizsei, United Nations Assistant Secretary General* [online]. [Accessed 16 August 2010]. http://europeandcis. undp.org/governance/show/A4CC97FB-F203-1EE9-B2064F449884D2F4.

UNDP. 2005. *UN General Assembly endorses new approach to Chernobyl challenge* [online]. [Accessed 3 May 2009]. http://europeandcis.undp.org/Home/show/A4CC9DD6-F203-1EE9-BDE97A4B5505EC78.

UNDP. 2006. Project draft *'Human Security for Individuals and Communities in Chernobyl-Affected Areas through Local Information Provision (International Chernobyl Research and Information Network)'.* Unpublished document.

UNDP. 2008. *Project Document 'The Area Based Development of the Regions Affected by the Chernobyl Accident'* [online in Russian]. [Accessed 17 August 2010]. http:// undp.by/pdf/Project%20Document%20ABD%20RUS.pdf.

UNDP. 2009. *Helping Chernobyl survivors face the future* [online]. [Accessed 6 September 2009].http://europeandcis.undp.org/hivaids/show/A4CC9D3A-F203-1EE9-B0F795A8E8 799601.

UNDP. 2010. *UNDP and Chernobyl: Q&A* [online]. [Accessed 10 August 2010]. http:// europeandcis.undp.org/Home/show/A4CCB4C3-F203-1EE9-B1046D84F8168040.

UNDP. 2013. *Knowledge product: Recovery from Chernobyl and Other Nuclear Emergencies: Experiences and Lessons Learnt* [online]. [Accessed 7 June 2014]. http://chernobyl.undp.org/english/.

UNDP and UNICEF (United Nations Children's Fund) with UN OCHA (United Nations Office for the Coordination of Humanitarian Affairs) and WHO (World Health Organisation). 2002. *The Human Consequences of the Chernobyl Nuclear Accident: a Strategy for Recovery* [online]. [Accessed 2 May 2009]. http://chernobyl.undp.org/ english/docs/strategy_for_recovery.pdf.

UN OCHA. 2000. *Chernobyl: a Continuing Catastrophe.* New York and Geneva: UN.

UNSCEAR (United Nations Scientific Committee on the Effects of Atomic Radiation). 2000. *Annex J. Exposures and Effects of the Chernobyl Accident* [online]. [Accessed 2 May 2009]. Available from: www.unscear.org/docs/reports/annexj.pdf.

UNSCEAR. 2008. *Report. A/63/46* [online]. [Accessed 16 August 2010]. www.unscear. org/docs/reports/2008/09-86753_Report_2008_GA_Report.pdf.

WHO. 2006. *Health Effects of the Chernobyl Accident and Special Health Care Programmes. Report of the UN Chernobyl Forum Expert Group 'Health'* [online]. [Accessed 16 August 2010]. http://whqlibdoc.who.int/publications/2006/9241594179_eng.pdf.

World Bank. 2002. *Belarus Chernobyl Review* [online]. [Accessed 16 August 2010]. http://www-wds.worldbank.org/external/default/WDSContentServer/WDSP/IB/2002/1 2/14/000094946_02120304004960/Rendered/PDF/multi0page.pdf.

Yaroshinskaya, A. 1994. *Chernobyl: the forbidden truth.* Oxford: Jon Carpenter.

Conclusions

> Foucault's work still lies before us, resistant and capricious, noncommittal where one expects firm argument, inquisitively questioning where one would have preferred a tactful silence, full of surprising turns and seductive in its doubts.
>
> (Visker, 1995: 1)

> I take care not to dictate how thing should be. I try instead to pose problems, to make them active, to display them in such a complexity that they can silence the prophets and lawgivers, all those who speak for others or to others. In this way, it will be possible for the complexity of the problem to appear in its connection with people's lives.
>
> (Foucault, 1994a: 288)

These last sections bring together and reflect upon some of the key positions and arguments, as well as opening some space for further engagement with policies, practices and effects of humanitarian governing drawing on Foucault's ideas on resistance, on 'how not to be governed *like that*' (Foucault, 1997: 44; original emphasis). After all, as the above quote suggests, posing problems is what Foucault's critical approach invites us to do.

Biopolitics, governmentality and the international

Michel Foucault has been and remains one of the most influential thinkers in many discipline areas (e.g. Downing, 2008; Neal, 2009; Ferguson, 2011; Koopman, 2011; Walters, 2012; Falzon *et al.*, 2013). Indeed, numerous engagements with his work amount to no less than 'the Foucault industry' (Bevir, 2011). Foucault's later thinking on biopolitics and governmentality has also been taken up by many scholars to examine a wide range of issues at a variety of levels, from the individual to the international. A close engagement with his later work and the secondary scholarship undertaken here has shown that, drawing on 'Foucauldian resources' (Falzon *et al.*, 2013: 6), it is possible to generate powerful and insightful accounts of different regimes of governing whose workings and effects often transgress national borders. Such exercises can be particularly successful when Foucault's theorising on biopolitics and governmentality is firmly positioned within a broader context of his thinking on power.

As has been emphasised, for Foucault biopower represents a new technology of power that evolved in two forms: discipline, focused on an individual body; and biopolitics, focused on the collective body of the population. Biopower did not replace sovereignty, and is distinct in its overall orientation and mechanism, as it is more concerned with care over living beings and relies on the improved knowledge of the body, both individual and collective. Indeed, knowledge of the population it its 'naturalness' and its relationship with its environment is essential for biopolitical governing. It is this attention to the continuing reiterative link between the development of the technologies of power over life and the development of life sciences that sets Foucault's account apart from the alternative accounts offered by Agamben and Esposito.

Importantly, if we follow Foucault, biopolitics appears to have a death function reliant on sovereign violence, with the positive biopolitical concern of 'care' used for its justification, and a death function, which has to do with 'letting die' rather than direct killing. The concept of racism is important for accounting for these biopolitical death functions. Foucault (2003: 254) understood racism as 'a way of introducing a break into the domain of life that is under power's control: the break between what must live and what must die'. In this sense, racism is a way of assaying the life of a population and dividing it into groups, with some of them to be protected, some disciplined (transformed) or abandoned, and others eliminated as representing threats to the security, health and well-being of a given population. The existence of external threats, often emanating from other populations, means that these processes are not contained within national borders. Thus, in the analysis of 'new' humanitarianism as a regime of governing, I have emphasised its role in sustaining the biopolitical divide between developed (insured) and under-developed (uninsured) populations (e.g. Duffield, 2007). Furthermore, as the two case studies of particular assistance efforts have shown, biopolitical abandonment is often reliant on creating conditions of invisibility for those abandoned, which can take different forms, from a lack of recognition of the suffering in the case of Chernobyl's 'ghosts', to a diversion of resources through the geographical targeting of aid in Afghanistan. At the same time, the reliance on sovereign violence justified by biopolitical concerns was more characteristic of 'humanitarian' interventions and especially of counter-terrorist and COIN strategies in Afghanistan. These practices highlight the dangers resulting from 'demonic' combinations of different technologies of power, e.g. sovereignty and biopolitics (Foucault, in Prozorov, 2007: 57). What the analysis undertaken in this book has shown is that while the purposes of humanitarian governing post-Cold War are specific to particular contexts, their promise of care is more often than not accompanied by sovereign and/or biopolitical violences (invisibility, containment, endangerment and abandonment). At the same time, biopolitical governing is not necessarily negative. This becomes especially clear when Foucault's theorising on biopolitics is placed within the broader context of his thinking on power. As with any power technology,

biopolitics can, and does, produce positive outcomes and has a productive potential. With respect to humanitarian action, when based on the humanitarian imperative, biopolitical technologies are more likely to generate positive biopolitical
effects.

Foucault's theorising on biopolitics is explicitly linked to his theorising on
governmentality. Furthermore, when we read Foucault's later work carefully,
and follow the lead of such scholars as Dean (1999, 2002), Walters and Haahr
(2005), Nadesan (2008), Rosenow (2009), Bröckling, Krasmann and Lemke
(2011), Weidner (2011), Collier (2009, 2011a, 2011b) and Walters (2012), we
can distinguish at least three different meanings, or 'faces', of governmentality
(as a particular understanding of government, as a theoretical perspective, and as
a historically specific rationality of governing), and we can appreciate that the
introduction of this concept calls for a re-evaluation of sovereignty and biopolitics and their global and local effects. While we may not fully agree with Collier
(2011a) that, without taking into account rationalities of government, there is
little to understand about biopolitical governing beyond that fact that all governments have to manage their populations, it is indeed important to study 'different
ways in which the government of living beings is made a problem of reflection
and intervention' (Collier, 2011a: 17). In turn, this only becomes possible when
we consider different formations of biopolitical government informed by different rationalities, which also means that biopolitics is not always neoliberal, as
the example of Soviet biopolitics demonstrates (Collier, 2011a; see also the discussion of tensions between neoliberal and Soviet-style biopolitics that characterised the Chernobyl-related assistance effort in Belarus).

In terms of the productive use of governmentality as a perspective, there are
clear advantages in considering it within the broader context of Foucault's thinking on power and, in particular, reconnecting it with such concepts as power/
knowledge and problematisation (e.g. Miller and Rose, 2008; Bröckling *et al.*,
2011) and such methodologies as genealogy (e.g. Walters, 2012; Koopman,
2013). In terms of operationalising governmentality as a perspective, following
Rose *et al.*, (2006), as well as Dean (2002), one can argue in favour of empirical
investigations. Such investigations benefit from productively combining the
topological analysis (Collier, 2009), which is attentive to different technologies
and rationalities of governing, and the analytics of government (Foucault, 1987;
Dean, 1999; Miller and Rose, 2008), which focuses on the relationship between
rationalities and technologies. Thus, the analytics of government (Dean, 1999)
invites critical examination of the following elements of any regime of governing: problematisations and underpinning systems of knowledge; strategies and
technologies of governing; and subjectivities. Identifying and analysing conflicting problematisations is the crucial first step, which also signals a close affinity
between this type of analysis and genealogy. Genealogical investigations reveal
what Koopman (2011) calls the double-contingency of discourses and practices:
first, by showing that the taken-for-granted is contingently produced, and,
second, by opening up possibilities for alternatives (see the final section for a
further discussion). Thus, in the analysis of 'new' humanitarianism in general

and of the two specific assistance efforts, I have considered both dominant and alternative problematisations of situations that required a humanitarian response and their implications for assistance provision.

In the last decade, Foucault's theorising on biopolitics and governmentality has informed investigations of the international domain, contributing the development of biopolitcs scholarship and of governmentality studies. In a critical overview of the former, close attention has been paid to the accounts focusing on the sovereignty-biopolitics nexus and contexts and conditions that produce negative biopolitical effects, which include studies of the biopolitics of the War on Terror (e.g. Dauphinee and Masters, 2007; Dillon and Reid, 2009; Bell and Evans, 2010) and studies of limit spaces, such as borders and limit figures (e.g. Amoore, 2006; Cairo, 2006; Salter, 2006; Doty, 2007, 2011; Isin and Rygiel, 2007). With respect to international governmentality studies, some key accounts have been examined with a view to identifying important insights and productive ways of using governmentality for the study of the international (global) domain. I have argued in favour of distinguishing between different 'faces' of governmentality (e.g. Joseph, 2010; Walters, 2012), avoiding totalising accounts (e.g. Rosenow, 2009), while being attentive to different rationalities and technologies of governing that characterise specific regimes of governing (e.g. Rosenow, 2009; Walters, 2012), which often traverse domestic/international boundaries. In an attempt to be attentive to specific characteristics of humanitarian governing, in line with suggestions by Rose *et al.* (2006) and Collier (2011a and 2011b), the analysis of 'new' humanitarianism has been combined with that of the two particular assistance efforts. At the same time, while it is both analytically unhelpful and empirically inaccurate to see neoliberalism as an all-encompassing, global and uncontested rationality of government, it can still be seen as a dominant and a globalising one (e.g. Nadesan, 2008; Vrasti, 2013). Thus, it played a crucial role in shaping 'new' humanitarian enterprise post-Cold War and in replacing the humanitarian imperative with the market rationality to decide 'who matters and who doesn't, who lives and who dies' (Giroux, 2008: 594). Furthermore, neoliberal rationality informed specific practices of humanitarian governing, as reflected in the pressures to foster self-reliance and entrepreneurism that characterised the post-2000 Chernobyl-related assistance effort in Belarus.

Understanding the nature of humanitarian governing

This research has been driven by the wish to better understand the nature of post-Cold War humanitarian governing, and, in particular, to account for its violences, which, on the face of it, may appear surprising, if not improbable, especially in the light of the humanitarian principles and high moral ground occupied by humanitarian entities. Humanitarian governing has been examined at both the international and the local level using the critical lenses of Foucault's theorising on biopolitics and governmentality. As far as the international level is concerned, it was not my intention to produce a comprehensive or overly detailed account, and I am all too aware of the inherent limitations of any such attempts. However, the most important and relevant post-Cold War developments in the international environment have been examined, including the unequal erosion of state sovereignty, increased disengagement of the North from the South accompanied by the policies of containment, 'new' interventionism and the War on Terror, and outlined the implications they had for humanitarian action in terms of both challenges and opportunities. In particular, the emphasis has been on the convergences between the opportunities and specific agendas, such as the 'coherence' agenda and the integrated approach to peace. It has been shown that the emergent humanitarian enterprise was an outcome of a set of shifts and convergences, which included: the proliferation of humanitarian actors; aid privatisation and an increased competition for funds; further institutionalisation of humanitarian action through the establishment of coordination structures; and a shift towards increased standardisation and professionalisation and increasingly technological nature.

I have argued that, as a regime of governing, 'new' humanitarianism is best understood as a biopolitical regime of neoliberal governmentality. This argument does not imply that this regime is the only form of humanitarian action in existence today or that it is in itself homogenous and free of conflicts and contestations, with all its practices producing negative, damaging or even violent effects. Rather, what has been attempted is mapping out 'new' humanitarianism as a dominant regime of humanitarian governing. In particular, the focus has been on: the importance of dominant problematisations of humanitarian situations and their implications; the role of 'new' humanitarianism in sustaining the biopolitical divide between the developed (insured) and the underdeveloped (non-insured) populations; and the ways in which the latter are constructed as targets of interventions (broadly conceived). While humanitarian action is essentially biopolitical, with 'new' humanitarianism positive imperatives are often substituted with negative ones, overriding its original logic of equality, unity and solidarity. It has been argued that 'new' humanitarianism's role in sustaining the biopolitical divide (or rather, in producing and sustaining a number of biopolitical divides) is informed by neoliberal rationality, which answers the question about how to govern underdeveloped populations effectively in a particular way, i.e. with minimal resources. Therefore, assistance that just makes people live can be understood as inferior biopolitics (Kelly, 2010), which only partially resembles that available to the developed populations. The predominantly non-material development is essentially an instance of biopolitical abandonment, as people in need are increasingly expected to take care of themselves by becoming self-reliant in the absence of real opportunities and necessary resources. Furthermore, while humanitarian biopolitics is inferior, during the War on Terror interventions it produced many negative biopolitical effects, as the humanitarian imperative was abandoned and assistance was used as an instrument of violent pacification, containment and management of threatening populations (Duffield, 2010; Reid, 2010; also Chapter 3).

Finally, I have argued that the biopolitical divide simultaneously produces and relies upon a particular construction of those to be assisted. People to be assisted emerge as a population, a product of processes of decontextualisation, biologisation, quantification and de-individuation through aggregation. They are only visible through statistics and needs assessments, with such limited visibility obscuring many types of suffering. More often than not, these are people who are counted, but who do not count.

The choice of particular assistance efforts was informed by the need for the cases to be representative of a larger group and to be theoretically decisive. In terms of the former consideration, the post-2001assistance effort in Afghanistan is an example of an assistance effort in a conflict environment, and the post-2000 Chernobyl-related assistance effort in Belarus is an example of an assistance effort in a non-conflict environment. However, each case has been treated as unique, with only limited generalisation. With respect to the latter criterion both assistance efforts are the least likely cases. Both assistance efforts can be seen as extreme, with the assistance effort in Afghanistan shaped by a high-profile external intervention, and the one in Belarus representing a very limited response to a forgotten emergency. The cases are also as different as possible, which allows mapping out and analysing very different combinations of rationalities and technologies of governing, as well as identifying any possible similarities.

Both assistance efforts have been investigated using a modified version of the analytics of government combined with the topological approach as a way of operationalising Foucault's theorising on biopolitics and governmentality. Overall, the analysis has supported the assumption that changes in the nature of humanitarian action associated with 'new' humanitarianism informed the ways in which particular assistance efforts were carried out in a variety of conflict and non-conflict environments by establishing the conditions of possibility for particular problematisations, policies and practices. At the same time, each assistance effort has been found to be shaped by its own localised constellation of rationalities and technologies of power. For instance, while both assistance efforts were reliant on biopolitical management of the assisted populations, the purposes and effects of such management were distinct. This finding justifies the methodological choices made and challenges reductionist interpretations suggesting that all one can expect to find at the local level is a reflection/replication of a single global project. This also points to the need for more empirical studies of particular assistance efforts. Furthermore, both assistance efforts chosen have a long history, and a fully detailed genealogical inquiry spanning several decades could have been incredibly powerful and insightful. The analysis in this book, however, has been limited to the previous decade. Each case study has a specific focus, which in the case of Afghanistan is aid securitisation and militarisation, and, in the case of Belarus, the health effects of the Chernobyl accident and related projects.

In the analysis of both assistance efforts, particular attention has been paid to the dominant problematisations, given their role in informing and shaping assistance strategies and technologies. In this respect, 'speaking with one voice' has been shown to be an important way sustaining dominant problematisations in both cases and an instrument of depoliticisation. More specifically, I have argued that the way in which the post-2001 situation in Afghanistan was problematised

– first as terrorism, requiring a counter-terrorist operation in a post-conflict context, then as an insurgency, requiring COIN and stabilisation – had a significant impact on the assistance effort in creating conditions for its securitisation and militarisation. With respect to the post-2000 Chernobyl-related assistance effort in Belarus, I have shown that the consistent 'erasure' of radiation effects undertaken in a number of reports by relevant international expert bodies and in the official discourse of influential organisations of the UN family, was crucial in making the accident and its victims 'disappear' from the radar of the international humanitarian assistance community. At the same time, in both cases problematisations have been shown to be sites of conflict and contestation.

Expert interviews have proven to be indispensable for understanding the dynamics of the chosen assistance efforts; expert interviews combined with further engagement with beneficiaries would be something to consider for painting an even more detailed and comprehensive picture of particular assistance efforts. As for policies and practices that characterised the assistance efforts, the biopolitics of invisibility and abandonment were significant in both cases, as reflected in the denial of the humanitarian crisis in post-2001 Afghanistan and in the denial of a link between the accident-related exposure and health effects in Belarus. In addition, the biopolitics of invisibility functioned at a more basic level by obscuring the suffering of those still alive, as well as individual suffering, emphasising the biopolitical violence of erasing individual bodies in the process of creating the collective body of population. Furthermore, in both cases the assisted populations were found to be 'lacking' in some respect, as they either had to be protected from the threats they presented to themselves and others (in Afghanistan) or to be saved from their dependency syndrome (in Belarus). In Afghanistan, this meant that the population was also exposed to sovereign violence. In both cases, the humanitarian imperative was undermined, and there were insufficient attempts/opportunities to identify and meet the existing humanitarian needs. Both assistance efforts were characterised by tensions between short- and long-term goals, which can be seen as a reinstatement of the traditional tension between humanitarian assistance and development (or deontology and consequentialism). These tensions were also reflected, to some extent, in the institutional conflict between UN OCHA and UNAMA in Afghanistan and UN OCHA and UNDP in Belarus. Importantly, both assistance efforts were marked by the shift towards non-material development and the emphasis on resilience, which maintains, rather than bridges, the biopolitical divide between the developed (insured) and underdeveloped (non-insured) populations.

Finally, it should be noted that the importance of understanding the dynamics of the assistance effort in Afghanistan is not limited to this case alone, given the implication for other assistance efforts in conflict environments and for the future of humanitarian action in general. The case of Belarus, on the other hand, serves as an example of a forgotten emergency with a limited involvement, something that we can expect to see more of.

In search of alternatives: the challenge of resistance

Crucially, Foucault's conception of power presupposes freedom. While freedom can be circumscribed under the conditions of domination, without it power relations cannot exist: '[a]t the very heart of the power relationship, and constantly provoking it, are the recalcitrance of the will and the intransigence of freedom' (Foucault, 1994b: 342). This suggests that, for Foucault, power relations are coexistent with resistances. Furthermore, in the power/resistance relationship, resistance is more important as a change-driving force (Kelly, 2008). Not surprisingly, then, Foucault insisted that we should start our analysis of power with the analysis of resistances, as it is the best way to achieve an understanding of power relations (Smart, 1985), which is also one of the main reasons for this discussion.

In turn, resistance depends on the existence of power relations, as when subjects do not have any freedom to act and are 'reduced to impotence' (Smart, 1985: 134), a relationship of power ceases to exist, replaced by a relationship of violence. Foucault's (1994b: 340) explanation of the difference between a relationship of power and a relationship of violence is important here:

> A relationship of violence acts upon a body or upon things; it forces, it bends, it breaks, it destroys, or it closes off all possibilities. Its opposite pole can only be passivity.... A power relationship, on the other hand, can only be articulated on the basis of two elements that are indispensable: ... that the 'other' (the one over whom the power is exercised) is recognized and maintained to the very end as a subject who acts; and that, faced with a relationship of power, a whole field of responses, reactions, results, and possible inventions may open up.

Pertinently, Agamben (1998) argues that, under biopolitical sovereignty, all subjects are reduced to 'bare life', which suggests that power relations are replaced with those of violence. While this argument is particularly relevant as far as provision of humanitarian assistance is concerned, given the position in which many of those to be assisted find themselves, we should question the extent to which all subjects are indeed rendered completely powerless. Furthermore, some scholars, who have suggested combining Foucault's and Agamben's insights, argue that opportunities for resistance continue to exist even in relationships of violence. These include resistance as the refusal of sovereign distinctions and resistance as the acceptance of bare life, with the latter strategy often involving using one's own body as the last site of protest (Edkins and Pin-Fat, 2004: 13, 15). An illustration of the former strategy can be found in Fassin's (2007) account of MSF workers who refused to leave Baghdad before the bombardment and, in that way, challenged the divide between the lives that do not count (Iraqis) and lives that do count (Western humanitarian agents), restoring parity between them as equally exposed/vulnerable. In fact, many aid workers still engage in similar strategies, and risk (and sometimes lose) their lives in the process, as illustrated by the story of Dr Karen Woo, a 36-year-old British aid worker, killed by the Taliban during an expedition to take medicines to a remote area of Nuristan in Afghanistan (McVeigh, 2011).

Importantly, 'resistance is ... always specific' (Kelly, 2008: 112), which suggests that strategies of resistance are also specific and local. As Coleman and Grove (2009: 503) stress, 'resistance is about particular sites of legibility – multiple potentially contradictory and overlapping social and spatial contexts within which exploitation is experienced and, importantly, recognized and resisted as such'. Indeed, according to Foucault, to take resistance seriously, in each specific case we should be addressing the questions of 'who is engaged in struggle, what the struggle is about, and how, where, by what means and according to what rationality it evolves' (Foucault, 1980b: 164). For this reason, what would constitute an effective resistance strategy within one context would not necessarily constitute one in another context; the same applies to agents of resistance. For example, while with respect to the post-2001 assistance effort in Afghanistan, resistance on behalf of humanitarian actors could mean refusing to blur the lines between them and the military actors by not using military convoys (as was the case of ICRC and MSF), with respect to the post-2000 assistance effort in Belarus, the unwillingness of beneficiaries to follow the complicated and burdensome radiation safety rules and guidance could be considered as an act of resistance against responsibilisation. Indeed, as Binkley (2009: 76–77) argues, 'counter-conducts within neoliberal governmentality might choose to practice differently certain tenets of neoliberal rule' (e.g. pressures to assume agency, to be responsible and enterprising) by 'recovering the capacity for inaction, irresponsibility and the refusal to seek out opportunity'.

Although mostly localised, resistances are multiple, and can join into global struggles. For Foucault (1994b: 330–331), such struggles against specific forms of power share a number of features: they are 'transversal' in a sense of not being limited to a particular national context or form of government; they target power effects as such and are 'immediate' in confronting power where it is exercised; they oppose processes of individualisation (one can also add the opposition to processes of totalisation); they challenge the privileges of knowledge (we can think of expertise) and the associated secrecy and mystification (we can add depoliticisation); finally, they are concerned with the question of who we are, which involves 'a refusal of a scientific or administrative inquisition that determines who one is'. With respect to the subject matter of this book, a question arises about possible 'transversal' strategies of resistance to 'new' humanitarianism as a biopolitical regime of neoliberal governing.

Thus, from its origins, humanitarianism was associated with the ideas of the indivisibility of humanity and solidarity with others. However, it is important to appreciate which understanding of humanity such ideas are predicated upon. Pupavac (2006: 268) suggests that '[h]umanitarianism is ultimately connected with affirming a universal humanity and recognising the humanity of every individual'. But, as Edkins argues after Campbell, we could envisage a different understanding of what it means to be human, the one that is not based on sharing 'an essential and universal matter', but rather based on us all being produced by relations of power (Campbell, 1998, in Edkins, 2003: 256), as, in Foucault's words, 'we are all governed and, to that extent, in solidarity' (Foucault, 1981, in Edkins, 2003: 256). On this reading, our bond with others is based on a protest against sovereign divides and not on a depoliticised and depersonalised idea of common humanity (Edkins, 2003). Duffield (2007) also endorses this idea. He argues that such solidarity would be political, as it would challenge the gap between the developed (insured) and underdeveloped (non-insured), along with policies and practices of transforming, or bettering, others, and would encourage learning from their struggles.

A more immediate strategy is a 'back to basics' approach, whose advocates suggest abandoning liberal peace (Donini, 2010), transformation and similar agendas in favour of a more limited and more independent humanitarian action (e.g. Rieff, 2002; Edkins, 2003). While suitable for 'Dunantist' humanitarian organisations, such an approach presents more of a challenge for many other humanitarian agencies, as not only would it threaten their survival, but could also have negative consequences for their beneficiaries. A further pluralism within the humanitarian enterprise itself (still mostly Western or Northern) (e.g. Donini, 2006; Davey, *et al.*, 2013), on the other hand, could facilitate emergence of alternative regimes of assistance provision, without necessarily causing adverse implications for aid beneficiaries.

It is important to appreciate, however, that even globalised strategies can never allow escaping from power as such, as one can never be 'outside' power, but this does not mean that we are trapped or should always accept defeat (Foucault, 1994a: 294), as both individual and collective strategies of resistance are always possible. Indeed, resistance should be approached as 'a complicated and heterogeneous phenomenon' (Medina, 2011: 10), and Foucault always emphasised the variety of forms of resistance, ranging from passive opposition to existing governmental efforts, to an active subversion of government and invention of alternative tactics and strategies based on the desire 'not to be governed like that, by that, in the name of those principles, with such and such objective in mind and by means of such procedures, not like that, not for that, not by them' (Foucault, 1997: 44). This means that resistance can be just about saying 'no': '[t]o say no is the minimum form of resistance. But, of course, at times, that is very important' (Foucault, in Kelly, 2008: 109). As far as humanitarian governing is concerned, such instances of saying 'no' can include refusal of food aid (Branch, 2009), refusal to stay in camps, or refusal to leave one's house as was the case with returnees in the Chernobyl-affected zone. However, resistance is more than just a negation, it is a creative, transformative process. The main challenge, therefore, 'is not to discover what we are, but to refuse what we are' (Foucault, 1982, in Hutchings, 1997: 107). An engagement in the process of becoming something else, can, in turn, be a starting point for producing a new commonality (Revel, 2009). Therefore, '[t]he common is not the reassuring starting point for the production of the political but its outcome ... the common is ahead of us' (Revel, 2009: 49–50), which further supports the ideas about a different kind of solidarity discussed above.

At the same time, Foucault recognised that not everybody has the ability to engage in the 'critical interrogation of power and productive self-creation' that is 'the model of active and political practice' (Tobias, 2005: 78). Indeed, many conditions (e.g. extreme pain or debilitating illness) and circumstances (e.g. extreme poverty and deprivation) may erode individual agency and result in des-ubjectification, which means that 'powerlessness may require the intervention of others with the objective of changing state policy' (Tobias, 2005). For instance, Foucault felt very strongly about the responsibility of offering assistance to those in need (Tobias, 2005), which has a direct relevance for the role of humanitarian actors.

However, providing assistance should not involve dictating objectives or strategies of resistance (Picket, 2005) or speaking for others, as this would risk replacing one form of domination with another. Furthermore, one can never know in advance the outcome of resisting, and this uncertainty is a part of the whole experience (Apperley, 1988: 48). Indeed, it is not unusual for resistances 'to fail to attain their goals and produce unintended effects' (Bröckling, Krasmann and Lemke, 2011: 19–20). In this respect, the role of genealogical inquiry cannot be overestimated. Indeed, not only does genealogy 'makes visible the conflicting forces, the breaches and modes of resistance provoking governmental efforts' (Bröckling *et al.*, 2011: 13), but can also provide a starting point for resistance. Genealogy produces an account that exposes conflicts between different forms of knowledge, some of which have become dominant, while others have been disqualified and subjugated (Smart, 1985; Medina, 2011). Subjugated knowledges are excluded from the dominant discourses, rendered invisible and cannot be easily accessed, which also obscures possibilities for resistance (Medina, 2011). As has been discussed, Foucault (1980a) distinguished between two types of subjugated knowledges: those that have fallen victim to various processes of systematisation and those that have been deemed insufficiently scientific. The analysis of the ways in which the humanitarian situation was problematised in Afghanistan and Belarus included bringing to the fore some subjugated knowledges of the first category. In the case of conflict-related assistance effort in Afghanistan, it was knowledges produced by humanitarian actors on the ground, including UN OCHA, who insisted that the situation could not be characterised as either post-conflict or as an absence of humanitarian crisis, and that urgent needs had to be more fully established and addressed. In the case of the Chernobyl-related assistance effort in Belarus, it was knowleges produced by national and international scientists and scholars, local medical doctors, government officials and humanitarian agencies. Marginalised by the 'speaking with one voice' stance of the Chernobyl Forum, they challenged the dominant problematisations of the accident and its health consequences and drew attention to the exclusionary nature and limitations of such problematisations, as well as offering alternative assessments of the impact of the accident. As far as the second category of subjugated knowledges is concerned, these are knowledges of 'ordinary' people, who, despite having an understanding of their circumstances and an ability to express themselves, are prohibited from doing so (Smart, 1985: 67). It is in this vein that I have considered some examples of disqualification and marginalisation of perspectives and voices of aid beneficiaries (e.g. health concerns of the people affected by the Chernobyl accident).

One of the tasks of genealogical inquiry is to challenge the dominant, exclusionary, taken-for-granted perspectives by resurrecting subjugated knowledges and, with them, memories of the struggles that produced the dominant perspectives. In this way, genealogies can provide a 'counter-memory' (Mahon, 1992; Walters, 2012). These counter-memories combine erudite and popular knowledges to offer alternative accounts (Foucault, 1980a) and, therefore, require a collaboration between 'genealogical scholars/activists and the subjects whose experiences and memories have been subjugated' (Medina, 2011: 11). As Foucault put it, genealogy is 'the union of erudite knowledge and local memories which allows us to establish a historical knowledge of struggles and to make use of this knowledge tactically today' (Foucault, 1980a: 83).

While my genealogies may fall somewhat short in this respect, they can hopefully inspire others and inform co-production of alternative problematisations of situations which give rise to humanitarian needs, which will then result in alternative responses.

At the same time, a genealogical inquiry does not aim to reveal the ultimate truth by producing a comprehensive account or to lay out a plan for reform; its task is to achieve a balance by drawing attention to the excluded knowledges and silenced voices (Smart, 1985). Crucially, in doing so, a genealogist does not attempt to speak for and in the name of those whose voices were silenced, because 'the interests of the oppressed are best expressed in their own words and these, too, are to be found in a submerged, invalidated mass of "documents"' (Sheridan, 1980:221). This can suggest focusing on individual stories and using them to challenge totalising perspectives on which biopolitical governing is reliant. I have shown that such a strategy can be productive by engaging in 'tracking' Chernobyl's ghosts and revealing conditions of their disappearance. A similar position was also advocated by a high-level UN official, directly involved in the coordination of the assistance effort in Afghanistan (at the time of the interview):

> Are the numbers large? [First], we do not know, because we do not have access everywhere; second, it is not significant if numbers are small or large, peoples' lives are at stake. Whether it is one person, or fifty people, or five hundred – the numbers are irrelevant in humanitarian assistance.
>
> (21 March 2010)

This comment also points to the appreciation of the fragility and vulnerability of the individual body, an appreciation that used to be at the heart of humanitarian action but which has been replaced with de-individualising statistical aggregates and risk factors. Maybe it is precisely in responding to others in the face of radical complexity and undecideability – and having realised violences and limitations that characterise established criteria, standards, policies, protocols and ready-made 'solutions' – maybe it is in this openness, and this very difficulty, that the possibility of another humanitarian politics lies?

References

Agamben, G. 1998. *Homo Sacer: sovereign power and bare life*. Stanford: Stanford University Press.

Amoore, L. 2006. Biometric borders: governing mobilities in the War on Terror. *Political Geography*, **25**(2): 336–351.

Apperley, A. 1997. Foucault and the problem of method. *In*: M. Lloyd and A. Thacker (eds). *The impact of Michel Foucault on the social sciences and humanities*. Basingstoke: Macmillan, pp. 10–28.

Bell, C. and B. Evans. 2010. Terrorism to insurgency: mapping the post-intervention security terrain. *Journal of Intervention and Statebuilding*, **4**(4): 371–390.

Bevir, M. 2011. Political science after Foucault. *History of the Human Sciences*, **24**(4): 81–96.

Binkley, S. 2009. The work of neoliberal governmentality: temporality and ethical substance in the tale of two dads. *Foucault Studies*, **6**: 60–78.

Branch, A. 2009. Humanitarianism, violence, and the camp in Northern Uganda. *Civil Wars*, **11**(4): 477–501.

Bröckling, U., S. Krasmann and T. Lemke. 2011. From Foucault's lectures at the *Collège de France* to studies of governmentality: an introduction. *In*: U. Bröckling, S. Krasmann and T. Lemke (eds). *Governmentality: current issues and future challenges*. London: Routledge, pp. 1–33.

Cairo, H. 2006. The duty of the benevolent master: from sovereignty to suzerainty and the biopolitics of intervention. *Alternatives: Global, Local, Political*, **31**: 285–311.

Coleman, M. and K. Grove. 2009. Biopolitics, biopower, and the return of sovereignty. *Environment and Planning D: Society and Space*, **27**: 489–507.

Collier, S.J. 2009. Topologies of power: Foucault's analysis of political government beyond 'governmenatlity'. *Theory, Culture & Society*, **26**(6): 78–108.

Collier, S.J. 2011a. *Post-Soviet social: neoliberalism, social modernity, biopolitics*. Oxford: Princeton University Press.

Collier, S.J. 2011b. Foucault, assemblages, and topology. Interview with Simon Dawes. *Theory, Culture & Society* blog [online]. March 23, 2011 [Accessed 10 November 2011]. http://theoryculturesociety.blogspot.com/2011/03/interview-with-stephen-j-collier-on.html.

Dauphinee, E. and C. Masters. 2007. Introduction: living, dying, surviving. *In*: Dauphinee, E. and C. Masters (eds). *The logics of biopower and the War on Terror: living, dying, surviving*. Basingstoke: Palgrave Macmillan, pp. vii–xix.

Davey, E., with J. Borton and M. Foley. 2013. *A history of the humanitarian system: Western origins and foundations* [online]. [Accessed 12 June 2014]. www.odi.org.uk/sites/odi.org.uk/files/odi-assets/publications-opinion-files/8439.pdf.

Dean, M. 1999. *Governmentality: power and rule in modern society*. London: SAGE.

Dean, M. 2002. Powers of life and death beyond governmentality. *Journal for Cultural Research*, **6**(1): 119–138.

Dillon, M. and J. Reid. 2009. *The liberal way of war: killing to make life live*. Abingdon: Routledge.

Donini, A. 2006. *Humanitarian agenda 2015: Afghanistan country study* [online]. [Accessed 11 March 2011]. https://wikis.uit.tufts.edu/confluence/display/FIC/Humanitarian+Agenda+2015+-+Afghanistan+Country+Study.

Donini, A. 2010. The far side: the meta functions of humanitarianism in a globalised world. *Disasters*, **34**(S2): 220–237.

Doty, R.L. 2007. Crossroads of death. *In*: Dauphinee, E. and C. Masters (eds). *The logics of biopower and the War on Terror: living, dying, surviving.* Basingstoke: Palgrave Macmillan, pp. 3–24.

Doty, R.L. 2011. Bare life, border-crossing deaths and spaces of moral alibi. *Environment and Planning D: Society and Space*, **29**(4): 599–612.

Downing, L. 2008. *The Cambridge introduction to Michel Foucault.* Cambridge: Cambridge University Press.

Duffield, M. 2007. *Development, security and the unending war: governing the world of peoples.* Cambridge: Polity Press.

Duffield, M. 2010. The liberal way of development and the development-security impasse: exploring the global life-chance divide. *Security Dialogue*, **41**(1): 53–76.

Edkins, J. 2003. Humanitarianism, humanity, human. *Journal of Human Rights*, **2**(2): 253–258.

Edkins, J. and V. Pin-Fat. 2004. Introduction: life, power, resistance. *In*: J. Edkins, V. Pin-Fat and M.J. Shapiro (eds). *Sovereign lives: power in global politics.* Abingdon: Routledge, pp. 1–22.

Falzon, C., T. O'Leary and J. Sawicki. 2013. Introduction. *In*: C. Falzon, T. O'Leary and J. Sawicki (eds). *A companion to Foucault.* Chichester: Wiley-Blackwell, pp. 1–7.

Fassin, D. 2007. Humanitarianism as a politics of life. *Public Culture*, **19**(3): 499–520.

Ferguson, J. 2011. Toward a left art of government: from 'Foucauldian critique' to Foucauldian politics. *History of the Human Sciences*, **24**(4): 61–68.

Foucault, M. 1980a. Two lectures. Lecture one: 7 January 1976. *In*: C. Gordon (ed.). *Power/knowledge: selected interviews and other writings 1972–1977. Michel Foucault.* Harvester Press Limited, pp. 78–92.

Foucault, M. 1980b. The eye of power. *In*: C. Gordon (ed.). *Power/knowledge: selected interviews and other writings 1972–1977. Michel Foucault.* Harvester Press Limited, pp. 146–165.

Foucault, M. 1987. Nietzsche, genealogy, history. *In*: M. T. Gibbons (ed.). *Interpreting politics.* Oxford: Basil Blackwell, pp. 221–240.

Foucault, M. 1994a. Interview with Michel Foucault. *In*: J.D. Faubion (ed.). *Power. Essential works of Foucault 1954–1984.* Volume III. London: Penguin Books, pp. 239–297.

Foucault, M. 1994b. The subject and power. *In*: J.D. Faubion (ed.). *Power. Essential works of Foucault 1954–1984.* Volume III. London: Penguin Books, pp. 326–348.

Foucault, M. 1997. What is critique? In: S. Lotringer (ed.). *The politics of truth.* Los Angeles, CA: Semiotext(e), pp. 41–81.

Foucault, M. 2003. *Society must be defended: Lectures at the Collége de France, 1975–76.* London: Penguin Books.

Giroux, H.A. 2008. Beyond biopolitics of disposability: rethinking neoliberalism in the New Gilded Age. *Social Identities*, **14**(5): 587–620.

Hutchings, K. 1997. Foucault and International Relations theory. *In*: M. Lloyd and A. Thacker (eds). *The impact of Michel Foucault on the social sciences and humanities.* Basingstoke: Macmillan, pp. 102–127.

Interview with a high-level UN official, directly involved in the coordination of the assistance effort in Afghanistan (at the time of the interview), 21 March 2010.

Isin, E.F. and K. Rygiel. 2007. Abject spaces: frontiers, zones, camps. *In*: Dauphinee, E. and C. Masters (eds). *The logics of biopower and the War on Terror: living, dying, surviving.* Basingstoke: Palgrave Macmillan, pp. 181–203.

Joseph, J. 2010. What can governmentality do for IR? *International Political Sociology*, **4**(2): 202–205.

Kelly, M.G.E. 2008. *The political philosophy of Michel Foucault*. London: Routledge.

Kelly, M.G.E. 2010. International biopolitics: Foucault, globalisation and imperialism. *Theoria*, **57**(123): 1–26.

Koopman, S. 2011. Foucault across disciplines: introductory notes on contingency in critical inquiry. *History of Human Sciences*, **24**(4): 1–12.

Koopman, C. 2013. *Genealogy as critique: Foucault and the problems of modernity*. Bloomington, IN: Indiana University Press.

Mahon, M. 1992. *Foucault's Neitzchean genealogy: truth, power and the subject*. Albany: State University of New York Press.

McVeigh, T. 2011. *The Observer. Film tracks doomed last mission of aid worker*. 15 May 2011.

Medina, J. 2011. Toward a Foucaultian epistemology of resistance: counter-memory, epistemic friction, and *guerrilla* pluralism. *Foucault Studies*, **12**: 9–35.

Miller, P. and N. Rose. 2008. *Governing the present: administering economic, social and personal life*. Cambridge: Polity Press.

Nadesan, M.H. 2008. *Governmentality, biopower, and everyday life*. London: Routledge.

Neal, A.W. 2009. Michel Foucault. *In*: J. Edkins and N. Vaughan-Williams (eds). *Critical theorists and international relations*. London: Routledge, pp. 161–175.

Picket, B. 2005. *On the use and abuse of Foucault for politics*. Oxford: Lexington Books (Rowman & Littlefield).

Prozorov, S. 2007. The unrequited love of power: biopolitical investment and the refusal of care. *Foucault Studies*, **4**: 53–77.

Pupavac, V. 2006. The politics of emergency and the demise of the developing state: problems for humanitarian advocacy. *Development in Practice*, **16**(3): 255–269.

Reid, J. 2010. The biopoliticization of humanitarianism: from saving bare life to securing the biohuman in the post-interventionary societies. *Journal of Intervention and Statebuilding*, **4**(4): 391–411.

Revel, J. 2009. Identity, nature, life: three biopolitical deconstructions. *Theory, Culture & Society*, **26**(6): 45–54.

Rieff, D. 2002. *A bed for the night: humanitarianism in crisis*. London: Vintage.

Rose, N., O'Malley, P. and M. Valverde. 2006. Governmentality. *Annual Review of Law & Social Sciences*, **2**: 83–104.

Rosenow, D. 2009. Decentring global power: the merits of a Foucauldian approach to International Relations. *Global Society*, **23**(4): 497–517.

Salter, M.B. 2006. The global visa regime and the political technologies of international self: borders, bodies, biopolitics. *Alternatives: Global, Local, Political*, **31**: 167–189.

Sheridan, A. 1980. *Michel Foucault: the will to truth*. London: Tavistock Publications.

Smart, B. 1985. *Michel Foucault*. London: Routledge.

Tobias, 2005. Foucault on freedom and capabilities. *Theory, Culture & Society*, **22**(4): 65–85.

Visker, R. 1995. *Michel Foucault: genealogy as critique*. London: Verso.

Vrasti, W. 2013. Universal but not truly 'global': governmentality, economic liberalism, and the international. *Review of International Studies*, **39**(1): 49–69.

Walters, W. 2012. *Governmentality: critical encounters*. London: Routledge.

Walters, W. and J.H. Haahr. 2005. *Governmentality and political studies*. *European Political Science*, **4**: 288–300.

Weidner, J.R. 2011. Governmentality, capitalism, and subjectivity. *In*: N.J. Kiersey and D. Stokes (eds). *Foucault and International Relation: new critical engagements*. Abingdon: Routledge, pp. 25–49.

Index

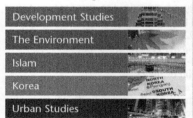